BURT FRANKLIN: RESEARCH & SOURCE WORKS SERIES
Philosophy and Religious History Monographs 121

THE BEGINNINGS

OF THE

TEMPORAL SOVEREIGNTY
OF THE POPES

A.D. 754—1073

𝔑𝔦𝔥𝔦𝔩 𝔬𝔟𝔰𝔱𝔞𝔱.

JOSEPH WILHELM, S.T.D.,

Censor deputatus.

𝔍𝔪𝔭𝔯𝔦𝔪𝔦 𝔭𝔬𝔱𝔢𝔰𝔱.

✠ GULIELMUS,

Episcopus Arindelensis,

Vicarius Generalis.

Westmonasterii,

die 30 *Aprilis* 1907.

THE BEGINNINGS

OF THE

TEMPORAL SOVEREIGNTY
OF THE POPES

A.D. 754–1073

BY

Mgr. L. DUCHESNE, D.D.

(DIRECTOR OF THE ÉCOLE FRANÇAISE AT ROME)

AUTHORISED TRANSLATION

FROM THE FRENCH BY

ARNOLD HARRIS MATHEW

(DE JURE EARL OF LANDAFF, OF THOMASTOWN, CO. TIPPERARY)

BURT FRANKLIN
New York, N. Y.

Published by LENOX HILL Pub. & Dist. Co. (Burt Franklin)
235 East 44th St., New York, N.Y. 10017
Reprinted: 1972
Printed in the U.S.A.

Burt Franklin: Research and Source Works Series
Philosophy and Religious History Monographs 121

Reprinted from the original edition in the Rutgers University
    Library.

Library of Congress Cataloging in Publication Data

Duchesne, Louis Marie Olivier, 1843-1922.
    The beginnings of the temporal sovereignty of the popes, A. D.
754-1073.

    Reprint of the 1908 ed., which was issued as v. 11 of International
Catholic library.
    Translation of Les premiers temps de l'État pontifical.
    1. Papacy—History. 2. Popes—Temporal power. 3. Papal states—History. I.
Title. II. Series: The International Catholic library, v. 11.
BX1070.D83 1973   945'.6   73-185937
ISBN 0-8337-4079-2

TRANSLATOR'S NOTE

MONSIGNOR DUCHESNE'S volume on the beginnings of the temporal power of the Popes appeared to me to be the most accurate and concise of any of the treatises on this important question which have hitherto appeared. I accordingly sought his permission to translate the work into English, feeling assured that it would prove interesting to a very wide circle of readers.

For the kindness and readiness with which the learned author acceded to my request, I desire to record here my sense of gratitude.

I have endeavoured to express the meaning of the original, rather than the actual words or idioms of the author, in order to avoid the awkwardness and clumsiness of diction, which a literal rendering would have involved.

ARNOLD HARRIS MATHEW.

CHELSFIELD, KENT.

TRANSLATOR'S PREFACE

THE learned author of this volume is well known, and deservedly esteemed, by a very wide circle of appreciative students of ecclesiastical history. His honesty and trustworthiness in publishing the results of his laborious investigations earned for him the praise and encouragement of Pope Leo XIII.

In the hope that this short treatise may be of service in an English version, I have ventured to translate it, and for his permission to me to undertake this work I must express my thanks to Monsignor Duchesne.

ARNOLD HARRIS MATHEW.

CHELSFIELD, KENT.

AUTHOR'S PREFACE

THIS book is the outcome of a course of lectures given at Paris some twelve years ago. They made their first public appearance, collected and printed, in a Review, and, afterwards, a fairly large selection of them was placed at the disposition of the public. As the first edition of the lectures is now exhausted, I am, in accordance with request, bringing out another. This, however, is rather out of deference to the advice of my publisher, than to any deep sense of the book's importance. So many people have written on the subject, and with so much erudition! At least, I suppose so; but not being a person of unlimited leisure, I have, as a rule, confined myself to the study of original documents, without unduly troubling myself about the lucubrations to which they have given rise. Few foot-notes will be found in these pages, for I have been chary of references, even with regard to my own first-hand investigations. Many details are explained in my notes on the *Liber Pontificalis*, to which the learned and conscientious reader is respectfully referred. Small works of this kind are intended for the average reader.

For the benefit of the latter, then, I have tried to explain the formation of the little pontifical state in the eighth century, and how the conditions under which it worked during the first three centuries of its existence are connected with the great religious conflicts in the time of Gregory VII. It is true that the subject may appear remote, but as long as it is a question of the Church and of Italy, its interest can never pall.

CONTENTS

THE TEMPORAL SOVEREIGNTY
OF THE POPES

CHAPTER I

THE SITUATION IN THE TIME OF KING LIUTPRAND

Lombard and Byzantine Italy—Progress of the Lombards—Leo the
Isaurian, Liutprand, and Pope Gregory II.—Roman politics under
Gregory III.—Zachary, the peace-loving Pope.

THE unity of Italy was first established by the
Romans, who, in the second century before our era,
conquered Cisalpine Gaul, and reached the barrier of
the Alps.   This unity really consisted in unfailing
submission to the Romans and to the masters who
were appointed by them.   Next to the senate and
the magistrates of the Republic came the Italian
and provincial emperors, and then the Gothic kings
of Ravenna.   These were replaced, in the middle of
the sixth century, by a re-establishment of the imperial
rule, under the auspices of the Emperor of Constantinople.   All these revolutions had taken place without
any parcelling out of the land, for although there had
been frequent change of authority, it had always been
of the same nature.   The last change resembled the
close of a long and disastrous war.   Now, however,
people were beginning to forget not only the
prosperous reigns of Theodoric and Amalasontus,
but even the miseries of the Gothic war, and con-

gratulated themselves on living peacefully under the distant though unmistakable rule of the Emperor Justinian: *Erat enim tota Italia gaudeus.*[1]

This happy state of affairs was interrupted in 569 by the Lombard invasion. At the same time the unity of Italy received a mortal blow, from which it took many centuries to recover. Not that Alboin wished to harm it, for he would willingly have supported it could he have done so to his own advantage. But his people had neither military power, nor unity of purpose enough, to set themselves against the whole of Italy, nor could they hold the same position of authority as the Goths had done. Besides, the Byzantine empire, suffering from the inroads of the Avaris in the north, and the Persians and Arabs in the east, were no longer in a condition to live up to the high ideals of Justinian. The dilapidated state of its military and financial power enabled it to offer but a desultory opposition to the attacks of the German barbarians. Towards the close of the sixth century the Roman defence was represented by two efforts not tending in the same direction. One—that of a boundless, unconquerable, but impotent hopefulness—was embodied in the person of the Exarch Romanus—a lieutenant of the Emperor Maurice. The other, that of local interests and practical claims, was led by the diplomatic Pope Gregory. This last effort was the only one which, under the circumstances, had any chance of success. It resulted in peace, but at the same time, in the loss of Italian unity, for the imperial rule was divided with the Lombards.

Henceforward there were two Italies — the Lombard and the Byzantine. The former was

[1] *Liber Pontificalis,* Life of John III.

subject to the barbarian masters of Northern
Tuscany and the Valley of the Po, and the latter
to the Roman Emperor of the East. The Byzantine
power in Italy was steadily declining, and, being
driven from the interior, was with difficulty sustained
on the coast of Genoa, the Venetian lagoons, and the
southern peninsulas. The two parties were never at
peace for long together, and the Lombards did not at
all agree with the Byzantines, who considered that
they had yielded enough. The Lombard power
became more and more firmly established in the
conquered territory, and they finally found themselves in a position to accomplish issues for which
the strength of Alboin and his followers had been
inadequate. On all sides their plans of conquest were
renewed, and they were rapidly gaining control of
the coast. As early as the seventh century Rotharis
had annexed the Ligurian sea-coast as well as the
remaining imperial territory at the end of the
Adriatic. The duchy of Beneventum was rapidly
increasing its power; it took possession of Salerno,
the Lucanian coast and maritime Apulia, and, following in the wake of the retreating Byzantines, extended
its sway as far as Otranto and Calabria. In the time
of St. Gregory it was still possible to journey from
the Venetian islands right down to the Straits of
Messina without leaving imperial ground. But
now things were changed. The Lombard power
was making itself felt all along the line of Byzantine
possession, attacking any undefended positions, and
breaking up the imperial domain. The possessions
that remained in the far south—Otranto, Gallipoli,
and Reggio—looked to Sicily for help, and, thanks
to the friendly sea, the promontories of Sorrento,
Naples, and Gaeta held out with fair success. The

island of Rialto, on which Venice was beginning to
rise, became the centre of the lagoons of the north.
Rome and Ravenna, though but poorly equipped,
were engaged in a painful struggle in mid-Italy.
While Rome, on her side, enjoyed a religious
deference inspired by her sanctuaries, Ravenna's
only protecting influence lay in the majesty of the
frail and distant empire.   Liutprand, evidently at
deadly enmity with them both, was gaining great
successes.   Sutri, Narni, Sora, Cumes, Osimo,
Ancona, Bologna, Cesena, and even Ravenna's own
port, Classis, all yielded to the Lombard king, or
to the Dukes of Spoleto and Beneventum.   Negotiations, and even strategical manœuvres were essayed,
not always in vain.   The Pope tried the effect of
entreaties and offers of money, but in spite of an
occasional success it was obvious that the country
surrounding Rome and Ravenna would soon be
completely subjugated, and that finally the cities
themselves would be obliged to yield.

Affairs in Italy were already going badly enough,
when the Byzantine government contrived to quarrel
with the Holy See.   They disagreed on the fiscal
question, and, what was more important still, on
religious matters.   Pope Gregory II., as the defender
of the Church's patrimony, thought fit to protest
against certain new impositions.   This opposition
had an adverse effect upon the emperor's financial
plans, for the Church of Rome owned valuable property in Sicily, Calabria, and the other Byzantine
districts, and the Pope was the richest contributor
in Italy.   But the final blow was the quarrel about
images, in which the government interfered with the
services of the Church and tried to impose upon the
Pope religious regulations which had not even been

submitted to his approval. Gregory II., in alarm, protested, and all Italy, Romans and Lombards alike, rallied round him.

He was, however, always a faithful subject of the empire, and though he organised resistance, he did not for a moment intend it as an act of rebellion. It must be admitted that the Byzantine officials tried his loyalty severely, for, from their point of view, it was the Pope, and not the Lombards, against whom they had to fight. They were under orders to despatch him, and if the worst came to the worst, they did not mean to stop short of assassination. The Exarch Paul even sent troops to Rome, which was on the side of the Pope. But the Lombards came to their assistance, and Paul had to retreat to Ravenna. There he soon found himself in an unpleasant position, for the Venetian and Pentapolitan troops refused to obey him, and even threatened to announce the fall of Leo the Isaurian, to proclaim another emperor, and to lead him to Constantinople. The Pope, however, managed to calm this undue enthusiasm.

The unfortunate Exarch perished at Ravenna, in a riot, brought about by the general discontent. Another, Eutychius by name, was sent by the emperor to take his place. He was the last of the Exarchs. Having been furnished with the same instructions as his predecessor, he at first adopted the same tactics; but the resistance which he encountered led him to try to break through the bond, which religious defence had established between the Pope and the Lombards. From the Byzantine point of view this alliance was most undesirable. There was no great harmony between the Lombards of the kingdom and those of the two duchies of Spoleto and Beneventum. These duchies had, from the first, enjoyed the privilege of self-government, a privilege which had only strengthened as time went on. They were, it is true, attached to the Lombard State, but with ties as loose as those which, on the other side of the Alps, bound the duchies of Aquitaine, Alamanny, and Bavaria to the Frankish kingdom. King Liutprand sought every opportunity of making his authority felt in these detached provinces. He responded to the overtures of the new Exarch, and they both united in an effort to restore Spoleto and Beneventum to the royal dominion, and Rome to that of the imperial representative.

This amiable alliance gave general satisfaction, though the result was hardly what the emperor would have desired. The king entered Spoleto and received the submission of the two dukes; then, accompanied by the Exarch, he went on to Rome, or rather to St. Peter's, where they were received by Pope Gregory. Liutprand was a Christian prince, as well as an experienced politician, and he and the Pope agreed to sacrifice the aggressive policy of the emperor against the Holy See. There seems to have been much interchange of courtesies, and the king overwhelmed St. Peter's with gifts. Then, to show that they harboured no ill-feeling towards the Emperor of Constantinople, the Romans, headed by the Exarch, set out under the imperial banner to put down a rival of Leo the Isaurian, who had seized a favourable opportunity to land in a corner of Roman Tuscia. This Petasius or Tiberius, as he was called, was killed at Monterano, and from that time the Exarch of Ravenna ceased his machinations against the Roman pontiff. The emperor, if not the empire, was practically ignored, and the administrative power was distributed in such a way as enabled them to arrange matters among themselves without asking the imperial opinion.

The situation soon became clear. As a result of the iconoclast dispute the patriarch Germanus of Constantinople (730) was compelled to resign. Gregory II. not only refused to recognise his successor, but severely reprimanded the prince who was the cause of all these disturbances. The Pope died soon after (731), but his policy was continued by Gregory III., who came after him. He even added force to his convictions by sending ambassadors to Constantinople, but Leo, far from giving way, managed to rid himself of these unwelcome guests by means of bribery and intimidation. Most often they were stopped on their way by the cruisers of the Sicilian patrician. The property of the Holy See in Sicily and in the other Byzantine possessions in the south of Italy was seized, and the bishops of these districts were despatched to Constantinople. Once there they could not go to Rome for consecration, and they were regarded as subject to the authority of the patriarch of the imperial city.

The Exarch's reconciliation with the Pope did not tend to increase his popularity with his chiefs, and availed but little against the Lombard attacks. Gregory II. had almost succeeded in protecting the Roman territory against his enterprising neighbours. Liutprand had yielded to his claims upon Lutri, though Narni was still in the grip of the Duke of Spoleto. Round Ancona and Ravenna the imperial power was decreasing to such an extent that Ravenna herself succumbed to the Lombards, and the Exarch Eutychius was obliged to take refuge at Venice. In compliance with the wishes of Gregory III. the

Venetians soon sent him back to Ravenna, and the Exarchate continued for some years longer.

Just then the tranquillity of the situation was almost upset by a political indiscretion. The Dukes of Spoleto and Beneventum reasserted themselves, and assumed an independent attitude towards King Liutprand. Their neighbours at Rome, who could no longer resist the temptation to take an active part in Italian affairs, were unfortunately inspired to interfere in the quarrels which ensued. The king invaded Spoleto, expelled Duke Trasimund, and installed another in his place. The outraged duke sought refuge at Rome, and when the Romans refused to give him up to Liutprand, the latter seized upon Ameria, Orte, Bomarzo, and Blera, four places in the north of the duchy. Being now at open enmity with the Romans, his followers organised a series of pillaging expeditions in their domains, pushing their depredations even to the very gates of Rome.

Their interference seemed likely to cost the Romans dear. Gregory III. in this extremity besought Liutprand to restore the four towns that he had taken. This request being, not unnaturally, refused, the Pope had recourse to the extreme measure of imploring help from France. Relays of messengers, charged with eloquent letters and presents, and bearing the Keys of the Confession of St. Peter, were despatched to Charles Martel. Special attention was called by them to the plundering of the Roman territory, which was exhausting the revenues of St. Peter to such an extent that the illumination of the apostolic sanctuary had to suffer curtailment. Charles received the Pope's representatives with due respect, and even sent an embassy in return. The Romans, however, could expect but little help from this quarter, for the relations between Charles and Liutprand were too harmonious to be disturbed. Only a short time before, the young Frankish prince, Pepin (the future conqueror of Astolphus) had been sent by his father to have his head shorn by Liutprand, in token of military adoption. In the same year (739), the Lombard king had, in response to Charles's appeal, united with him against their common enemies, the Saracens, who were invading Provence. Besides, the Franks were not ignorant of the state of affairs in Italy, and they realised that the Romans had themselves to blame, in some measure at least, for the position in which they found themselves. If they were in difficulties, they must get out of them as best they could, such was the Frankish opinion.

In time, the Romans succeeded in overcoming the difficulty, but not without bloodshed. With unwonted and commendable energy, they undertook to subjugate the duchy of Spoleto, not for themselves, but for their confederate, Trasimund. One division of the army fell upon Abruzzo, while the other devoted its attention to the despoiling of Rieti and Spoleto. An entry was easily secured, and Trasimund, after giving orders that Duke Frederic, Liutprand's protégé, should have his throat cut, established himself in his place. This was in December 740.

After this, it seemed that the least he could do was to show his gratitude to the Romans by helping them to regain the places they had lost in supporting his cause. There were, however, difficulties in the way. Trasimund saw that he would have his work cut out to maintain authority in his duchy, and apparently he did not feel equal to engaging in operations so far from home. Liutprand, meanwhile, was leisurely preparing to bear down upon his refractory vassal of Spoleto, his ally, the Duke of Beneventum, and their good friends of Rome. The year 741 was passed in expectation. The Romans in vain demanded their towns from the helpless Trasimund. In the midst of all this, in the month of December, the Pope died, just a year after the triumphal entry into Spoleto. The same year also witnessed the passing of the two great Princes of the East and West, Leo the Isaurian (June 18), and Charles of France (October 22).

The Romans were in sore need of a man of wisdom who would guide them with his counsel. Pope Zachary, who was immediately elected, had no difficulty in explaining to them their situation and prospects. Liutprand and his army were about to descend upon them, secure that no opposition was to be feared on that side of the Alps. Had not Spoleto and Beneventum already twice succumbed to the king of the Lombards, and was it probable that the Roman forces, though not to be despised, could hold out against him? There seemed every chance that they would be defeated, and it was hardly likely under the circumstances that the king would yield to the Pope's petitions that Rome should be spared. Their best course would be to forsake their faithless ally, Trasimund, and enlist themselves on the stronger side. They might then have occasion to render the king some service, which would redound to their advantage.

So it was arranged. The king, being approached by the Pope, promised not to molest the duchy of Rome, and further, to restore to them their lost towns.

As soon as he drew near to Spoleto the Roman army advanced to his assistance. Trasimund made an unconditional surrender, and the Pope, fearing that the king's promises might be as easily broken as those of the Duke of Spoleto, sallied forth to remind him of them, and at the same time to come to an understanding with him on other matters, ecclesiastical as well as political. The interview, which took place at Terni, was most satisfactory. The king agreed to keep peace with the duchy of Rome for twenty years, and restored not only the four towns, but also the imperial prisoners and the estates of the Holy See which had been annexed in the foregoing years.

The Romans were not alone in experiencing the truth of the saying that persuasion is often more effective than force. The following year Liutprand, not content with Bologna and Imola, seized upon the town of Cesena and even upon part of the land belonging to Ravenna. In response to the terrified appeal of the Ravennese, Pope Zachary hastened to their help, leaving the government of Rome to Stephen, patrician and duke. On 29th June, 743, he interviewed Liutprand at Pavia, and once more the Lombard king yielded to the peaceful tactics of the Pope, and Ravenna, for the time being, remained under the Byzantine sway.

At the beginning of the next year, 744, the long and glorious reign of Liutprand came to an end. Impertinently enough, Zachary's biographer attributes his death to the prayers of the Pope, who had had so much reason to be grateful to him. We must, however, for Zachary's honour, look upon this as the slander of an unprincipled eulogist. Be this as it may, the new king, Ratchis, at first appeared as

well disposed as his predecessor.   Like him, he
granted the Pope's request for a twenty years' peace.
But this was only to affect the duchy of Rome, and
the Lombard king soon resumed the war against the
emperor, in the neighbourhood of Pentapolis and
Perugia.   He was besieging the latter when he was
surprised by the Pope.   Once more was the king
obliged to yield to his irresistible eloquence, and
deliver up the prey that he had already grasped.   Indeed, Zachary's blandishments were so effectual that
Ratchis not only abandoned the siege of Perugia
but he actually abdicated the Lombard throne (749)
and entered upon a religious career.   He, with his
whole family, withdrew to St. Peter's at Rome, and
finally settled at Monte Cassino.

Zachary's ambition had overleapt itself.   He
might have been thankful at having to deal with
such kings as Liutprand and Ratchis, instead of
rejoicing at their deaths or driving them into convents.   The new king, Astolphus, proved himself
less amenable to the Pope's influence, and matters
began immediately to assume a threatening aspect.
He began by settling the affairs of Ravenna and
Pentapolis, and at Zachary's death, in March 752, the
imperial rule was definitely abolished in those regions.
In fact, to the north of the Apennines, the lagoons of
Venice alone acknowledged the dominion of the
Byzantine emperor.

CHAPTER II

THE DUCHY OF ROME

Political position of the Pope, in Rome, in Italy, and elsewhere—The radius of his immediate influence—The Duchy of Rome, its limits and its autonomy—The moral and the political authority of the Pope in this province : the people of St. Peter—Relations with the Greek Empire

St. Gregory the Great was, in modern parlance, an excellent patriot, in spite of the fact that he was the chief representative of the submissive policy which assented to the division of Italy between the Lombards and the empire. In theory his sorrow was as keen as the hopes of the Exarch Romanus, but in practice he was as much interested as anybody in the safety and prosperity of the empire. Fortunately for the imperial progress, his successors were animated with the same spirit. 'The Pope, indeed, was a mighty moral power which, had the boundary line between the spiritual and the temporal sphere been less jealously defined, would probably have become a powerful political factor. Over the frontiers he held communication with other races—the Franks, the Visigoths, the Anglo-Saxons, the Bavarians, and, in particular, with the Lombards, who heard him the more willingly as their converts increased in number. He held quite an exceptional situation in the interior of Byzantine Italy. It is a mere theological quibble to speak of the Bishop of Rome at any time as of an ordinary bishop. It is an historical quibble, in connection with a Pope of the sixth, seventh, or eighth century, to lay stress on his subordinate relation to the Emperor of Constantinople. Undoubtedly, from a theoretical point of view, he was a subject, for the emperor was supreme ruler of the empire. But in reality the Pope was elected by the Romans at Rome, and his appointment received the imperial sanction, merely as a matter of form. He was in this way distinguished from the highest dignitaries, particularly from the Exarch. His authority was independent of the emperor, and though his renown shone forth both within and without the empire, it was certainly with no reflection of Byzantine glory. Indeed he really owed his prestige and position to the influence of St. Peter. The succession of St. Peter, the See of St. Peter, the authority of St. Peter, the tomb of St. Peter — all these counted for much in the atmosphere of respect and admiration which surrounded the apostolic representative.·

The Papal influence was by no means confined to the Church. The Pope's experience, his moral authority, his sound financial position, and his powers of administration were a valuable help in the conduct of temporal affairs. We see him concerning himself, apparently in no meddlesome spirit, with war operations, the arrangement of treaties, the appointment of officials, the management of the State exchequer, as well as with municipal enterprises, such as the repairing of ramparts and aqueducts and schemes for the public food supply.·

But, in spite of the solicitude for the general welfare, the Pope's influence was more particularly concentrated on his own immediate surroundings— above all on Rome. He certainly busied himself in both the political and military affairs of Ravenna and

Naples, but it was the needs, temporal though they might be, of his spiritual flock which specially claimed his attention and sympathy. As might have been expected, the result of this condition of affairs was the creation around the apostolic sanctuary of a kind of holy ground, whose limits spread beyond the city, even to the boundary line of the duchy of Rome.'

The extent of the duchy, which was the province of the duke [1] and other military authorities who resided at Rome, had been defined by the limits of the Lombard invasion. In Liutprand's day it included, between the Tiber and the coast, part of ancient Tuscia, called Roman Tuscia, to distinguish it from Lombard Tuscia, now Tuscany. The most northerly places on this side were Centumcellae (Cività Vecchia) on the sea, and Orte on the Tiber, and, between the two, Blera (Bieda), Sutri, and Bomarzo. On the other side of the Tiber, not very far from Orte, on the line between Perugia and Rome, was the town of Amelia, which was under Roman jurisdiction. Except for this one place, the left bank of the Tiber, as far as the outskirts of Monte Rotondo, belonged to the duchy of Spoleto.[2] The first Roman towns were Nomentum and Tilsur ; then the frontier line followed the mountains behind Prenesto, Anagni, Alatri, and Veroli as far as the Liris, where it turned off to Terracina.[3]

---

[1] The Commanders-in-Chief formerly bore other titles ; that of duke is used for the first time in 712.

[2] This had not been the case for long. Narni was taken about 725, and Sabina, properly speaking, twelve years earlier. (*L. P.*, t. i. p. 403, 428.) If the first two parts of the Farfa register were authentic (which is not the case), the taking of Sabina was rather earlier.

[3] For an account of the administration and politics of this town, see the Memorandum by M. J. Gay, *The Papal State*, &c., in the mélanges of the *École de Rome*, t. xxi. (1901), p. 487.

This *ducatus Romanus* had originally been merely a military province, like the duchies of Naples or Venetia. The duke was subject to the Exarch, and the *exercitus Romanus* was a division of the Byzantine army commanded by the vice-emperor of Ravenna. But these relations did not last very long. There arose divisions, induced by the peculiar configuration of Byzantine Italy, the difficulties in the way of communication, and the differences of outlook fostered by such conditions. Matters were worse still when, about the year 727, in virtue of their resistance to the iconoclastic *fiats* of Leo the Isaurian, the commissioned officials were banished to Constantinople, and native dukes elected in their places. Henceforth each duchy was practically independent, though there was a kind of federation among them. This state of affairs was all the more unavoidable as the superior authority, the Exarch, had apparently freed himself from the imperial power, and was disporting himself, like an ordinary duke, in the province of Ravenna, which was visibly disappearing as the Lombard conquests increased.

Under these circumstances it is far from surprising that Rome should embark on a political career of her own. We see her concluding alliances, declaring war, and signing treaties. She it is and not the Exarch with whom Trasimund,[1] Duke of Spoleto, negotiates at different times, and with whom King Liutprand arranges the Peace of Terni in 742. Ravenna is treated in quite a different manner. Without so much as asking permission the prince seizes upon her lands, towns, and even her capital. On the other hand, if he feels inclined to annex parts

---

[1] *L. P.,* t. i. p. 420 (*Affaire de Gallese*), 426 (treaty for its restoration to Spoleto).

of the duchy of Rome, Sutri, Blera, Bomarzo, Orte, or Amelia, he restores them without much difficulty. This was, undoubtedly, an idiosyncrasy, for the Duke of Spoleto, who in his reign took possession of both Narni and Sabina, was by no means so easily prevailed upon to part with them. Still there is no doubt that Rome was treated very differently from Ravenna. The real reason for this favouritism was that Rome was under the protection of St. Peter and his vicar, and not that the Lombard king considered that they had any special claim upon his good will. Owing to the repeated solicitations of the Pope, who spared neither pains nor money in the cause, Sutri was restored, after an occupation of several months. The king intended it as a gift to the Apostles Peter and Paul.[1] Gallesa,[2] on which the Duke of Spoleto had long cast a covetous eye, was finally included again " *in compage sanctæ reipublicæ atque corpore Christo dilecti exercitus Romani.*"[3] But this was really due to a money arrangement entered into by Pope Gregory III.[4] It was Pope Zachary with whom Liutprand, on two different occasions, both directly and indirectly, settled the question of restoring the four towns by

[1] This document is lost, and we derive all our information on the subject from the *L. P.* We cannot therefore thoroughly understand the terminology used, and we do not know whether or not it was a question of the duchy of Rome or of the empire. The biographer, whose account is, above all else, practical, simply wishes us to understand that if Sutri was recovered it was owing to the Pope.

[2] A village not far from Viterbo.

[3] These subtle expressions denote the imperial domain (*sanctæ reipublicæ*) and the military command (*exercitus*) or duchy of Rome.

[4] According to his biographer it would appear that the Pope bought the place and gave it back to the duchy of Rome : *annecti precepit in compage,* &c.

official charter.   There is no mention of any military representatives accompanying the Pope to Terni. He and his clergy were alone, and, under these circumstances, a twenty years' truce was concluded with the duchy of Rome.   Again, it was with Pope Stephen II. that Astolphus negotiated, before making war on the Romans.

In keeping with all this is the form by which the inhabitants of the duchy of Rome were introduced to the foreign princes, whose aid was sought.   They were called the " peculiar people (*peculiaris populus*) of St. Peter and the Church." [1]   Apart from any rhetorical exaggeration, this expression seems to be typical of the relations between the Pope and his people.   There was a very strong feeling among the Romans that they must look for help and sympathy in the approaching crisis to the Pope and St. Peter rather than to the distant empire of Constantinople.

Peaceable relations with the latter were now resumed.   Following upon the iconoclastic quarrel, there had been a series of disagreements, one counterbalancing the other, the final effect of which had been to produce a kind of equilibrium. True, the emperor's decision had been opposed, his representatives banished, and his authority reduced to a mere name.   But to have no relations at all with the Romans was surely better than to have disagreeable ones.   The emperor had been obliged to relinquish the Pope's help in his plans for religious reform, but, on the other hand, the imperial treasury had been considerably augmented by the confiscation of the papal patrimonies in Sicily.   The union, in brief, was not dissolved, but there was no longer any intimacy between the parties.   The result made for peace.

[1] Letters from Gregory III. to Charles Martel.

There was even an exchange of amities. Pope Zachary sent envoys with letters to his contemporary, Constantine V., with intent as much personal as ecclesiastical. These letters, unlike the despatches of Gregory III., arrived safely, but the messengers, on reaching Constantinople, found a revolution in full swing. This was brought about by the claims of one Artavasde to the imperial throne. Constantine, the legal heir of Leo the Iconoclast, was himself an iconoclast, while his rival held orthodox views. There ensued a sharp and exciting struggle, in which Constantine hastened to besiege Artavasde in his capital, and finally succeeded in gaining the upper hand, 2nd November 744. The envoys were treading on delicate ground, but as soon as Constantine was reinstated at Constantinople they appeared before him and were graciously received. He acceded to the Pope's request that, to make up for the loss of his Sicilian estates, he should be granted at least the two domains of Norma and Nimfa, in the neighbourhood of Rome. The envoys, after this satisfactory interview, returned home with a substantial present.

• The effect of the iconoclastic struggle upon Italian affairs has been greatly exaggerated. Certainly there were at first a few critical years to be passed through, but, as the imperial power in the north and centre of Italy was practically extinct, its interference in religious affairs was no longer to be dreaded. The necessary declarations had been made by the Popes Gregory II. and Gregory III., and constant reiteration would have been futile. It was no longer an Italian but an Eastern question. The Holy See was particularly involved, not only because all religious matters, however distant, were her peculiar province, but also because the forfeiture of her Sicilian patrimonies and the dividing up of her ecclesiastical department which ensued [1] affected her very deeply. Again, as was shown by the gift of Norma and Nimfa, certain mitigations might be hoped for. After the embittered attitude of the first few years, a new phase of a more or less diplomatic nature had been entered upon. ,

The Roman duchy, in brief, was about to become a self-governing state, nominally subject to the Greek empire, but really attached to it by very loose bonds. Venice and Naples were in the same position. In both places a local autonomy was being organised on the strength of their strong maritime positions. Naples could also rely upon efficient support from the Patrician of Sicily. That island was being organised under a military government, presided over by the local duke.'

These three autonomies contrived to exist for many a long year. That of Naples received its death-blow at the hands of the Norman King Roger in 1139. The other two were much longer lived. As late as 1797 they were attacked by Buonaparte, and again in 1870 by General Cadorna. Indeed, these officers might almost be said to have fired on the Roman empire.

Let us now turn our attention to the duchy of Rome, to its situation at the death of Zachary (752), and to the series of events which, while delivering it out of the hands of the Lombards, yet indirectly strengthened the opposition of the other two.

---

[1] As a matter of fact, these consequences survived the reconciliation of the two Churches. The Byzantines retained Calabria and the Sicilian patrimonies, and the bishoprics of these countries were not restored to the Roman rule till after the Norman conquest.

CHAPTER III

THE SOVEREIGNTY OF THE POPE AND THE FRANKISH INTERVENTION

King Astolphus seizes on Ravenna—He threatens the Roman Duchy—
The Annexation from a Religious Standpoint—Roman National
Attitude Antagonistic to Lombards—Roman Autonomy could only
be organised under the Pope's direction—How the Franks understood the Question.

ASTOLPHUS, who succeeded Ratchis in 749, did not
long leave Ravenna in peace. The exact date of his
seizure of the town is not known, but there is no
doubt that the Exarchate came to a miserable end,
so miserable, indeed, that we have no record of its
last moments. All that we know is that, from the
month of July 751, the Lombard king was established in the Exarchal palace, and that thenceforward
his sway extended over the whole of the ancient
imperial territory between the Po, the Adriatic, and
the Apennines. Even Gubbio, the other side of the
mountains, had succumbed to him, but Perugia, Todi,
Amelia, and the duchy of Rome were not yet captured. Astolphus was meditating a descent on the
latter, when the newly elected Pope, Stephen, despatched ambassadors, who succeeded in bringing
about a peace which was to last for forty years. They
were Ambrose, the chief (*primicerius*) of the notaries,
and the Pope's own brother, Paul. These negotiations took place in June 752, but, by the following
autumn, the treaty was violated. The Pope's biographer does not enlarge upon the fact, and the

Lombard king's reasons for perjuring himself are not given.

Hostilities, however, were not renewed, and Astolphus seems to have contented himself with levying a poll tax of a gold sou on the inhabitants of Rome. He further proposed, greatly to the consternation of the Romans, to extend his jurisdiction over Rome and its dependencies, thus creating a sort of protectorate. The Pope, not thinking it discreet to send any of his own ambassadors to the king a second time, despatched two Lombard subjects, the abbots of Monte Cassino and St. Vincent of Vulturno. These could, of course, represent things from a religious point of view only. They had no effect on Astolphus, who sent them back to their convents, with orders not to return to Rome.

The situation was becoming serious. The Romans and the Pope, preoccupied with the dangers which threatened them at home, naturally did not give much thought to the late Exarchy. At Constantinople, on the other hand, they could not realise the changes that were taking place in Italy, and innocently imagined that a little diplomacy was all that was required in order to insure the return of the annexed provinces. An important dignitary, John the Silentiary, was sent to Rome with one imperial letter for the king of the Lombards; and another to the Pope, invoking his good offices. Stephen, therefore, deputed his brother Paul to support the Silentiary at his interview with Astolphus. The king was then at Ravenna, and, though his reply was somewhat vague, he gave orders that a Lombard ambassador should accompany John back to the emperor. On his way through Rome, the Byzantine envoy acquainted the Pope with the non-success of his errand, and the latter entrusted him with letters explaining the position of affairs once more, and urging the emperor to take definite steps in the matter.

With the approach of winter, the outlook became still more gloomy. The most alarming rumours sprang up and grew apace. Astolphus, it was said, meant to have all the Romans beheaded. The protection of religion was sought. The most sacred mysteries were carried in procession, in particular the great acherophite picture of the Saviour, which is still preserved in the Lateran. The Pope was prolific in prayers, litanies, and exhortations, and a copy of the treaty, broken by the terrible Lombard king, was fastened to the stational cross.

So far, however, Astolphus had confined himself to threats. The only noteworthy event of the war seems to have been the seizure of the Castle of Ceccano, part of the ecclesiastical patrimony. This castle was situated close to the southern frontier, on the side of the duchy of Beneventum, and was a somewhat important centre of agricultural operations. Astolphus was, at this time, awaiting the return of his ambassador from Constantinople, and the seizure of Ceccano was probably due less to his efforts than to those of the duke.

What was to be the result of these negotiations, and what could be expected from the Pope's representations to the emperor of the need for his intervention? Constantine had so much to do at home, that he could not effectually enter into the affairs of these distant provinces. He would probably advise them to get out of their difficulties as best they could. It would not be the first time that this attitude had been adopted towards the Romans. From

the beginning of the Lombard war the Emperor
Tiberius II. had maintained it.

， If the goodwill of the Lombard king could not be
counted on, the only solution of the problem was
either to resign themselves to the annexation, or to
prevent it by calling in the help of the Franks. ，

There was, apparently, no insuperable religious
objection to the annexation. There is certainly no
sign of it, either in the papal correspondence, or in
the other documents of the time. We must not be
misled by the frequent evangelical allusions to the
" lost sheep " (*oves perditæ*) which the Pope, like a
good shepherd, wishes to wrest from the wolf, or, in
other words, the Lombard king. The sheepfold in
question was a political, rather than a religious one,
and there was nothing to fear for the sheep from an
ecclesiastical point of view. The Pope had often to
deplore the Lombard depredations in the Roman
territory, but these were merely the accidents of war,
or psychological means, similar to the bombardments
of modern times. The Lombards, to defend themselves against the Romans, or to effect their surrender, laid waste the country by fire. They followed
the universal custom and plundered, in order to live,
and also to gain some advantage from the war. In
more than one case the havoc made among church
property savoured of sacrilege, but, at that time,
warriors with any respect for ecclesiastical belongings
were few and far between. The followers of Astolphus are accused of having stolen some sacred corpses
from the Catacombs, in order to cherish them in
their monasteries. The theft of relics in the eighth
century and since, has been, all over Christendom, a
very common and readily condoned sin.

These unpleasant occurrences were, however, all

connected with the conditions of war. The ordinary
relations between the Lombards and their Roman
neighbours were by this time again of a tolerably
friendly nature. The Aryan and pagan element
brought into Italy by the Conquest had long been
absorbed. The Lombards were all Catholics, and
had recently proved their faith by helping to defend
Pope Gregory II. against the proceedings of the
Exarchs. Their princes, Liutprand, Ratchis, Aistulf,
and Didier, far from being infidels, were men of
piety, with a taste for founding monasteries and
supporting churches, and full of the deepest respect
for the sanctuaries of Rome and the apostolic See.
The Romans, indeed, would not have lost much,
in passing from the Byzantine to the Lombard rule.
Even as part of the Lombard kingdom, Rome
would have remained a holy city and a living link
with the rest of Christendom. She would still have
been the resort of pilgrims, and the Pope could have
continued his somewhat restricted interest in the
religious affairs of both the East and the West.
Astolphus had his traditional capital at Pavia, and
he had just conquered Ravenna, the capital of the
Exarchs and of the Gothic kings. It was, therefore,
improbable that the seat of government would have
been moved to Rome. From the conditions which
the Lombards wished to impose upon the Romans,
we gather that the latter would in some measure
have retained the power of self-government, under
the protection of their pontiff, and that it would have
been a case of ordinary annexation.

The stumbling-block in the way was that the
Romans in general, and the Pope in particular, did
not wish to be Lombard subjects. They considered
as derogatory any alliance with a people whom they

regarded as barbarians, and who were personally distasteful to them. All kinds of rumours concerning the Lombard inferiority obtained credence. It was said that leprosy flourished among them, that they were malodorous, and so on. Their laws, as well as their manners and customs, were uncongenial to the Romans; the Lombard law was strongly imbued. with German tradition, while the Roman law had been religiously preserved from the tables of stone up to the time of Justinian. Then again, the Lombards and the Romans had quite a different way of dressing, and of wearing their hair and beards. Any change of nationality, such as was bound to accompany an annexation of this kind, would immediately be followed by a modification of these habits. In those days the barber followed closely in the wake of the conqueror and the diplomat. ·

These are but trifles, we say. Truly, but one might go far to seek the Englishman who would not object to wear the pigtail and flowing garb of the Chinese, or the Chinaman who would willingly adopt our national habits. Apart, too, from these material considerations, there was a certain subtle and sacred prestige attached to the mere fact of being a Roman. It was no mean thing, they thought, to be a member of the Holy Republic, and the subject of a man who was, after all, the heir of Augustus and Constantine.

This question of escape from the Lombards was, therefore, a vital one for the Romans of the eighth century. The Pope and the clergy were at one with their compatriots in this matter, fortunately for the maintenance of the ecclesiastical influence. They espoused the cause of the autonomy without any coercion, but from no particular religious feeling in the matter.

`The main point, however, was, not that the autonomy should be established under the protection of any outside monarch, but that its interior organisation should be under the supervision of none other than the Pope himself. ` Although at Naples and Venice the bishop was of some political importance, it was the Byzantine duke who was governor of the little republic. At Rome, too, they had a duke whose title corresponded precisely with that of his Venetian and Neapolitan colleagues. Like them he was, at one and the same time, civil chief and military governor; it was upon him that depended the whole administration and the whole staff of the *Judices*. The whole military body—the *exercitus Romanus*, as it was called—including the aristocratic cavalry, the urban foot soldiers, and the garrisons with their tribunes—all these were under his command. He was undoubtedly a most important personage. But besides the *felicissimus exercitus*, the *venerabilis clerus* was no inconsiderable figure. He, too, had his district organisation, his aristocracy, his *proceres Ecclesiæ*, his deacons, his cardinal priests, his *chefs de service*, and his suburban bishops. This hierarchy culminated in the apostolic Lord, the Vicar of St. Peter, the High Priest of the Roman sanctuaries, the Primate of the bishops of the whole world, and doctor of the Church Universal,[1] *i.e.* a dignitary who, even apart from his religious importance, exercised over Italy a moral and political influence beyond compare. For the Pope to have been subject to the duke as the Venetian Patriarch was subject to the Doge would have been an incongruous and untenable position.`

---

[1] Formula of the Pope's Ordination, in use at that time. See *Origins of Christian Worship*, 3rd edition, p. 363.

As a matter of fact, even at the first, affairs apparently showed not the slightest tendency towards this attitude.   True, the Holy See had come into collision with the Emperor of Constantinople, during the monothelite crisis; again, at the time of the Council in Trullo, and also at the beginning of the iconoclastic struggle.   These were, however, but passing attempts at tyranny, and not the result of regularly organised institutions.   In ordinary practice, the Papal authority certainly tended in the direction of sovereignty, as may be seen from the documentary evidence concerning Gregory II., Gregory III., and Zachary.   We have already seen the latter in his outside transactions, on behalf of the duchy of Rome.   A strong light is shed upon his position at home through a significant remark made by his biographer in speaking of his journey to Ravenna and Pavia.   He set out, it is said, "leaving the government of Rome to Stephen, patrician and duke."   The duke is governor, during the absence of the Pope !   It is not thus that one could have spoken of either the Doge of Venice or the Duke of Naples.

The natural and traditional trend of affairs pointed, then, towards the solution required by the pontifical dignity ; and, it may be added, this solution was the only acceptable and imaginable one for the Frankish princes, with whom explanations were to ensue.

It was not the first occasion upon which the Romans had thought of invoking the help of the Franks.   At the instigation of the emperor and the Exarch, the Austrasian Franks had made several descents on Italy, during the reign of King Autharis.   Pope Pelagius II. was careful to explain to King Gontran that, as the Franks were Catholics like the Romans, they ought to look upon the Lombards as their common enemy, instead of entering into an alliance with them. St. Gregory, in his correspondence with the heirs of Gontran and Childebert, refrains from this attitude. Besides, in his day, the empire had left off inciting fresh Frankish incursions into Italy, having found them expensive and unprofitable. There was still stronger | reason for discouraging them in the eighth century, when Liutprand's victories were threatening the safety of Ravenna and the Exarchy. Charles Martel and Pepin were, on the whole, fairly well disposed towards the Lombard king, and recked little of his disputes with the Greeks. This political archæology affected them not at all.

But the interests of the Roman ex-empire and of the apostolic sanctuary were quite another matter. This was obvious to everybody in France and in Rome. As Christian princes, the Frankish monarchs felt bound to listen to the common Father of the Faithful, and to support him in time of need. To neglect what appeared to them a pressing necessity would be to incur serious personal risks. St. Peter is the chief of the apostles, and he is also the doorkeeper of Heaven. Present-day politicians are not greatly affected by this fact, but it was weighty enough to give food for reflection to a Carlovingian prince, and even to influence his politics.

We get an excellent idea of this state of mind from the History written by the Venerable Bede, a renowned writer of that period.

The English King Oswy (664) had been summoned to arbitrate in a great religious discussion,

which affected the organisation and general progress of his people. The subject of dispute was the
Easter offertory. The Irish party, on the one hand,
laid stress on the patronage of their great Saint,
Columba, while the Romans pinned their faith on
the Apostle Peter. They had gone as far as quoting
the celebrated Gospel passage: "Thou art Peter
. . . I will give unto thee the keys of the kingdom
of heaven," when the king stopped the discussion,
and asked the Irish if they admitted that these words
had been addressed to St. Peter. On their replying
in the affirmative, he remarked, " Well, then, he is a
doorkeeper with whom I should not like to have
dealings; for on my arrival at the portals of heaven,
if I happened to be in bad odour with the keeper of
the keys, he would very likely shut the doors upon
me!".

Bede was only half English, and we may perhaps
allow something for his somewhat humorous way of
looking at things. The Pope's letters to Charles
Martel and Pepin, though written in a different style,
breathe the same spirit: " Let us work for St. Peter,
and then we shall prosper in this world, as well as
the next."

It was not to be supposed that the Franks would
risk a quarrel with the Lombards, with the object of
procuring for the Romans the pleasure of remaining
under Byzantine rule, and of enabling the military
staff of the Palatine to enjoy this advantage in peace.
The conditions of the Frankish intervention would
obviously be as follows: The Lombards should leave
the Roman territory alone; the Romans should be
under the protection of the Franks, instead of under
the now enfeebled imperial power; in dealing with
the Greek monarch, everything inconsistent with the

new relations should be suppressed; and, finally, the Pope should be supreme at Rome and in the duchy.

But " there is many a slip 'twixt the cup and the lip," and what Gregory III. had proposed, Charles Martel had refused. It is true that the danger was not as imminent as the Pope imagined, and the Frankish prince had good reasons for not interfering. Nevertheless, the pontiff's proposal had created a great sensation, and the chronicler who succeeded Fredegarius and wrote under the direction of Childebrand, brother of Charles Martel, speaks of it with visible pride and pomp. This is all the more striking because, like his patrons, he usually displayed but a mild interest in the affairs of the Church.

Though Pope Zachary was constantly brought into contact with Pepin and Carloman, either personally or through the medium of St. Boniface, it was always in connection with ecclesiastical affairs in France, the mission to Germany, and internal reform. There had never been any question of the Lombards and their quarrels with the Romans. The Pope was quite capable of managing Italian affairs, without any help from the Franks. Indeed, it was the Franks who required his advice and assistance in their political affairs; and not until the papal sanction was obtained did they take the important step of substituting the family of Austrasian parvenus for the ancient royal race. ·

From this fact we see the majesty of the position held by the Roman pontiff in relation to the Franks. As far as the new dynasty was particularly concerned, it was a service of no importance. It was still quite recent when the turn of events compelled Pope Stephen II. to avail himself of it.

CHAPTER IV

STEPHEN II

The Pope's journey to Pavia and to France—Interview at Ponthion—
Negotiations concerning Rome and Ravenna—Dignity of Patrician
Order bestowed on Frankish Kings—Attempts at Conciliation—
Assemblies at Braisne and Kierzy—Pepin in Italy—Peace signed
and then broken—Astolphus besieges Rome—Pepin's second expe-
dition—Gift of the Exarchy and Pentapolis—Death of Astolphus—
Negotiations with Didier.[1]

THE Pope had not been idle during the winter of
752–753. After a long period of consideration, the
time for action had arrived, and Stephen began
negotiations with the Frankish king. Everything
was carried on with the greatest secrecy, a peasant
acting as the medium of communication between
the two parties. The first letters have been lost,
but from the account in the *Liber Pontificalis* we
gather that it was purely a question of the Roman
province and its escape from the Lombard yoke.
Pepin appeared well-disposed, and despatched without delay, one after the other, two confidential
messengers—Oroctigang, Abbot of Jumièges, and
another of his intimates. They soon returned to

[1] Documents are scarce; there are none of Byzantine or Lombard origin; on the Roman side we have the Life of Stephen II.
in the *Liber Pontificalis,* and this is our best source of information, as
the writer seems to have accompanied the Pope to France. There
are also two letters from Stephen II. addressed in 753 to Pepin
and to the Frankish dukes. On the Frankish side, the successor
of Fredegarius is about our only informant. In common justice,
we must remember that it is the winning side from whom we hear
most, and that the others have not a fair chance of stating their
case.

France with a verbal message, requesting Pepin to send a reliable escort through the Lombard kingdom for the Pope, who was anxious to come to France. Two letters, conveyed by the Abbot of Jumièges, were inserted in the *Codex Carolinus;* they are couched in very general terms, and merely call upon the Frankish leaders to aid in furthering the interests of the Apostle Peter.

Pepin, rising to the occasion, sent off two august persons—Chrodegang, Bishop of Metz, and Duke Autchaire, the Oger of legendary fame. On their arrival at Rome, they found Stephen quite ready to set out. The Lombard ambassador and the Silentiary John had returned from Constantinople, with orders for a personal interview between the Pope and Astolphus, to arrange about the restoration of Ravenna. Stephen had already obtained a permit for a journey to Pavia, so his way was clear before him. There was a public leave-taking at St. Peter's attended by many of the neighbouring citizens, as well as by the Pope's own people. The whole caravan set out together on 14th October 753. The papal retinue included representatives of the military aristocracy, *ex militiæ optimatibus,* a certain number of clerks of high degree, the two Frankish envoys, and the imperial legate.

Autchaire, going on in front, was the first to arrive at Pavia. Astolphus, when he heard of the Pope's approach, sent to meet him, begging that he would refrain from any allusion to the Exarchy and the other imperial possessions (*reipublicæ loca*) which he or his predecessors had conquered. The Pope, emboldened by the presence of the Frankish envoys, declared that he would not comply with this request. The Lombard king was beset on all sides ; the Pope, aided by tears and presents, addressed him on the subject. The imperial legate and the emperor himself (by means of his letters) also said their say. All in vain was Astolphus warmly exhorted to "give back the Lord's sheep which he had carried off, and the estates, to their owners," *ut dominicas quas abstulerat redderet oves et propria propriis restitueret.* He remained obdurate, and would concede nothing.

In this affair Stephen II. was acting in the interests of the empire and as a subject of the emperor, under whose commands he had gone to Pavia. But, however great may have been his zeal for the Exarchy, there can be no doubt that his keenest sympathies were centred in the duchy of Rome. This fact is beyond question, although his biographer abstains from mentioning it. At Pavia the Pope was playing two rôles. The one, which was perfunctory and lacking in confidence, was that of the imperial representative, demanding the restitution of Ravenna. The other, whole-hearted and sanguine, was that of the Roman pontiff, whose desire was to secure the independence of his fellow-citizens with regard to the Lombards, and his own independence with regard to his fellow-citizens.

Having thus disposed of the question of Ravenna, the Pope, without more ado, begged permission to enter France. Astolphus did his best to deter him, but was overcome by the united representations of the pontiff and the Frankish ambassadors.

Stephen's presence in France did not require the presence of the lay aristocracy, still less of a Byzantine diplomat. The latter, therefore, returned to Rome under the escort of the *optimates militiæ*, the clerks alone remained with the Pope. They started forth on 15th November, and soon arrived at the entrance to the Aosta valley (*Francorum clusas*); they were then on Frankish ground, and the Pope, beginning to breathe more freely, offered up thanks to God. Their journey was nearly ended, for the king had promised to meet them at the Abbey of St. Maurice, just on the other side of the St. Bernard pass. Their hearts were filled with a great joy, for they were conscious of the fulfilment of a grand task—the salvation of Rome : *in Roma salvanda petebant regno Francorum*,[1] says the crude epitaph of Dean Ambrose, one of the party. He died at St. Maurice, the toils of the journey, which, for him, was not the first, having proved too much for him.

When they arrived at the abbey they found that Pepin had not come to meet them, but had sent in his stead two ambassadors, Duke Rotard, and Fulrad, Abbot of St. Denis, who were to conduct the party to the royal palace of Ponthion. Near Langres, about a hundred miles from the palace, they encountered one of the king's sons—Charles, the future Charlemagne. Within three miles of the royal residence, on the Feast of the Epiphany, appeared Pepin himself, together with his family. He greeted the Pope with much ceremony, getting off his horse and prostrating himself on the ground. Then, taking hold of the stirrup, he walked for some time by the side of the pontiff's horse. This is the oldest example of that *officium stratoris* which later on became compulsion, and thus gave rise to severe quarrels. To the accompaniment of psalms and chanting the procession continued its way, and at last reached the palace of Ponthion. At the first official interview, which took place in the palace oratory, the Pope with tears besought the king to

[1] *Liber Pontificalis*, t. i. p. 458.

intervene "peacefully in order to arrange the affairs of St. Peter and the Roman Republic," *ut causam beati Petri et*[1] *reipublicæ Romanorum disponeret.* The king promised to satisfy the Pope, and in due season to procure the restoration of the Exarchy and the rights or possessions of the republic, *ut illi placitum fuerit exarchatum Ravennæ et reipublicæ jura seu loca reddere.*

So far we have followed the account of the *Liber Pontificalis.* But the French chroniclers are also well worth consulting. From the *Moissac* chronicle we learn that the Pope's entreaties were environed with a good deal of pomp and circumstance. The pontiff and his clerks, clothed in sackcloth and ashes, cast themselves on the ground, imploring the mercy of God, and calling to witness the blessed Apostles Peter and Paul. Nor could they be prevailed upon to rise until Pepin, his sons and his nobles, had extended their hands in token of cooperation and deliverance.

From the biographer we get a different impression, but it is probable that his statements are not altogether reliable. He passes lightly over these doleful formalities, calling attention to the prostrations of the king rather than to those of the Pope. In his anxiety to give prominence to Ravenna, it is to be feared that he takes a somewhat distorted view of Stephen's claims. Probability and the quasi-official chronicler of Moissac alike incline us to believe that it was Rome, and not Ravenna, which was the leading theme of this interview.

It is, however, not to be denied that, in his conference with the Frankish king, Stephen either claimed or accepted what is called the "restitution"

---

[1] The *et* is doubtful.

of Ravenna, together with the Exarchy, Pentapolis, and other territories conquered by Astolphus. This "restitution" was, in fact, brought about, or at least agreed upon, after Pepin's first Italian campaign. But they did not restore *propria propriis*, for neither the duchy of Rome nor the Roman Church had the slightest claim to be regarded as holding any right of sovereignty over these provinces. The Emperor Constantine alone could claim this right, and he alone could be made the "subject" of a "restitution" in the strict sense of the term. Stephen's biographer treats the matter in a way which reveals his anxiety to gloss over anything at all questionable in the manner of the Pope's succession to the emperor. This attitude was also maintained among the pontifical officials.

From our own point of view, as well as from that of the Franks, the right was unquestionable, being founded upon the basis of conquest. Astolphus had conquered the imperial provinces, and they belonged to him in the same way as Liguria, Friuli, and the duchies of Spoleto and Beneventum. But Pepin had conquered Astolphus, and could impose upon him what conditions he chose, one of these conditions being the surrender of the provinces in question. They were thus the legitimate property of the Frankish king, who presented them to the Pope, or rather to St. Peter, for this patron saint was considered capable of owning and governing them by means of his Church and his successors.

All this is obvious enough. If the Roman chroniclers have given us confused accounts of the affair, it is for two reasons. To begin with, they found it hard to divest themselves of the notion that any part of Italy which did not belong to the

Lombards must somehow or other be the property of the Romans. Their expression "*respublica*"[1] is a most unsuitable one, for it ought to be applied only to a definite state, governed directly by the Roman emperor. As a matter of fact, it is applied to the various conditions of the Roman nationality, whatever their link with the imperial power. In the pontifical world, on the other hand, there was a strong and pardonable objection to admit any responsibility for a disloyalty to the empire, exacted by circumstances; for Rome apart from the Roman empire; Rome ceasing to be Rome; this was indeed a political profanation. And yet there seemed no way of escape. Now, if ever, was the time to call upon the resources of literary style to deaden the compunction awakened in the national conscience by this violation of all loyal tradition.

The idea of St. Peter as sovereign of the Exarchy naturally presupposes that he was sovereign of Rome; for he who rules over the affairs of others may, not unreasonably, be expected to rule over his own as well. As far as the Carlovingian princes were concerned, at least, the papal dominion over Rome seems to have been accepted as an incontrovertible fact. At any rate they never sought to interfere (in early times at least) either with his position at

---

[1] This term is also employed by the successor of Fredegarius in expressions concerning the misdeeds of Astolphus : *quod nequiter contra rempublicam et sedem Romanam apostolicam admiserat . . . quicquid contra Romanam ecclesiam vel sedem apostolicam contra legis ordinem fecerat . . . ulterius ad sedem apostolicam Romanam et rempublicam hostiliter numquam accederet.*" There is no reason to suppose that the chronicler was referring particularly to the Exarchy of Ravenna. His interests centre on the Pope and the Holy See, and though whatever there may be of "*respublica*" around the apostolic throne is mentioned at the same time, it is in an indefinite manner, which points to lack of any great interest.

home or with his relations with Constantinople. They seem to have contented themselves with promising him their protection and assuring him of their good will in the most general terms, relying in return on his friendship, and leaving him to do the best he could for the papal prosperity. To assert that Pepin recognised the duchy of Rome as an independent state is rash, for we have no proof, not even an indirect one, that such was the case. Pepin always kept on good terms with the empire, and although he and his sons were honoured by the Pope with the title of "*patricius Romanorum*," he never made use of it in his documents. Neither does his chronicler, the successor of Fredegarius, ever invest him with it.[1]

On the other hand, in the documents which emanate from Rome, whether drawn up in the name of the Pope or of others, the title is always used.[2] There has been much discussion as to its origin and meaning. In the empire the title of "patrician" was merely an empty distinction, and had been borne by exarchs, dukes, and strategists. In France it was bestowed on the governors of Provence, *e.g.* Mummolus and Dynamius in the sixth century, and Abbon in the eighth. But the title in question is not that of "patrician" in general, but of "Patrician of the Romans," for the word *Romanorum* is never

---

[1] The title is used in the *Clausula de Pippino*, which is a private document.

[2] It must, however, be remarked that the biographer of Stephen II. makes no mention of it. In the life of the next Pope, Paul, a dead silence is maintained on the subject of the Franks and their prince. This is evidently intentional, for they would have naturally been referred to in the account of the translation of Saint Petronilla. To the author of this life, the Greek Emperors Constantine V. and Leo IV. are paramount, and the title of "patrician" only appears in the life of Stephen III.

absent. Later on, after the year 744, Charlemagne
made use of it in addition to his former titles of *rex
Francorum* and *rex Langobardorum*, which all served
as an expression of his rights over the Franks, the
Lombards, and the Romans—the Romans of the
Pope, be it understood, not the others.   It is evident,
then, that the term *patricius Romanorum* was of
Roman rather than of imperial origin.

It seems extremely probable, if we may venture to
say so, that the title was given by Stephen to the
Frankish princes, first of all as an expression of their
protectorships over the new order of things in
general ; and secondly, to avoid reviving the Exarch
at Ravenna, and to maintain the duke at Rome.
In fact, after the year 754, there is no mention of
the *Duke of Rome;* there are *dukes* of Rome, in the
plural, the title being used in either an administrative
or a military sense ; but the δοὺξ 'Ρώμης no longer
existed.   With these two exceptions all the former
offices are preserved, and it must be noted that the
patriciate had been conferred on the holders of both
the extinct titles.   The Pope could henceforth dispense with Exarch and duke ; and, in order to re-
press any inconvenient desire for reassertion on their
part, he did his best to replace them by a *patricius
Romanorum*, whose influence, though remote, was
rendered important by the spell of his power and the
memory of services rendered in past days.

Before speeding the Pope on his homeward way,
Pepin was anxious to form some idea of the direction
affairs would take, as a result of their amicable interview.   Besides, the time of year was not suitable for
a long journey, especially in the case of a venerable
old man.   The king, therefore, established his guest
at the Abbey of St. Denis, taking advantage of the

occasion to confirm his title to the crown by a second coronation ceremony, which included not only himself, but his wife and sons. Soon afterwards, the Pope, worn out by travelling, and tried by the rigours of the winter, fell so seriously ill that his life was despaired of. He recovered, nevertheless —an event which was attributed by the monks to the influence of their patron saint.[1]

Meanwhile, the negotiations were proceeding. In vain did Pepin's ambassadors surround the Lombard king with incessant and urgent petitions. Stephen's biographer tells us that they had been sent *propter pacis fœdera et proprietatis sanctœ Dei ecclesiœ reipublicœ restituenda jura.* This curious expression, which is employed several times in these accounts, seems to contain incongruous elements. We get a much more coherent account from Fredegarius's successor, who asserts that Pepin requested Astolphus to avoid any display of enmity to Rome (*in partibus Romœ*) out of respect for the Apostles Peter and Paul, and for his (Pepin's) sake, to abstain from unaccustomed impositions. History does not relate the Lombard king's reasons for refusing, but we know that he despatched to France an ambassador of sacred calling—no less a person than Pepin's own brother, Carloman, formerly king of the eastern part of the Frankish empire, and at that time a monk of Monte Cassino. This reverend personage proved as unsuccessful with the Pope and the Frankish king as the latter's envoys had been with Astolphus. Indeed, Italy saw him no more, for the Frankish authorities considered that he would more worthily fulfil his vocation in their own territory, and established him

---

[1] The *Liber Pontificalis* does not mention the intervention of St. Denis.

in a convent at Vienna, where he soon afterwards
died.

A great national convocation was held on 1st
March 754 at Braisne, and another at Easter (14th
April) at Kiersy-sur-Oise. It was decided, though
not unanimously,[1] to make war upon Astolphus, and
force him to yield to the Pope's demands. One
last fruitless appeal was made to him, when the
Frankish army was already on the way to Italy.
The united letters of Pepin and the Pope produced
no effect. The Frankish army continued its way
towards the Mont Cenis pass. On both sides the
passes were in Frankish territory, and the somewhat
feebly garrisoned valley of the Susa was reinforced
in order to prevent the Lombards from taking possession. Astolphus made his appearance before he was
expected, but the Frankish vanguard presented such
a good front that the Lombards, in alarm and dis-
order, fled back towards their capital. Pepin, followed
at no great distance by the Pope, calmly crossed the
Alps and laid siege to Pavia.

Astolphus, utterly defeated, was obliged by
solemn treaty[2] to deliver up Ravenna and the other
conquered provinces ; he even agreed to yield Narni,
a town in the north of the duchy, which had been
seized by Liutprand. Pepin was quite satisfied,
and gave no heed to Stephen II., who, having
some reason to distrust the Lombard king, would
have preferred a more reliable guarantee of good
faith, and wanted the Frankish king to insist on

---

[1] Eginhard is responsible for this statement. (*Vita Karoli* 6 :)
*Stephano papa supplicante, cum magna difficultate (bellum) susceptum est.
Quin quidam e primaribus Francorum, cum quibus consultare solebat,
adeo voluntati eius renisi sunt ut se regem deserturos domumque redituros
libera voce proclamarent.*

[2] *L. P.*, vol. i. p. 403.

the immediate restoration of the provinces in question.[1]

Pepin provided the Pope with the escort of his brother Jerome,[2] and other persons of consequence, as far as Rome, which he entered at the end of October 754. The clergy and the people[3] welcomed him with open arms, and thanks were rendered to God for His great mercies.

These rejoicings were but of brief duration. Astolphus, plausible enough, had allowed the Frankish army to return home, and even began to carry out his promise of restoring Narni. But no sooner was Pepin at a safe distance than the faithless monarch absolutely refused any further concessions, and actually resumed his former plundering expeditions in the country round Rome. The Pope wrote two letters[4] of complaint to Pepin; one was entrusted to Wilchar, Bishop of Nomentum, and the other to Abbot Fulrad, who had possibly been one of the return escort. Meanwhile Astolphus, no longer concealing his animosity, prepared to invade the duchy of Rome. On 1st January 756 there arrived at Rome itself three military divisions. The first, which came from Tuscany, established itself before the gates of St. Pancratius; the second, with the king at its head, passed over the left bank of the Tiber, and threatened the gate of Salaria; while the third, which hailed from the duchy of Beneventum, blockaded the gates of the Lateran and St. Paul's. The surrounding country was ravaged and laid waste in a pitiless manner. The

---

[1] Reference is often made to these representations of the Pope in the letters of Stephen II.; Jaffé, 2322, 2323, &c.

[2] One of the numerous illegitimate children of Charles Martel.

[3] The biography speaks only of the military aristocracy.

[4] J., 2322, 2323.

troops pressed closely around the city, but the Pope continued to smuggle out fresh ambassadors, who proceeded by sea to France, to seek help from Pepin. These were George, Bishop of Ostia, Thomaricus and Comita, two Roman nobles, and one of Pepin's own legates, a Frankish abbot named Warneharius. This latter had taken part in the Roman defence, wearing a suit of armour over his monastic habit, and mounting guard in the ramparts. Three letters [1] were entrusted to these messengers; the first in the name of the Pope alone; the second in the name of the Pope, the suburban bishops, the Priests, Deacons, Dukes, Registrars, Counts, Tribunes, the whole people, and the army. This was of the same import as the first, and was addressed not only to Pepin, but also to his two sons, and to all the Bishops, Abbots, Priests, Monks, Dukes, Counts, and the whole Frankish army. The third is addressed to the same persons as the foregoing, but it is supposed to be written by the Apostle Peter: *Ego Petrus apostolus.* It contains, in this strange form, the ingenuous expression of the idea likely to prove most effective: the Prince of the Apostles, the doorkeeper of heaven, was threatened in his sanctuary; to come to his assistance was a sacred duty, and those who responded to the call would have special claims on his gratitude and patronage.

These cries of distress were heard. The Frankish army again turned towards Mont Cenis, and Rome was immediately set free. The Franks and the Lombards engaged in deadly warfare, and the vanquished Astolphus was driven to take refuge once more in Pavia. Meanwhile, John the Silentiary reappeared at Rome, in company with another worthy,

[1] J., 2325, 2326, 2327.

the great secretary George (*proto a secreta*). They were entrusted with a mission to the Frankish king, and the Pope provided them with a confidential escort as far as Marseilles. On arriving there, however, they found that Pepin was already in Italy. The Byzantine diplomats, much perturbed at this discovery, made arrangements to detain the papal delegate at Marseilles, while George hastened to Pepin, whom he found in the neighbourhood of Pavia. His entreaties that Ravenna, the Exarchy, and the other contested cities should be restored to the imperial government (*imperiali concederet ditioni*)[1] were fruitless. Pepin protested that he had only undertaken the campaign out of love for St. Peter, and to gain the remission of his sins, and that no amount of bribery could have any effect on him. Thus dismissed, the crestfallen envoy returned to Rome, on his way to Constantinople.

Astolphus soon found himself obliged to enter into a treaty, the terms of which were rather more stringent than the first time. Comacchio was added to the list of territories to be yielded, and Pepin not only imposed a heavy war tax, but revived the tribute which the Lombard kings had in former times paid to the Franks.

To ensure the proper carrying out of this compact, the Abbot Fulrad, who had stayed behind in Italy with a military detachment, made a tour of the towns with the Lombard commissioners, everywhere

---

[1] The biographer uses this term in quite a different sense from the word *respublica* which, up to the end of the life of Stephen II., he employs, under circumstances in which it obviously cannot be applied to a country in submission to the empire. Thus Didier promises, in 757, to give back *reipublicæ*, the cities conquered by Liutprand; Pope Stephen, who died during the course of this transaction, ended *rempublicam dilatans*.

demanding the delivering up of the city keys, hostages and delegates from the aristocracy. Then, together with these representatives of the conquered territory, he proceeded to Rome, and deposited in the Confession at St. Peter's, not only the keys of the towns, but the deed by which King Pepin made them over to the Apostle, to his Vicar, and to all his successors.

The exact wording of this deed of gift is no longer preserved to us, but in the life of Stephen II. we have the list of territories given up to the Holy See. They include, first of all, Comacchio and Ravenna, and then the tract of land between the Apennines and the sea, from Forli in the north as far as Jesi Sinigaglia in the south. There is no mention of Ancona and the remains of what was known later as the Marches, nor of Faenza, Imola, Bologna, and Ferrara. The papal State had still therefore much to acquire north of the Apennines. To the south of the chain, Eugubium (Gubbio) alone appears to be included. Perugia, which was a near neighbour, still belonged to the Romans.

With the exception of Narni, which had formerly been annexed by the duchy of Spoleto, and which was restored in 756, the Lombard king's "restitutions" were what he himself had seized. Rome, though at first satisfied, had not forgotten the time when these provinces had other limits. It was hardly thirty years since the annexation of Bologna in the north and Osimo in the south, and now the Romans began to consider the possibility of recapturing Liutprand's conquests in the same way as those of Astolphus. They had not long to wait for their opportunity. Only a few months after the departure of the Frankish army, Astolphus met his death

through a hunting accident. There was great rejoicing among the Romans, who thought they saw
the hand of Providence in the fact of the king's
dying only a year after his last expedition. To make
matters still more cheerful, the possession of the
throne was disputed by two rivals, neither of them
very formidable. They were Desiderius, Duke of
Tuscany, and Ratchis, brother of the former king,
and at that time a monk of Monte Cassino. Desiderius intimated his willingness to acquiesce in all
the Pope's wishes, so Stephen sent him a deputation,
consisting of his own brother Paul and the Councillor
Christopher, together with the Abbot Fulrad. Desiderius promised to restore to the "republic" the
cities which were lacking, *civitates quae remanserant*,
i.e., Faenza, Imola, and Ferrara, to the west of the
Exarchy, and Ancona, Osimo, and Umana to the
east of Pentapolis. An agreement was signed under
Fulrad's supervision, and, with a little persuasion,
Desiderius promised to give up Bologna as well.

Stephen was beside himself with delight, and
poured forth his soul in a letter to Pepin written
in March or April 757. Thanks to the Frankish
protection and Fulrad's vigorous action, the Pope
already looked upon himself as the sovereign dis-
poser of Italy. Desiderius, the new king, begged
his good offices in recommending him to the favour
of the Frankish monarch. The inhabitants of the
duchy of Spoleto, who had just elected a new duke,
and even those of the duchy of Beneventum, approached him with the same end in view. We may
add that the Dukes of Spoleto and Beneventum were,
in theory at all events, officially connected with the
Lombard kingdom.

The Byzantine empire, however, did not join its

note to this chorus. It was no longer in a position, as in Zachary's time, to benefit by the diplomatic successes of the Holy See, which, by the way, were not as complete as they had hoped. It was for the Pope to yield first. He sent one of his priests, Stephen, to Ratchis, exhorting him to go back to his monastic life. The Abbot Fulrad sallied forth at the head of his Frankish troops to support the eloquence of the legate. The Roman army was ready to follow him. Ratchis did as he was bidden, and Desiderius was proclaimed king of the Lombards.

The situation once conquered, he appeared in no hurry to divide up his kingdom. It is true that Faenza and Ferrara [1] were restored to the Exarchy, but as far as Pentapolis was concerned, no change took place.

[1] With the two little towns of Bagnacavallo (*Castrum Tiberiacum*) and Gabello, the former between Faenza and Ravenna, the latter in the lagoons of Adria.

CHAPTER V

PAUL

Monumental Souvenirs—The Chapel of St. Petronilla—The Monastery of the Via Lata—The Abbey of Nonantola—Relations between the Pope, the Frankish King, the Lombard King, and the Greek Empire.

POPE STEPHEN was, however, spared this disillusionment, for soon after the accession of Desiderius, on 26th April 757, he was gathered to his fathers. He was immediately succeeded by his brother, the deacon Paul, in spite of opposition from a section who desired the appointment of the Archdeacon Theophylact. These two brother Popes, under whose auspices the temporal power began to rise, were members of an aristocratic family who dwelt at the end of the Via Lata, the rich quarter of that time. Paul turned the paternal mansion into a monastery, so that they were, in all probability, the last of their race.

We must here make mention of the religious monuments which, at Rome and elsewhere, consecrate the memory of many events of this time. One of the most important of these is the Chapel of St. Petronilla.[1] In the cemetery of the Ardeatine way at Rome, the tomb of St. Petronilla[2] was venerated, who, according to the fabulous records

[1] For further details on this subject see De Rossi, *Bullettino*, 1878, 1879.

[2] There seems to have been a kind of revival of the worship of St. Petronilla in the eighth century. Pope Gregory III. (*L. P.*, i. p. 420), established a yearly " station," to be celebrated in the cemetery of the Ardeatine way.

of the saints Néreus and Achilles, was considered to be the daughter of St. Peter. Pepin, whose interest in this cult had been by some means aroused during Stephen's stay in France, requested that the body of the saint should be removed to the Vatican, near to the tomb of her putative father. For her resting-place was chosen one of two circular mausoleums, constructed in the fifth century for the Theodosian family; the first, which had probably never been used for purposes of interment, had been dedicated to St. Andrew by Pope Symmachus (498–514), while the other became the temple of the saint beloved by the Franks. The necessary alterations were speedily completed, and on 8th October 757, the Pontiff Paul presided over the removal of the remains. Not long after, Rome became possessed of an important memento of the Carlovingian family, which was solemnly deposited by the Pope in the new sanctuary. It was nothing less than the sabanum[1] of Gisèle, Pepin's baby daughter, to whom Paul had accepted the office of god-father. Thenceforward in his correspondence with the Franks, Paul always styles himself the " compère " (or fellow-father) of King Pepin. His brother Stephen, before him, had made use of the same title, though in his case it was probably an empty one, for there is no record of any children being born to Pepin during the preceding years.

Thus, through these family ties, represented by Petronilla and Gisèle, a close union was brought about between the Frankish princes and the heads of the Church—St. Peter and his successors. In

---

[1] *i.e.* the linen cloth in which the child was wrapped after her baptism.

this connection we must also mention St. Sylvester and St. Denis.

In the imposing legend of St. Sylvester, which dates from the fifth century, the vivid Eastern imagination had symbolised the remarkable effect produced on the world by the conversion of Constantine. One of the most prominent topographical features of this old story was Mount Soracte. This beautiful mountain, which towers over the course of the Tiber and Roman Tuscia, had, from early times, been the haunt of monastic colonies. In the eighth century the highest peak was crowned with a church dedicated to St. Sylvester, and lower down were three other convents in connection with the superior monastery. This was at one time the abode of Pepin's brother, Carloman, who had resigned his temporal position. The monastery and all its dependencies had been presented to him by Pope Zachary. Later on, however, Paul made over the rights of the property to Pepin, who immediately assigned it to the Roman Church.

Paul proceeded to affiliate this royal gift to the monastic foundation which he had just established in his paternal mansion in the Via Lata. He named it in honour of the two saints, Stephen and Sylvester. The former was a third century Pope, who had left his mark on the legendary lore of the time, and with whose name were bound up memories of Stephen II., formerly joint owner of the estate to be consecrated. His remains were taken from the catacombs; those of St. Sylvester were brought from his basilica in the Salarian way, and those two sainted Popes were installed in the interior church of the monastery. The convents of Soracte, St. Sylvester, and others, were annexed to the monastery in the Via Lata. Furthermore, the larger of the two churches of which the monastery boasted, the external basilica, to which the public had access, was dedicated to St. Denis of Paris.[1]

This was evidently to commemorate the Pope's visit to the royal abbey of St. Denis, whose abbot was distinguished by a burning enthusiasm for the Holy See. Pepin, Carloman, Stephen II., Fulrad, and all the other prominent names of latter years were to be found there under the rival protection of the saints of Rome and of Paris. The Via Lata monastery might, indeed, be called a memorial of the foundation of the early Roman State.

But that St. Sylvester did not confine his patronage to memorials of this kind will be seen from the following. King Astolphus had married the daughter of one of the principal Lombard dukes Anselm. This latter, like his contemporaries, Hunald of Aquitaine, Carloman of France, and Ratchis of Italy, had devoted himself to a monastic life, and his royal son-in-law bestowed on him a large estate to the north of Modena, in the district of Nonantola, as the site for a monastery. This was in 751, shortly after the capture of Ravenna. The following years (752 and 753) when the relations between Astolphus and the Pope were already somewhat strained, the Bishop of Reggio first, and then the Archbishop of Ravenna, proceeded to consecrate the churches and oratories. The monastery had not long been established when the Lombard king undertook his expedition against Rome. The Abbot Anselm followed his king as far as the walls of the holy city, and though there is no

---

[1] In connection with this name, see my *Mémoire, St. Denis in Via Lata*, in the *Mélanges* of the *École de Rome*, t. xx. p. 317.

evidence that he actually engaged in fighting as did such other well-known monks as Hunald [1] and Warneharius, there is no doubt that he received his share of the spoils. Among the treasures that he brought away from Rome was the body of St. Sylvester. Now, as this holy relic was preserved in a church in the Salarian way, just where the Lombard army had taken up its position, its removal to Nonantola may safely be reckoned among those depredations condemned as sacrilegious by the biographer of Stephen II. The idea that it may have been a gift from the pontiff is scarcely worth entertaining. The monks, later on, tried to gloss over the misdeed by manufacturing letters of transfer, very difficult to reconcile with the foundation of St. Sylvester in the Via Lata.[2]

This is no place in which to investigate the authenticity of the relics claimed by the two convents. It is of no great moment whether the Lombards or the Romans were mistaken as to the tomb, or whether an unequal division was the result of a theft on the one hand, or of a pious appropriation on the other. The point to be accentuated is that the Abbey of Nonantola and its local worship of St. Sylvester, perpetuated in the Lombard district, and in an essentially Lombard style, the memory of the Roman crisis of 756, and the beginnings of the temporal power.

No sooner was Paul elected than, without waiting to be ordained, he announced to Pepin the facts of his brother's death and of his own succession, assuring

[1] See *L. P.*, t. i. p. ccxxvii.
[2] On this question, see the Memoirs of P. Bortolotti, *Antica vita di S. Anselmo,* Modena, 1892.

him at the same time of his readiness to carry out faithfully the engagements made by his predecessor. A Frankish envoy, Immo by name, had just arrived at Rome, and he was detained by the Pope, in order that he might attend the ordination ceremony. A few weeks later letters arrived from France; one of them was addressed to the aristocracy and the lay population, and urgently enjoined loyalty to the new Pope.[1]

We will come back later to a consideration of home affairs. Outside, serious transactions were taking place. The Pope continued to clamour for the towns that Desiderius had promised, but the Lombard king was by no means eager to respond. His reluctance was undoubtedly intensified by Paul's curious interference in the affairs of Spoleto and Beneventum. In demanding the Frankish protection for these two duchies, the Holy See was encroaching upon the political domain of the Lombard kingdom. It was going back twenty years to the schemes of Gregory III., afterwards abandoned by Zachary,[2] under the pressure of circumstances.

Obviously it was not for Pepin to follow the Pope's example, and involve himself in these perilous political affairs. He must have thought it odd that Paul should have enlisted himself on the side of the Dukes of Aquitaine and Bavaria, who were continually in rebellion against the central power of the Frankish kingdom. He, therefore, refused the protectorship, and gave no support to the Romans in their increased claims upon the Exarchy and Pentapolis. Desiderius imagined that he had a free hand in the matter, and

---

[1] See the answer to this letter in the *Codex Carolinus*, No. 13 (JAFFÉ).

[2] See *L. P.*, vol. i. p. 426.

began operations by starting forth to quell the rebellious dukes. In order to reach them he had to pass through Pentapolis, most probably by way of Gubbio, and the ravages committed by his soldiers on the way created great indignation among the Romans. The Duke of Spoleto, Alboni, was taken prisoner with several of his "satraps," but the Duke of Beneventum managed to take refuge at Otranto. Desiderius installed another in his place, and then proceeded to Rome. The Pope met him outside the walls of St. Peter's, and pleaded persistently for the restoration of the promised towns. His eloquence, however, had no effect upon the king, who undertook to surrender Imola alone, and that only on condition that Pepin should deliver up the Lombard hostages who had been taken to France. The Pope, seemingly resigned, wrote to the Frankish king to this effect, but at the same time he contrived that Pepin should receive another letter from him, cancelling the contents of the first, maintaining all the Roman claims, and urging him to insist on a complete fulfilment of all the promises made by the Lombard king.[1]

Pepin despatched to Italy his brother Remedius, Bishop of Rouen, and the Duke Autchaire, and they succeeded in arranging matters on the basis of *uti possidetis*. Desiderius was to yield no other town, not even Imola; the Pope was adjudged possessor of the remainder; the damage done by either party was to be repaired; and many trifling questions concerning boundaries, customs, and patrimonies were affably settled. Pepin did his utmost to persuade the Pope to submit, and even to cultivate the friendship of the Lombard king. Paul, there-

---

[1] J., 2340, 2341.

fore, resigned himself, though not without grief and recriminations, to the dispelling of his dreams. It was, nevertheless, extremely evident that the Frankish king could neither undertake to place himself at the disposal of the Romans and their plans, nor to cross the Alps every time that there was a frontier skirmish between the Romans and the Lombards.

Moreover, it was to the interest of the Lombards to cultivate peace; henceforth they had a common enemy, the Byzantine empire, which was quite ready to take advantage of their disagreements. Constantine V., disappointed in his hopes of the Frankish intervention and the diplomacy of the Pope, continued his designs on Ravenna, and sought to regain a footing in central Italy. His efforts were mainly directed against the Pope, who at that time held Ravenna, and was responsible for the emancipation of the Romans. Instead, however, of entering into direct communication with him, he began by making friendly overtures to Desiderius. On the other hand, he considered that the ecclesiastical disunion produced by the images dispute was pretext enough for approaching the Frankish king. The iconoclastic reform did not, of course, affect the dwellers on the other side of the Alps to anything like the same extent as those of Byzantine Rome. Not only had they taken no part in the papal demonstrations, on behalf of the use of images and symbols in worship for thirty years, but the worship itself, in spite of the great decline of Frankish Christianity, did not appeal to them at all seriously. An attempt might be made to engage them in a struggle against what the empire proscribed as a religious perversion. Piety, thus understood, would provide a substitute for ground lost in the political arena. One proof that this ground was well selected is to be found in the fact that the Frankish Church, under Charlemagne and Louis the Pious, far from sharing the Pope's attitude towards the image question, rather supported the views of the iconoclast emperors.

At Rome they were quite cognisant of this danger. Indeed, Pope Paul spent the whole of his pontificate in listening to rumours from the south, and quaking before the dread of a political alliance between the Greeks and Lombards, or a religious compact between the emperor and the Frankish court.

But Pepin, who was a man of ability and common sense, did not let himself be beguiled by the half-theological diplomats who were sent to him from Constantinople. Nor did he allow himself to be led away, like the Romans, into constant plans for the re-division of the Italian territory. He saw at once that the important point was to bring about a reconciliation between his two allies, the Pope and the Lombard king, and with tact and energy he set about producing this result without wounding the feelings of either party. In spite of the Pope's demands for a Frankish *missus* to be in permanent residence at Rome, Pepin confined himself to supplying temporary legations, deputies entrusted to arrange transient or special difficulties. If there was any need for the Frankish king to be represented in Italy as the Pope's protector, it was on Desiderius himself that the office devolved. The latter was induced to give up the intrigues formed with the Greeks at the beginning of his reign, and the Pope was persuaded to come to an understanding with him, and, if necessary, to claim his support.

Towards the religious question, Pepin's attitude

was just as sane and simple. He listened to the Pope's continual exhortations against the imperial unorthodoxy, and always acted in accord with him, both at Constantinople (by means of their respective ambassadors), and in France in the event of any dispute. The Byzantines finally recognised their mistake; in Italy, Pepin's friendly relations with the Pope and the Lombards were an effectual hindrance to their political schemes, while, as far as the Franks were concerned, their loyalty to the great Head of religious affairs of the west was deep enough to discourage any further attempts on the part of the orientals to arouse ill-feeling against their powerful protector.

This is the impression that we get from the letters written by Paul to King Pepin, and preserved to us in the *Codex Carolinus*. Unfortunately we have no means of correcting or supplementing this correspondence, and, as the dates are lacking, it is often difficult to arrange the letters in their chronological order. Details on the subject are not easily obtained, for, from the *Liber Pontificalis* we learn nothing, and from the Frankish chronicles, but little, of these events. But there is conclusive evidence that the two Byzantine diplomats of 756, John the Silentiary and George, the chief secretary, continued their mission in the following year. The former installed himself at the Frankish court, and the latter in Italy, where he combined with the Lombard king in plotting against Ravenna. Later on, in 763, Pepin and Paul united in sending two ambassadors to Constantinople, where they stayed the winter. The pontiff's chief adviser at that time was Christopher, *primicerius* of the notaries. Among the people of Constantinople he bore the reputation of taking an undue part in the writing or editing of the papal letters, and he was popularly accused of trying to corrupt the Frankish and Byzantine envoys. The imperial government was anxious to do away with the papal legates, and to transact business directly with the Frankish court, but their endeavours in this line were apparently unsuccessful. We hear of a conference held at Gentilly early in 767, where, according to the annalist of Lorsch, there was a discussion *inter Romanos et Græcos de sancta Trinitate et de sanctorum imaginibus.* From the presence of the Romans on this occasion, we conclude that Pepin continued to persevere in his principle of referring all religious discussions to the Pope.[1]

Very soon afterwards, on 28th June 767, Pope Paul breathed his last. Affairs at Rome itself were quiet, though with a superficial quietness which was speedily and seriously to be disturbed. Let us now glance at the ecclesiastical and military organisation of the little Roman State and at the beginnings of the contest which might have been observed or foretold even at that time.

---

[1] The mention of the Trinity is strange. From that time there seems to have been no difference of opinion between East and West on the subject of the Holy Spirit. At the Roman Council of 769 no Trinitarian question was discussed.

CHAPTER VI

ROMAN INSTITUTIONS IN THE EIGHTH CENTURY

The military *scholæ* and the staff of the Palatine—The Cardinal Clergy—
The Lateran Palace and the general services of the Roman Church
—The Recruiting of the Clergy—Pontifical Finances—*Domus cultæ*—
Charitable offices—Monasteries.

THE military organisation of Rome was as follows :—
The population was divided, according to district,
into twelve groups or *scholæ*, and at the head of
each *schola* was a *patronus*, afterwards called a
decarco. The whole of the town on the left bank
of the Tiber was included in this arrangement, but
beyond this the inhabitants of the island (*insulani*),
and the Trasteverians [1] formed at that time, or later,
two other sections. We must also mention the
Greek section, *schola Græcorum*, which corresponded with the Byzantine quarter *par excellence*,
the Palatine and its neighbourhood. Finally,[2] there
were in the unfortified suburbs of St. Peter's *scholæ*
made up of foreign colonies; there were four of
these (if not just at that time, very soon afterwards) belonging to the Saxons (Anglo-Saxons),
Frisians, Franks, and Lombards.

The headquarters were at the Palatine, in the old
imperial palace, which was again officially repaired
towards the close of the seventh century.[3] This was

[1] See *Les Régions de Rome au moyen age,* in the *Mélanges* of the
École de Rome, vol. x.; *cf. L. P.,* vol. ii. p. 253, note 7.

[2] *L. P.,* vol. i. p. 36, note 1.

[3] *L. P.,* vol. i. p. 386, note 1.

the residence of the emperor on his one and only
visit to Rome (663), and of the Exarch, who appeared
there more often, as well as of the duke and the
military staff. In connection with this palace there
was an official chapel,[1] St. Cæsar *in Palatio*, the place
of receptacle for the image of each emperor on his
accession. St. Cæsar,[2] of which there is no trace left,
was situated within the precincts of the palace itself;
while, at the bottom of the hill, was the church bearing the old priestly title of St. Anastasia. This had
become the headquarters of the Byzantine district.
In these times, when politics and religion were so
intimately related, the festivals in connection with
these churches were of the highest importance.
One of the Christmas masses was celebrated at
St. Anastasia, in honour of its patron saint; and
equally impressive was the festival of St. Cæsar,
which was celebrated on 1st November at the
Palatine, and distinguished by a grand procession.[3]

The superior degrees were those of duke, cartu-
lary, count, and tribune, and next below these in
dignity came the *patroni scholarum*, the *primicerii*,
domestici, and *optiones*. But we know very little
of the details of these offices, or, indeed, of the
military organisation in general.

---

[1] *Bull. Crit.*, vol. vi. p. 417; *L. P.*, vol. i. p. 377, note 12.

[2] The site indicated in the *Forma Urbis* of M. Lanciani is quite
out of the question; in fact it is outside not only the palace but the
Palatine also.

[3] We must not omit to mention here the Byzantine Church of
Sta. Maria Antica, which recent excavations have brought to light.
The flight of stairs connecting it with the Palatine is still to be
seen. Its officiating clergy seem to have been monks, speaking
the Greek tongue, and in the eighth century it was a very popular
devotional resort, probably in consequence of its pictures and inscriptions. We will not attempt to record the countless attempts
which have been, and are still being made, to trace its origin back
to the time of Pope Sylvester in the fourth century.

We hear no more of a chief duke after the time of Stephen II. As was mentioned before, the title of *patricius Romanorum* seems to have been conferred on the Frankish princes, in order that the Pope might be relieved from the presence in his neighbourhood of a superior dignitary. The Pope is the head of the government; and the army, like the rest, is subject to his command. He claims no other dignity than that which accrues to him from his ecclesiastical position, and it is as head of the *ecclesia Dei* that he, at the same time, assumes authority over the *respublica Romanorum*.

Then there were also the cardinal priests, who surrounded the Pope. They were generally about twenty-five in number, and constituted a kind of senate of the Church. At the present time they receive and manage the revenues of their churches, reside in the ecclesiastical establishments attached to them, and superintend the religious ceremonies. But, although they constitute the official council of the Pope, and are conspicuous in the pontifical ceremonial, they are really of less importance than the cardinal deacons.

These latter are always seven in number, and are the permanent assistants and ordinary servants of the Pope. Their special province is within their district limits. The archdeacon is the director of the ecclesiastical staff in general. Next below the deacons come the sub-deacons, who are divided into two groups of seven; some of them are specially attached to the district government, while others are in the more immediate service of the Pope.

The deacons lived at the Lateran, which was the chief centre of the ecclesiastical administration.

But there was, also, another papal palace, that of the Palatine[1]; it was erected about the beginning of the eighth century, at a time when the safety of the Lateran was not to be relied upon. During the pontificate of Gregory II. the ramparts of Rome were repaired, and the Lateran, thus protected, became, from the time of Zachary onwards, the usual residence of the Pope. To the diaconal administration were referred all matters connected with the ecclesiastical staff, the charitable arrangements, and, generally speaking, most of the temporal affairs of the Church. The Lateran was also the headquarters of the following :—

1. The government of the palace itself, controlled by the *vice dominus* (vidame), in conjunction with, or instead of whom appears, after the end of the eighth century, the *superista*. Below the vidame are the *cubicularii* (chamberlains), the *cellerarii* (cellarers), the *stratores* (equerries), &c. The *nomenculator* is the grandmaster of the ceremonies; the *vestararius*, or *prior vestiarii*, is the guardian of the stores of valuable furniture and other treasure.

2. The chancellor's office, where the clerks were known as *notarii* or *scriniarii*. These included the seven district notaries, the two most important of whom (the *primicerius* and the *secundicerius*) were numbered among the great ecclesiastical dignitaries. The *primicerius* of the notaries, together with the chief priest and the archdeacon, made up the triumvirate on which the government of the Roman Church devolved, in the event of the Pope's death or absence. He was also trustee of the archives

---

[1] Probably at the northern angle, above Sta. Maria Antica. The site is covered by a grove of evergreen oaks, and is one of the most delightful spots in Rome.

and manager of the library, though by this time the functions of librarian were beginning to be separated from those of the notaries.

As yet, there is no mention of the *primiscrinius* or *protoscrinius*, who, later, succeeded the *primicerius* as the real head of the chancellor's office.

3. The financial administration presided over by the *arcarius*, chief cashier, and the *saccellarius*, or paymaster-general. Connected with them were the advocates, who had to do with the courts of justice, and particularly with the execution of ecclesiastical sentences. They, like the notaries, possessed an aristocracy of seven district officers, with a *primicerius* at their head.

After the ninth century, some of these offices became secularised, while others remained in ecclesiastical [1] hands. These latter soon formed a special and distinguished category, the seven Palatine judges, viz., the *primicerius* and the *secundicerius* of the notaries, the *arcarius*, the *saccellarius*, the *protoscrinius*, the chief of the advocates, and the *nomenculator*.

There were also the functions of the *consiliarius* and the *ordinator*. That of *consiliarius*, sometimes entrusted to the clergy and sometimes to the laity, seems to have been of great importance. After the eighth century, however, we hear no more of either of them.

As a rule the Pope officiated at the Church of the Lateran, which was included, since the time of Constantine, in the *domus ecclesiæ*. He and his court, however, were often present at other ceremonies, either at Sta. Maria Maggiore or in some

---

[1] But generally, ecclesiastics who had not been promoted to the higher orders and were thus in no way bound to celibacy.

other of the city or suburban basilicas. The daily
religious service at the Lateran was presided over,
in turn, by the seven bishops in the closest vicinity
of Rome. It was through this system of papal
assistants that the class of cardinal bishops was
formed.[1]

The Roman clergy were recruited from two
sources, according to the social position of the candidates. Those belonging to the lower classes were
educated in a kind of seminary, the *Schola cantorum*,
which was situated not far from the Lateran. It
was also known as the Orphanage—*Orphanotrophium*.
The children of the nobility were received into the
papal palace among the *cubicularii*. Both classes
received the tonsure at the outset of their careers, a
rite which admitted them to the ranks of the clergy,
and gave them the much appreciated privilege of
decorating their horses with white saddle cloths.
During their novitiate they took the position of
acolytes; the other lesser orders, owing to their
practical disuse, had fallen into insignificance. The
acolytes were distributed among the priestly offices;
they constituted the whole assistant clergy of the
cardinal priests. These clerics took no vows of
celibacy, but, as a rule, indulged in matrimony. It
was not until several years later, after promotion
to the higher orders, that they bound themselves
to a celibate life. Even then, they only severed
their family relationships as far as was absolutely
necessary. The wives of the superior orders
of clergy were not sequestered in cloisters, and
they even shared, to a certain extent, in the

[1] See *Le sedi episcopali nell' antico ducato di Roma,* in vol. xv. of
L'Archivio Romano di storia patria.

promotion of their husbands, becoming *diaconæ*, *presbyteræ*, or *episcopæ*. On the day of the clerk's preferment to the priesthood, or the diaconate, their wives were also honoured with a kind of consecration ceremony, in celebration of this access of dignity.

Besides the ordained clerks, who, for the most part, had had time to found families, there was still a very large number who were not ordained, *e.g.* those engaged at the chancellor's office or in the administrative service, notaries, advocates, chamberlains, cellarers, &c. All these constituted a kind of clerical reserve, from which the *Schola cantorum* drew the necessary supplies. They also served to fill up ecclesiastical offices, and being strengthened in the *cubiculum sacrum* by the addition of an aristocratic element, they attained to the highest ranks of the sacred hierarchy, not excepting the pontificate itself. The temporal power once definitely organised, it fell to the lot of the hierarchy to manage many matters which were originally foreign to it. Its importance and prestige increased perceptibly, and at the Orphanage there was much competition for the *cubiculum* as the means of entry. As will be seen, this was a severe trial for the ecclesiastical spirit.

The pontifical finances [1] were still drawn, in the main, from the landed property of the Church. Owing to the confiscations by the Byzantine government, a large portion of the immense estates mentioned in the letters of St. Gregory had vanished. The ancient patrimonies of Sicily and Calabria no longer yielded any income, and it was only with

---

[1] *Cf.* Paul Fabre's book, *De patrimoniis s. Romanæ ecclesiæ.* Paris, 1892.

great difficulty that the Pope obtained a small profit from the domains which remained to him in Istria, and the neighbourhood of Naples, and Gaeta. The chief part of the papal revenues was drawn from the Church property around Rome. But even this source had been seriously affected by the long lease system. In spite of all this, however, the constant reception of gifts and legacies had enabled not only Paul's predecessors, but also some of his successors, to reconstitute an important department. In order to minimise the covert estrangement of property which was continually going on, and also to re-populate the sparsely inhabited country, the Popes undertook to cultivate certain extensive districts themselves without any outside help. This was called the *domus cultœ*. The peasants who worked for them were regarded as papal employés, and formed rural *militiœ*, which were not disarmed like the *militia ecclesiastica*. Thus the ecclesiastical revenues were being confirmed and strengthened, while, at the same time, a staff was being consti-tuted capable of military organisation, and having the advantage over the *exercitus Romanus* of repre-senting no tradition at variance with the *ecclesia Dei*. If properly developed and employed, this would be a valuable aid to the Popes in confront-ing the internal difficulties of their temporal govern-ment.

In closing this review of the Roman institutions in the eighth century, a word must be said of the charitable establishments and monasteries. The former were abundant, comprising hospices and hospitals (*xenodochia, ptochia, hospitalia*), asylums for foundlings (*brephotrophia*), for aged men (*gero-comia*), and benevolent societies or deaconries.

These establishments were founded on endowments, and, like the presbyteral churches, had their own incomes and official staff.

The same might also be said of the monasteries which abounded at Rome. A large number of them were occupied by Greek monks, while others sheltered Orientals, Syrians, Armenians, &c. As a rule, they were established in the neighbourhood of such sacred places as St. Peter's, St. Paul's, St. Lawrence's, or even the city basilicas. Each foundation had an oratory of its own, though most of the services seem to have been held in the neighbouring basilica, several monasteries sometimes having one common celebration in the same church. There were, for example, four or five congregations meeting in the basilica of St. Peter's. This was the origin of the chapters. The vicissitudes of the convent system led to the formation of congregations of canons, both regular and lay, the most important of which have survived to the present day.

As we mentioned before, the monasteries of Rome were of no great importance. The Popes seemed to have been warned by the ill-effects produced on ecclesiastical discipline by large bodies of monks in other places—Constantinople, for example. Thus, while they encouraged the religious profession, they did not favour the formation of powerful congregations. Moreover, when the monks were officiating in the basilicas it was much easier to keep them under control. The large convents were elsewhere. Monte Cassino, which had been revived under Pope Zachary, was situated in the Lombard domains. So also were the Abbeys of Monte Amiata, St. Saviour of Rieti, and Santa Maria of Farfa. The latter, however, had been founded on part of the territory which the Lombards undertook to restore to the Pope. It was transferred to the papal jurisdiction during Hadrian's pontificate, when it did not fail to become a subject of discord.

CHAPTER VII

CHRISTOPHER THE PRIMICERIUS

Government of Pope Paul—Divisions at the time of his death—Usurpation of Constantine II.—Reaction led by Christopher, with the assistance of Desiderius — Constantine is expelled from the Holy See—Election in the Forum—Stephen III.—Sanguinary retaliation —The Council of 769—Desiderius at Rome—Paul Afiarta—Assassination of Christopher and his son Sergius—Deception and death of Stephen III.

FROM the foregoing account of the institutions of the little Roman State, it is not difficult to understand that the existing conditions contained the elements of an important internal crisis. There were two great rival bodies, the clergy and the army, and the transfer to the Church of the political supremacy, hitherto enjoyed by the army, did not tend to sweeten the relations between them. Affairs seem to have gone on calmly at first, and we hear of no definite resistance during Paul's reign, except in the case of a priest called Marin. This man resided at the Frankish Court, and gave himself up to incessant plotting against the Pope. The latter might well have wished to be rid of him, through his promotion to a French bishopric, but when his parents were anxious to see him again, Paul formally requested that he should be sent back to Italy, promising to honour him with another ecclesiastical title. Marin, notwithstanding, remained in France during the rest of the Pope's lifetime, apparently to the complete satisfaction of the latter.

If order continued to prevail at Rome, it was because Pope Paul ruled with a high hand. Even his biographer, while lauding the papal virtues, refers to the molestations practised by his "iniquitous satellites," and relates that the prisons often harboured prisoners under sentence of death. The Pope was accused of many extortions,[1] and rapidly acquired a reputation for unjust severity. The power of the papacy, while having its advantages, was not without drawbacks. The army, ousted by the government, watched the flame of rebellion smouldering, and, if necessary, did what it could to fan it. In the early summer of 767 the Pope, who was living at that time in the neighbourhood of St. Paul's, was taken seriously ill. A reaction immediately followed.

Under these conditions any change of authority was not feasible, and the idea of a Byzantine restoration does not seem to have occurred to anybody. As at the accession of Stephen II., the emperor was too far away and the Lombards too close at hand to enable the Romans to dispense with the intervention of the Franks, who would hardly have consented to the transference of the political power from the Pope to the army. The best way out of the difficulty, they thought, would be to elect as Pope a member of the military aristocracy, who would be inclined to restore to the army at least part of what it had lost during the pontificates of the two brothers, Stephen and Paul. The clergy, realising that a crisis was at hand, had already taken precautions, and felt safe as to the result of the election, provided that it was conducted in an orderly manner, and among the Roman inhabitants of Rome.

[1] *L. P.*, vol. i. p. 463, 475.

At this time the most important person in the ecclesiastical world was Christopher, the *primicerius*. From the time of Stephen II. he had been a conspicuous figure, having accompanied the Pope on his Frankish mission[1] in 753, in virtue of his office as district notary, or advocate. We hear of him again, three years later, as one of those engaged in negotiations for an alliance between Pope Stephen and Desiderius,[2] the claimant to the Lombard throne. This time he bears the title of *consiliarius*. He was as devoted to Paul as he had been to his brother, and seems to have had no inconsiderable share in the most weighty transactions and correspondence of the time. At the court of Constantinople it was said that Pope Paul was nothing but a puppet, whom Christopher forced to dance to his piping, and that the latter was really responsible for the whole of the papal policy. It is, indeed, more than probable, that the *primicerius* was the chief promoter of the policy of the last few years, the instigator and mainstay of the Frankish alliance, as well as of the ecclesiastical supremacy.

The nobles, who were stronger in the outlying districts and the small towns than in the capital, promulgated the idea that as the Pope was now ruler of the whole duchy, it was only right that all his future subjects should have a voice in his election. *Qui omnibus præesse debet ab omnibus eligatur.* This old maxim of canon law was now applied to the episcopal instead of to the monarchical election. This was all the more natural, because the provincial governors formerly, and in later times the dukes, had gained their position by election.

---

[1] *L. P.*, vol. i. p. 446.
[2] *Ibid.*, p. 455.

How these ideas were translated into facts we shall now see.

Residing at Nepi, but also owning a house at Rome, was a certain Duke Toto[1] (Theodore). He arranged to confer with his three brothers, Constantine, Passivus, and Pascal, and some confederates, and together they plotted to hasten the Pope's death. Their evil designs were, however, thwarted by Christopher, who even succeeded in making Toto swear that the election should proceed in proper form. But the duke straightway broke his oath; he summoned around him all the troops of Roman Tuscia, and these, reinforced by a large number of peasants, presented themselves before the gate of St. Pancratius, which was not barred or bolted.

The rebellion was being organised in the city under the command of the new arrivals when the Pope suddenly expired on 25th June. A preliminary convocation was immediately held in the basilica of the Apostles, at which, thanks to Christopher's influence, the clergy and the army met in a friendly spirit, and overwhelmed one another with mutual pledges of good-will. The outlook seemed promising, and, according to custom, the election was put off for a few days, when Toto and his followers forced their way into the Lateran and proclaimed, as Pope, Constantine, the eldest of the three brothers. He was not a cleric, but a military man, for they had ignored the old Roman custom, often set forth in the canonical writings, and honoured by constant observance, which forbade such a choice.

---

[1] Our chief sources of information on these events are: (1) The letters of the *Codex Carolinus*; (2) the lives of Stephen III. and Hadrian in the *Liber Pontificalis*; (3) fragments of the Council of 769; see my edition of the *Liber Pontificalis*, commentary on the Life of Stephen III.

George, Bishop of Prenesto, whom they encountered in the *vicedominium*, was obliged, in spite of protests, to confer the tonsure on the newly appointed pontiff. Christopher was sought, in order that he might have a share in this usurpation, but he refused emphatically to have any connection with it.

The next day Constantine was ordained subdeacon, and then deacon and priest, in the oratory of St. Lawrence at the Lateran; he was then inducted in due form, with the administration of a solemn oath. On the following Sunday, 5th July, he was consecrated Pope at St. Peter's, again by the Bishop of Prenesto, who was assisted by his colleagues of Albano and Porto. After this ceremony, Christopher, and the most faithful of his adherents, were alone in refusing to recognise Constantine's promotion. But Christopher was a force to be reckoned with. His influence over the two preceding Popes had been marked, and now the victorious party hoped to get rid of him and his followers. Duke Gregory, one of the latter, was assassinated, and the *primicerius*, feeling his own situation to be precarious, fled with his children to seek refuge at St. Peter's. Nor could they be induced to emerge from its friendly shelter, until Constantine himself assured them that their lives were not in danger. In return, they undertook to remain quiet until after Easter, when they were to retire into monastic life. There was some slight amount of local opposition, but it was speedily overcome, and this severe treatment of Gregory and of Christopher and his family was the only conspicuous case of the kind. Those who had scruples awaited a safer opportunity to declare them. It was, however, related, with some consternation, that the Bishop of

Prenesto, who was paralysed in the right hand, had not been able to use it since he had stretched it forth at the consecration of Constantine. His death, which occurred shortly after, was looked upon as a token of divine displeasure.

The gratitude of the Frankish king had still to be procured. Constantine immediately[1] wrote to him to announce the fact of his accession, but Pepin, who must have had some inkling of the state of affairs, seemed in no haste to reply. A second letter[2] was despatched in September, ostensibly to inform the prince of the arrival of oriental communications connected with the veneration of images. Constantine then proceeds to the subject of the election, attempting to plead extenuating circumstances. He speaks of his unworthiness, of the violence offered to him, of the decrees of Providence, in short, of all that might be urged in a parallel case. Pepin, at that time, was very much engaged with his war in Aquitaine, and although it is certain that he took no active measures against Constantine, there is no evidence that he made any exertions on his behalf. He appears to have held aloof from the whole affair, or, at least, not to have taken any serious notice of it. The Lombards, for their part, lay low, and made no attacks on the Roman State, a sign that they regarded the Frankish protection as including, if not the person of the new Pope, at any rate the domain consecrated to the Prince of the Apostles.

About the middle of April (768) Christopher the *primicerius* and his son, Sergius, who, under the last Pope, had held the office of *saccellarius*, were left

---

[1] J., 2374. [2] J., 2375.

free to embrace a religious career. For this purpose they selected the monastery of St. Saviour at Rieti, in the duchy of Spoleto. The abbot was sent for, and undertook the custody of the two novices. Once outside the Roman frontier, however, they succeeded in eluding his vigilance, and, upon reaching Spoleto, called on the duke for an escort to Pavia. Their plans were successful, and they came to an understanding with the Lombard prince without the intervention of their protectors on the other side of the Alps. Desiderius was delighted at the chance of profiting by the disordered state of affairs, and assured the Roman dignitaries of his sympathy and support. He had them escorted back to Spoleto, bearing a message to the duke, who, acting upon his instructions, put an army at the disposal of Sergius. The latter, accompanied by the priest Waldipert, a Lombard ambassador, set out at the head of it, and they arrived at the Salarian Bridge on the evening of 7th July, exactly thirteen months after Constantine's promotion to the Lateran. The next day they crossed the Anio and the Tiber, then, after an ineffectual attempt on the St. Peter's gate, they tried the gate of St. Pancratius, which is at the top of the Janiculum, and commands a view over the whole town. Here confederates were awaiting them, the gate was opened, and Waldipert's troops passed through into the city of Rome.

The Lombards had been in Italy for two hundred years. They had besieged Rome many times, but never before, even by treason, had they succeeded in gaining admittance to it. The new arrivals, consequently, hardly daring to believe in their good fortune, remained in trepidation on the fortifications, without venturing to descend into the town.[1] Their hesitation gave the Romans time to flock together. Toto and Passivus went up to the gate of St. Pancratius and succeeded in making the Lombards beat a retreat. But treachery stepped in for the second time. Duke Toto was struck down from behind, and his death threw the defending party into disarray. Passivus hastened to the Lateran, and the unfortunate Constantine, quite broken-spirited, sought refuge in chapel after chapel; he was discovered with his brother Passivus, and the Bishop Theodore, his vidame, cowering in the oratory of the sacristy.

Christopher had stayed behind, evidently detained by some Lombard conspiracy. Waldipert, taking advantage of his absence, managed to divert the attention of Sergius, and the next day, which was Sunday, proclaimed, as Pope, a venerable priest named Philip, the superior of a monastery near the church of St. Vitus. He was not a cardinal, but the Lombards evidently thought him a suitable candidate for the papacy. He was acclaimed with the customary ceremony, conducted to the basilica and palace of the Lateran, and even followed the custom of giving a banquet to the most important of his electors, clerical or military.

This, however, was the only act of his pontificate. Christopher, who had arrived before the walls of Rome during the day, had another candidate in view; and he sent a message to the Romans, saying that he would not set foot in the town so long as Philip was at the Lateran. They submitted, and

[1] The biographer of Stephen III. seems to feel strongly about this; in spite of his devotion to Christopher, he does not hesitate to describe as *nefandissimi proditores* those who opened the gate to the Lombards.

one of Toto's assassins, Gratiosus, undertook the difficult task of conveying the Lombard Pope back to his monastery of St. Vitus.

Christopher was now master of the situation. The next day, 1st August, he assembled the clergy and the lay aristocracy, in fact, the whole population of Rome, *in Tribus Fatis*, *i.e.* the ancient Forum, near the church of St. Hadrian. After some discussion, they finally settled to appoint the candidate of the *primicerius*. This was Stephen, priest of St. Cecilia, a man of about fifty years of age. He was a native of Sicily, and his knowledge of men and things had been limited to an experience of life within the monasteries, the episcopal palace, and the churches. His piety was an undoubted recommendation, and the weakness of his disposition was sufficient to justify Christopher and his family in their intention of holding the reins of power in their own hands. He was escorted to the Lateran, of which he took formal possession, and his episcopal consecration was celebrated on the following Sunday, 7th August.

But the victorious party did not wait for this ceremony before engaging in the most revolting acts of revenge. Those who had been captured on 30th July in the sacristy oratory were brought forth from their prison. Bishop Theodore and Passivus were incarcerated in monasteries, after having had their eyes put out. The wretched Constantine had first to undergo the humiliation of taking part in a mock cavalcade, and then, on the evening before Stephen's consecration, he was brought before an ecclesiastical tribunal, and declared to have forfeited the papal dignity. Finally, a few days later, some of his enemies forced their way into the monastery of St.

Sabas, where the unfortunate wretch was imprisoned, dragged him outside, and put out his eyes. The same fate befell others, among them the tribune of Alatri, Gracilis, and Waldipert, the Lombard priest. The latter in vain sought refuge at Sta. Maria Maggiore behind a sacred image; he was torn from the sanctuary and cast into one of the Lateran prisons. Finally he was dragged to the open space in front of the palace, where his eyes were taken out. They took him to a neighbouring hospital, but he expired almost immediately.[1]

Such were the edifying circumstances under which the new Pope, Stephen III., entered upon his pontificate. For lack of further victims the disturbances were at last calmed down, and the victors now hastened to acquaint the Frankish king with their success. Sergius, who was chosen as the delegate, was well adapted to represent things in their most favourable light. When he arrived in France, he found that the great Pepin had just passed away, so he presented himself to Charles and Carloman, the two Frankish princes, and succeeded in convincing them of the urgent need for repairing the breach of canon law caused by the election of Constantine.[2] In accordance with his demand, a deputation, consisting of certain members of the Frankish episcopacy, was sent to Rome. They were chosen for their familiarity with the Scriptures, and the "ceremonies of the holy canons." First of all came Wilchar, the former Bishop of Nomentum, at that time Bishop of Sens, and bearing the title of Archbishop of the Gauls. Then came the Metro-

[1] We gather from this attack on a representative of King Desiderius that the Lombards had already left Rome.

[2] As a matter of fact they were not without qualms as to the validity of the election of Stephen III.

politan Bishops of Mainz, Tours, Lyons, Bourges, Narbonne, and Rheims; and finally the Bishops of Amiens, Meaux, Worms, Würzburg, Langres, and Noyon. On their arrival in Rome these thirteen dignitaries met, together with about forty Italian bishops, both from Lombardy and the Roman district. After the Easter festivals (769) the council assembled in the Basilica of the Lateran. The first to appear before them was the unhappy Constantine, *jam extra oculos*. His defence turned upon the violence to which he had been subjected, and the reaction against Paul's severity, which had culminated in his own election. The breach of ecclesiastical law upon which so much stress was being laid, had often occurred before for the benefit of others, he maintained. Prostrating himself on the ground, he implored mercy and forgiveness, but the priests were not to be moved. Following in the footsteps of Caiphas rather than of St. Gregory, they struck the poor blind pleader across the face, cast him outside, and ordered that his writ of election should be burned. Having performed these graceful acts, Pope Stephen, with his clerks and his faithful followers, abased themselves on the ground, confessing the sin they had committed in accepting Constantine, and beseeching penance for their misdeeds. The very angels must have smiled at the hypocritical litanies which were chanted over them.

But this was not all. The ordinations and enactments of Constantine were declared illegal, and he himself was condemned to a life of penance within a monastery.

In order to prevent any recurrence of these disturbances, it was decreed by the Council that cardinals or deacons should alone be eligible for election, and, moreover, that "laymen, both military and civil," and in particular, persons not belonging to the city of Rome, should henceforth be excluded from the electoral body, strictly speaking; though, after the Pope's election and installation at the Vatican, the Roman laity would be allowed to go in and greet him, and confirm, by their signatures, the act of his election. This provision introduced a most important change, but though, as will be seen, it was in force for some time, it was eventually annulled.

Finally, the convocation ratified the veneration of the images, and reprobated the decisions of the iconoclastic Council of 754. All these decrees were made public, with much solemnity, at St. Peter's, before a large audience of the clergy and people.

Between France and the Holy See, harmony was again established. The military party was subdued, and the lay aristocracy excluded from the papal elections. But Christopher and Sergius, the Pope's advisers, and the virtual wielders of the papal authority, had given King Desiderius very grave cause for complaint. It was in virtue of his support that they had succeeded in overthrowing Constantine II., and in return for this friendly help, they had not only debarred his candidate from the papacy, but they had permitted the assassination of his envoy, Waldipert. It was no wonder, therefore, that Desiderius took umbrage. Besides, they did their utmost to strengthen the Frankish alliance by their influence on the papal policy. A good deal of correspondence bearing on the subject is preserved in the *Codex Carolinus*.[1] In it the Lombards are constantly accused of disregarding the satisfactions (*justitias*) due to St. Peter. One of these

[1] J., 2380, 2381, 2386, 2387.

letters [1] is written with the object of deterring the Frankish princes from a family alliance with King Desiderius. The popular gossip as to the leprous and malodorous conditions, and so on, obtaining among the Lombards, is brought forward as an argument against the match, which took place notwithstanding. Desiderata was the first legitimate, or rather official, wife of Charlemagne, though, after she had enjoyed the honour for a very short time, she was cast off by her royal consort.[2] Bertrade, the Queen-mother, had herself come to Italy, to arrange the affair; she had even penetrated as far as Rome, where she seems to have reported to the Pope some favourable remarks of the Lombard king concerning the litigation between them.

Stephen III. was beginning to weary of Christopher's continual supervision. Desiderius, whose path had been prepared, more or less consciously, by Queen Bertrade, made up his mind to confer with the Pope in person. In Lent 771, he undertook a pilgrimage to Rome, *orationis causa*. He had some confederates in the pontifical circle, in particular a chamberlain, named Paul Afiarta. The news of the Lombard king's pious intentions, did not fail to arouse the suspicions both of Christopher and Sergius. Summoning to Rome troops from the country, and even from the duchy of Perugia, they reinforced the gates, and prepared to show a good front. Carloman, the one of the two

---

[1] J., 2381.

[2] Eginhard, *Vita Karoli*, 18 ; *cf. Vita Adalardi*, c. 7 (M. G., SS., t. ii. p. 525. Eginhard says " one year " later ; but this is not possible. In 770 Desiderata was already replaced by Hildegard. See *Julien Havet, Bibl. de l'École des Chartes*, vol. xlviii. p. 50.

Frankish kings whose estates bordered on Italy, had at Rome a *missus* named Dodo, who took their part with great zeal. It was pretty well known against whom Desiderius's animosity was directed. On his arrival at Rome, he took up his position near the Vatican, begging the Pope to come and confer with him. But instead of complying, Stephen proceeded to St. Peter's, and then went back to the Lateran without taking any notice of the Lombard king. This was the signal[1] for a most bitter contest.

Afiarta and Christopher were already at daggers drawn, and, as a result of their quarrels, Rome had for some time been divided into two factions. On the Pope's return, Christopher and Sergius, suspecting treason, appeared at the Lateran with a strong escort, declaiming against their enemies. The Pope succeeded in pacifying them, and even swore a solemn oath in their favour. But no sooner had the agitators taken their departure, than he went back to the king, and by means of fresh promises on the *justitiæ S. Petri*, he basely delivered over to him those to whom he owed his election. At his instigation two bishops repaired to the nearest gate, and called upon Christopher and his son Sergius to come to St. Peter's, to yield themselves into the Pope's hands. The two Roman nobles learned that day to what lengths cowardice and treachery can go. Their adherents forsook them, in order to listen to the voice of

---

[1] Besides the *LiberPontificalis* and the letter by which Stephen III. acquaints Queen Bertrade and Charlemagne with these events, we get valuable details in a Bavarian chronicle (in bad preservation, it is true) from which I have quoted in note 58 of the life of Stephen III.

the Pope, who was morally a Lombard prisoner. The first to desert Christopher was no less a person than Gratiosus, the traitorous assassin of Toto (768), the initiator of attempts on the person of Constantine II., as well as of many other crimes, a man who owed his elevation in rank to the one against whom he now so ignobly turned. To hasten to the Pope's summons he forced open the Porto gate, and this action gave a decisive turn to affairs. Sergius and Christopher, aghast at this sudden change of front, were misguided enough to commit themselves into the hands of the enemy. This took place in the middle of the night.

The next day the Pope celebrated mass in the presence of King Desiderius, and then returned into the city, leaving Christopher and Sergius in the basilica of St. Peter. According to his biographer, Stephen's wish was that they should adopt a religious career, but he must have been aware that, in neglecting to bring them back with him, he was delivering them over to the discretion of those who bore them ill-will. Indeed, before nightfall Afiarta and his supporters had united with the king in a design against them. Christopher and Sergius, dragged from the most revered sanctuary in Christendom, were taken to the bridge of St. Angelo, where their eyes were torn out. As a result of this inhuman treatment, Christopher died, only three days later. Sergius was cast into the great prison of the Lateran, where he survived for more than a year. A week before the death of Stephen III., Afiarta, and John, the Pope's brother, had him brought out of prison and assassinated. After being half strangled, he was buried, while still alive, under an arcade in the Via Merulana, quite near to the palace. Afiarta probably got rid of him thus, in the fear that he might be set free after the Pope's death.

The unhappy Stephen III., after having betrayed his benefactors, realised with grief that he was being made a dupe of by Desiderius, who refused him the least compensation. " What," said the king, " surely the Pope can expect no further concessions when I have relieved him of his guardians ! He had better mind his own business and not fall out with me ! Carloman is the champion of Christopher and Sergius, and he will require an explanation of their treatment. If I do not take Stephen's part he will be ruined." [1]

The Pope undoubtedly recognised the correctness of this reasoning, for he refrained from writing to Carloman, who was little inclined to listen to him. But he wrote to Charles and the Queen-mother a letter which is still extant, setting forth the above-mentioned sad events, from the standpoint of his mentor Afiarta and the Lombard king, whom he describes as being full of enthusiasm for himself, as well as for the temporal concerns of the Holy See. He lays great stress on the part played by Dodo, basely making the most of the discord between the two brothers, although two years before it was he who exhorted them to reconciliation.[2]

At the beginning of December (771) Carloman died, somewhat to the relief of the Pope and his new advisers. But their contentment did not last long. Only two months later, 3rd February 772, Stephen joined Christopher and Sergius, his sometime friends, in the unseen world. They had not

[1] J., 2388.   [2] J., 2380.

been mistaken in their expectation of finding in him a submissive agent. But such agents, however convenient they may be, require much discretion in handling, and are by no means always to be relied upon.

CHAPTER VIII

HADRIAN AND DESIDERIUS

Pope Hadrian—Restorative Measures—The Politics of King Desiderius—
His attempts against Rome—Overthrow of Afiarta and the Lombard
party—Appeal to Charlemagne—Charles in Italy—Siege of Pavia—
Central Italy and the Pope—Charles at Rome for the Easter
Festivals, 774—Donation of Charlemagne.

FORTUNATELY for the honour of the Holy See, the
election resulted in the appointment of a man of
probity, energy, and capability, the deacon Hadrian.
This new Pope was a scion of one of the noblest
families of Rome. Having been early deprived of
his father, he was entrusted by his widowed mother
to the care of his uncle, Theodotus, consul and
duke, afterwards *primicerius* and "father" of the
diaconate of St. Angelo. Hadrian had been trained
at the Lateran, and was distinguished for his piety,
high principles, and learning. His supporters hoped,
by electing him, to get out of difficulties, and to
please both the Church and the nobility, by giving
them a Pope who was at once a member of the
ecclesiastical profession and of the aristocracy. They
also wanted a man of action, who would avenge,
without delay, the iniquitous proceedings which had
disgraced the pontificate of Stephen III.

The attack on the unfortunate Sergius was not
the only offence of its kind. The death of Carloman
seemed to have let loose the evil passions of Afiarta's
adherents. Exalted members of the clergy and the
military had suffered banishment in the last days of

the deceased Pope. Hadrian lost no time in repairing their wrongs, but, immediately on his election, gave orders that they should be recalled. He at once resumed negotiations with the Lombard king, and awaited a favourable opportunity of bringing the assassins and their accomplices to justice.

Since Carloman's death, the situation had become complex. He had left behind him only young children, one of whom was little Prince Pepin, born in 770. The aristocracy of his kingdom decided, by a large majority, to amalgamate under the authority of Charlemagne. The latter was at Corbeny, near Laon, and thither were despatched deputies, empowered to endow him with the kingdom of his brother. Gerberga, Carloman's widow, fled with her children to Italy, accompanied by a few faithful followers; conspicuous among them was Autchaire. Desiderius welcomed them with open arms; by extending his encouragement and protection to these fugitives, he thought to undermine the formidable power which was springing up on the other side of the Alps. There was, at least, good reason to hope that the time would come, when a diplomatic interchange might be profitably arranged. Great stakes were at issue, but Desiderius was to be on the losing side.

He was not relying on this means of action when, on Hadrian's succession, he sent him greetings by the Duke of Spoleto, and two other officials, who urged the Pope to renew the agreement made with Stephen III., undertaking, in return, to render to the Holy See all the compensations (*justitiæ*) that it unceasingly demanded. Hadrian responded by sending him a deputation, conducted by Paul Afiarta. By this means, he succeeded in getting rid of the latter, while, at the same time, he was giving the Lombard king a pledge of his amiable intentions, by despatching to him a *persona grata.*

But no sooner had the papal legates quitted Rome than disquieting news arrived. Desiderius had made himself master of Ferrara, Comacchio, and Faenza, and was now meditating a descent on Ravenna. There was no mistaking his political attitude, for he publicly posed as the supporter of Carloman's children, and claimed that the Pope, by his solemn consecration of the young princes, had declared himself on their side. Afiarta was of the king's opinion, and undertook, at any cost, to bring about a meeting between Desiderius and Hadrian. The *sacellarius* Stephen, who had accompanied him on his mission, seems also to have been of the same mind.

They were, however, deluded. Hadrian having got wind of their designs, changed Stephen for another envoy, and Afiarta's temporary absence became permanent, under the following circumstances. The Pope was determined to get to the bottom of the mystery surrounding the assassination of Sergius the *secundicerius.* The enquiry, which followed, resulted in the arrest of the criminals, three Campanini,[1] the chamberlain Calventzulus, the priest Lunisso, and Leonatius, the tribune. These maintained that they had been but tools in the hands of others, and denounced, as the instigators of the crime, Paul Afiarta, the Duke John, brother of the late Pope, a district advocate named Gregory, and another chamberlain, Calvulus. Concerning the fate of John and Gregory we know nothing, but Calvulus, and the three Campanians, were handed

[1] The *Ciociari* of the present day.

over to the criminal judge, the Prefect of Rome, who now reappears, after an interval of more than a century and a half. Calvulus spent the rest of his life in prison, while the other three were banished to Constantinople.

According to the Pope's instructions, Afiarta was to be arrested on his return, by the Archbishop of Ravenna, who, after communicating to him the result of the inquest on the murder of Sergius, and having verified his guilt, would condemn him also to exile at Constantinople. Hadrian even caused a letter to be sent to the Emperors Constantine V. and Leo IV., acquainting them with what had occurred, and recommending them to keep a strict watch over the banished culprit.

On receiving these instructions, the archbishop had Paul arrested, on his way to Rimini, and placed in charge of the *consularius* of Ravenna, who, after making him listen to the reading of the indictment, received his depositions and admission of guilt. The archbishop and his party were greatly incensed against Afiarta, whom they justly regarded as an adherent of the Lombards. Maurice, Duke of Venice, was to have acted as intermediary between Ravenna and Constantinople, but, as his son was, at that time, a Lombard prisoner, the archbishop dreaded that he might be exchanged for Afiarta, and therefore wrote to the Pope, dissuading him from entrusting his captive to the Venetian duke.

At this, the Pope, not without good grounds, feared that the Ravennese might adopt a more expeditious method of getting rid of their prisoner. He therefore despatched another envoy to the Lombard king, with instructions to fetch Afiarta on his return through Ravenna, and bring him back to Rome. Arrived at Ravenna, this new ambassador solemnly informed the archbishop and his circle of the commission which he had to fulfil on his return journey. But no sooner had he set out on his way to Pavia than the *consularius*, at the archbishop's behest, had the prisoner executed. The Pope disclaimed any part in the matter, but, for all that, he was well rid of a most troublesome subject. As for Christopher and Sergius, they received an honourable burial in the basilica of St. Peter.

Tradition was renewed, and the Pope withdrew from the Lombard alliance. It must be admitted that Desiderius did his best to promote ill-feeling between them, and to throw the Pope back upon the Franks. Not content with plotting against Charlemagne, and seizing upon Exarchal territories, which had been ceded fifteen or sixteen years before, he set the Dukes of Spoleto and Tuscany to lay waste Pentapolis and the duchy of Rome. Hadrian, in alarm, tried to come to terms, and kept a constant succession of envoys going between Rome and Pavia. The Abbot of Farfa, escorted by twenty venerable monks, was among them. But it was all in vain; no treaty could be made. The king, remembering his success with Paul and Stephen III., was most anxious for a personal interview with the Pope. He hoped to induce Hadrian to unite with him against Charlemagne. The former agreed to a meeting, but only on condition that the recently annexed territories should be first restored to him.

At the same time he despatched a letter to Charlemagne by an envoy named Peter, who arrived at Thionville some time in the winter of 772–773. His welcome was not enthusiastic, for the king had been prejudiced by Desiderius, who had spread reports in

France that the Pope's lamentations were without cause, and that he had received no injury. The continual plaints with which the Frankish court had been beset in the times of Paul and Stephen III. made these declarations the more credible. But that this time the case was really serious, was demonstrated by the fact that Desiderius set out for Rome, accompanied by Autchaire and some of Carloman's sons. The aim of this expedition was merely to obtain audience of the Pope, and not, as in the case of Astolphus (756), the conquest of the city. As Hadrian declined to meet them at Pavia, Perugia, or anywhere else, Desiderius did what he had done several times before, under former Popes, and went forward in the direction of Rome.

But Hadrian viewed things in a different light. He imagined that he saw, or perhaps really did see, in the pilgrim king an invading foe. He therefore summoned the military forces from the neighbouring towns to Rome; had the suburban basilicas stripped of their valuables and closed; and the ramparts made ready for the defence. These precautions taken, the Pope stationed at Viterbo (at that time the nearest Lombard town) three bishops, charged to prohibit Desiderius, under pain of excommunication, from entering into Roman territory. This seems to have had a quenching effect on the king's spirit, for he retreated in the direction of Pavia.

Just at this time the Lombard king had to contend not only with the papal displeasure, but also with the diplomacy of Charlemagne. George, Bishop of Amiens (formerly of Ostia), and Gulfard, Abbot of St. Martin, came over to Italy to satisfy themselves of the state of affairs. First of all, they paid a visit to Rome, from which they brought away urgent letters; then they proceeded to Pavia, where they made fruitless attempts to obtain concessions from the king.

Charlemagne, on being informed of what was taking place, sent fresh ambassadors to Desiderius, charging him to restore what he had taken from the Pope. He himself offered to pay down a sum of fourteen thousand gold sous, as compensation. But again the Lombard king remained obdurate.

It was now about the middle of the year 773. Charles assembled his followers at Geneva, sending two military divisions to Italy. One of these, under command of his uncle Bernard, went by way of Valais and the Aosta valley, while the other crossed the Mont Cenis. History again repeated itself, and, as in the last campaign, there were summonses *in extremis*, an encounter, then defeat of the Lombards, and a siege of Pavia. This time, however, there was a second revolt at Verona. It was led by Adelchis, son of Desiderius, and the Frankish Duke Autchaire, who had taken refuge there with the family of Carloman. But Charles, after having established his camp in front of Pavia, marched against Verona, and soon succeeded in subduing the rebellion. Autchaire and his royal comrades cast themselves upon his generosity, and Adelchis took refuge in Byzantine domains. The other towns in the north of Italy also surrendered.

The days of the Lombard kingdom were numbered. The struggle was soon recognised to be an unequal one, and it was evident that the patience of the Franks was nearly exhausted. The people of Spoleto, always on the watch for a chance to assert their independence, took advantage of their Duke Theodicius' departure for the Cluses, and sent to Rome some of their most important inhabitants (*utiles personæ*) to proclaim their allegiance to the Pope, and to receive the civil tonsure of the Romans. After the overthrow of the Lombard army the whole duchy presented itself, followed by the people of Ancona, Osimo, Fermo, and Citta di Castello (*castellum Felicitatis*). So that, while Charlemagne was conquering the northern towns, the Pope was taking possession of the important districts of central Italy. He bestowed legal rights upon Hildeprand, the new Duke of Spoleto, elected by his subjects, and the latter in the beginning of his office certainly regarded himself as in subordination to the pontiff.

The siege of Pavia was protracted. Charles spent the winter in camp, having sent to France for his young wife, Hildegarde, to bear him company. When spring came he made up his mind to go to Rome for the Easter festivals. The Pope, although not aware until the last moment of the approach of such a distinguished visitor, found time to send a deputation of *judices*, *i.e.* army officers, with their banners, as far as Lake Bracciano. On the Saturday before Easter the king, with this additional escort, arrived at the meadows of Nero. There, drawn up before them, were to be seen the Roman militia under arms; the school children, palms in hand, singing *laudes;* and, finally, the district crosses. It was in this ceremonious manner that the Exarchs[1] had been received in bygone days. The king dismounted from his horse and advanced on foot towards the basilica of St. Peter's. The Pope, surrounded by his clergy, was awaiting

---

[1] The emperor himself was treated with greater pomp. In 663 Pope Vitalian himself, escorted by his clergy, went to meet Constantine II. six miles from Rome.

him at the top of the great staircase leading to the atrium. Charles ascended this on his knees, kissing each step on the way. Arrived at the top, he embraced the Pope, accepted his right hand, and accompanied him into the atrium or paradise, and then into the church.

The succeeding days were spent in religious festivals and official banquets. Nevertheless Charles and his Frankish subjects did not enter Rome until he and the pontiff had bound themselves by a mutual oath. On 6th April, the Wednesday after Easter, the great political agreements were drawn up. A meeting was held in the basilica of St. Peter, at which the Pope presented Charles with a document made out in 754 at Kiersy-sur-Oise, in the names of Pepin, Charles himself, and his brother Carloman. It was on behalf of St. Peter, Stephen II., his vicar, and successors, and contained a promise to surrender to the Pope a certain number of Italian territories. Hadrian begged the king for its fulfilment, and the latter, after re-reading it, had drawn up another document of the same purport (*ad instar anterioris*), and introducing the same cities and territories. These are indicated with great precision by Hadrian's biographer. It was, manifestly, not merely a question of the donation of the Exarchy and Pentapolis, placed by the Abbot Fulrad on the tomb of St. Peter, in 756. The new agreement, we are told, embraced, like that of Kiersy, the duchies of Spoleto and Beneventum, the whole of Tuscany, Corsica, Venetia, and Istria. Between Venetia and Tuscany, the Exarchy, which had greatly enlarged its borders in the north and west, included Parma, Reggio, Mantua, and Montselice, to the south of Padua.

If this promise had been carried out, the Lombard kingdom would have been reduced to very narrow limits. Indeed, almost the whole of Italy would have belonged to the Pope.[1]

Several copies of the document having been drawn up, it was invested with much solemnity. One copy was placed on the altar and confided to the Pope; another was deposited by Charles in the most sacred spot of the apostolic sanctuary. He then returned to Pavia, which surrendered shortly afterwards. The Lombard king and his queen, Ansa, were confined at Corbi, where they seem to have flourished for many years. Charles returned to France, leaving behind him at Pavia a garrison and a provisional government.

[1] In the introduction to the *Liber Pontificalis,* vol. i. p. cclxii, we have tried to explain the treaties of Kiersy (754) and Rome (774) by proceeding on the supposition that Pepin and Charles desired to produce in Italy a Roman state strong enough to hold its own against the Lombard kingdom. It would have allowed the latter a separate existence, but only within such narrow limits as would render it no longer formidable. M. P. Kehr, in the *Historische Zeitschrift,* vol. lxx. p. 385 *et seq. (cf. Göttingische gel. Anz.,* 1895, p. 694), has lately proposed a more fundamental theory which is worthy of consideration. According to his view, these conventions were plans of distribution for an expected contingency, the suppression of the Lombard kingdom. The Frankish kingdom would have taken possession of the whole of northern Italy as far as Magra and the neighbourhood of Venice, thus comprising the best part of the plain of the Po, as well as all the watercourses of the Alps; the remainder would have constituted a separate state under the protection of the Pope.

CHAPTER IX

THE PONTIFICAL STATE IN THE TIME OF CHARLEMAGNE

The Pope's authority at Ravenna—The Archbishops Sergius and Leo—
Spoleto and Beneventum—Charles, King of the Lombards—Re-
linquishment of the Peace of 774—Arrangements of 771, in relation
to Terracino, the Duchies of Spoleto, Tuscany, and Sabina—Concessions of domains in Tuscany and Campania (787)—The patriciate
of the Frankish King, and sovereignty of the Pope—Election of
Leo III.—The Lateran *triclinium*.

IMMEDIATELY after the fall of Pavia, Charles had
commanded the Lombard authorities to evacuate
the cities of Emilia, which, by the treaty of 756,
Desiderius had made over to the Pope, but which
he had since either retained or retaken. Among
the latter were Comacchio, Ferrara, and Faenza,
while Imola and Bologna had remained in his
possession all along. The Frankish king would,
for the moment, make no further concessions to
the Pope, and even these were not likely to afford
much satisfaction, considering the aggressive influence
of the Archbishop of Ravenna.

The honoured founder of the Church of Ravenna
was the martyr saint Apollinarius, reputed to have
been a loyal disciple of St. Peter. His successors
were not always characterised by the same fidelity,
for their pride in the importance of their town soon
made them conspicuous by their greed for titles and
precedence, and by a marked inclination to resent
what they, of their own accord, called the yoke of
Roman servitude — *jugum Romanorum servitutis.*

The Popes of the seventh century had hard work to keep them under proper discipline. Old quarrels were continually being revived, for the resistance proceeded, not so much from the archbishops themselves, as from the Ravennese clergy in general, and indeed from the whole population without distinction of class.

In the last days of the Exarchy, when the Lombards were about to descend on Ravenna, the Pope's intervention was hailed with gladness. Zachary, when he passed through the town on his way to Pavia, was welcomed by the Ravennese as a deliverer and the father of the country. There was less enthusiasm, however, in 756, when the Abbot Fulrad and Pope Stephen II. inaugurated the new régime. The first consequence of this was the utter decapitalisation of Ravenna. If the Lombards had retained their supremacy, Ravenna would have retained its importance. Its inhabitants might hope that, as in the days of Theodoric and Honorius, it would become the residence of the Lombard kings, or that they would, at least, sojourn from time to time among the splendour of its historic palaces. They would still be citizens of a royal city, though no longer subjects of the emperor. But Pepin's donation caused the prospect to fade away. They would have to pass under the yoke of the pontiff and his Romans, and that without any redeeming feature, for it was impossible that St. Peter's successor should leave the palace of his seat and tomb. The *servitus Romanorum* already made itself felt in the spiritual domain, and now it was getting involved in a temporal affair. The Pope claimed the right to ratify the appointment of the archbishop, to consecrate him with his own hands, to summon him to his councils, 'and to veto his decrees. There was nothing for it but to submit. Officials were already arriving from Rome, furnished with a papal commission, and with instructions to superintend the administration of the towns, the government of the province, and the collecting of the taxes. This was really a severe infliction.

The Archbishop Sergius took a prominent position from the very first. The meaning conveyed to him by the donation of Pepin was, that although St. Peter was undoubtedly to enjoy possession of the Exarchy and Pentapolis, it was in the person of his disciple, St. Apollinarius. Without waiting for the approval of the Romans, he took upon himself to appoint officials, and placed himself at the head of the government in the provinces surrendered by Astolphus. Stephen II., annoyed at these proceedings, summoned the archbishop to Rome, and, thanks probably to the Abbot Fulrad, his command was obeyed. He even succeeded in detaining him for a time, and meanwhile the papal officials established themselves in the transapennine provinces.[1] In 758, as Sergius was still being kept at Rome, King Pepin, who liked to encourage harmonious relations among his Italian protégés, interfered.[2] He arranged matters with Pope Paul, with the result that Sergius was allowed to return to Ravenna. He was invested with a certain authority over the Exarchy and Pentapolis, but the right to receive taxes and appoint functionaries was reserved for the Pope alone.[3]

[1] J., 2408.   [2] J., 2338.
[3] J., 2408. We must compare with this letter the information evolved from the confused memories of the life of Sergius, collected by Agnellus (157, 158, 159). This Agnellus was aware of the archbishop's detention at Rome, in the latter days of Stephen II.,

After this Sergius and Paul continued on fairly good terms with one another. From a letter written by the Pope [1] we learn that the archbishop remained loyal to the new order of things, and did not fail to keep him informed of the intrigues which were growing up around him, in view of a Byzantine restoration. He sent a deputation to the Roman Council of 769.

Pope Paul had been wise in his generation. It was absolutely necessary to keep on friendly terms with so weighty a personage as the archbishop of Ravenna. Since the dissolution of the Exarchy there had been no centre in the Adriatic provinces to compare in importance with his episcopal town, and no body so influential as his clergy. The difficulty with the Ravennese was that if they were given an inch they showed a strong tendency to take an ell, and thus to reduce the pontifical authority to little more than a name.

This soon came to pass. On the death of Sergius, 25th August 769, the people of Ravenna appointed in his place one Michaelius, *scriniarius* of his state, and perhaps tonsured, but not a priest, or in holy orders. Pope Stephen III., in conformity with the recent decree of the Roman Council, strictly forbidding this kind of preferment, refused to acknowledge him. But Michaelius, supported by at least a part of the populace and King Desiderius, who seems to have had an aptitude for conspiracy,

his understanding with Paul (he reverses the names of these two Popes), followed by the remittance of considerable sums of money (wrongfully acquired), from the ecclesiastical treasury of Ravenna, to the Pope, or, rather, to his representatives; the disapproval accorded to this deed by the Ravennese; the punishment of certain leaders; finally the supreme magistracy conferred on the archbishop.

[1] J., 2358.

succeeded in retaining his position for a year. That the Pope did not eject him was from lack of power, rather than from lack of will. This gives some idea of the weakness of the pontifical authority in the Exarchy. Eventually some envoys who had been sent to Rome by Charlemagne were led by Stephen to take an interest in the affair. Their united efforts resulted in producing a revolt at Ravenna, and Michaelius was ousted from his seat and despatched to Rome. In his place the Ravennese elected their Archdeacon Leo, whose confinement at Rimini by the rebels had, from the outset, procured him much sympathy. Immediately upon his promotion he came to Rome, and was consecrated by the Pope.[1]

This was the same Leo who had been so anxious to get rid of Paul Afiarta, the friend of Desiderius. He had excellent reasons for not feeling amiably disposed towards the Lombard king, who appears to have taken some part, or, at any rate, shown great interest in Charles's expedition into Italy.[2] He therefore considered himself entitled to the spoils, and claimed all the surrendered cities of Emilia, Bologna, Ferrara, &c., as the property of St. Apollinarius. He even went so far as to dismiss the papal officials from other parts of the Exarchy, and would doubtless have done the same in Pentapolis if the inhabitants had not risen in resistance. The Pope, annoyed at this impudent interference, wrote to Charlemagne,[3] but the archbishop, nothing daunted, betook himself to the

[1] Hadrian's letter, J., 2467, mentions a *missus* called Hucbald. This, with the *Liber Pontificalis* (Stephen III.), is our only source of information on the subject.

[2] This we gather from a very incomplete account by Agnellus.

[3] J., 2408, 2414, 2415, 2416.

Frankish king in person, and came back more bumptious than before. We do not know how this affair ended, but in 775 Hadrian became convinced that Leo was playing Charlemagne false, and did not hesitate to denounce him as a traitor. Soon after this Leo died, in 777 or 778, and his successors appear to have maintained peaceful relations with Pope Hadrian.

But the pontiff had other sources of worry besides those connected with the archbishop of Ravenna. Duke Hildeprand, of Spoleto, was adopting an independent attitude, which ill accorded with the promises of 773 or with the origin of his power. Neither was Duke Aricio of Beneventum above suspicion, and the Pope feared his entering into conspiracy with the former king, Adelchis, who had taken refuge in the Byzantine territories of the extreme south. Finally, the Patriarch of Grado wrote to inform him of preparations for revolt that were taking place at Friuli. Even the Duke of Chiusi was plotting in Tuscany. Discontent grew into conspiracy.

Towards autumn 775 two Frankish ambassadors, the Bishop Possessor and the Abbot Rabigaudus, visited Spoleto, Beneventum, and Rome, and endeavoured in vain to bring about a reconciliation between the Pope and Hildeprand. Finally they returned to Charlemagne with such disturbing reports that he felt it his duty to intervene. In the spring of 776 he arrived in northern Italy, where Rotgaud, Duke of Friuli, had proclaimed his attitude and raised his standard. Unfortunately for his cause he perished in the first battle, and his followers were farther disconcerted by the death of the Emperor Constantine V. (14th September 775). Charles was thus enabled to begin his homeward journey, and even to conduct an expedition into Saxony.

The Pope was desirous that he should come to Rome, and especially that he should undertake to carry out the Kiersy programme. But Charles, upon his entry into Pavia in 774 (30th May–2nd June) had assumed the title of king of the Lombards, and was now in nowise disposed to divide up a state which he looked upon as his own property. Hadrian did his utmost to bring him to his own way of thinking, but with very small success.

In 780 Charles again visited Italy; after spending the winter in Lombardy, he proceeded to Rome for the Easter celebrations of 781. In preceding years the Pope had been very much occupied with Terracina. He had taken possession of this place, which had apparently been hitherto in the hands of the Greeks of Gaeta and Naples, but the latter, led by the Patrician of Sicily, had recaptured it and laid waste the Roman Campagna. Hadrian had undoubtedly succeeded in repulsing them, but they had returned to the fray. In this affair the Romans saw clearly the influence of Duke Arichis. As a matter of fact, the Pope did not lay great store by Terracina, which was difficult of access, except by way of the sea or through the territory of Gaeta. He would willingly have exchanged it for the privilege of enjoying his patrimonies in the Byzantine portion of ancient Campania.

Some arrangement of this kind ought to have been made during Charlemagne's stay at Rome. He had at that time all sorts of reasons for wishing to be on good terms with the Greeks. An alliance was being arranged between his daughter, Rotrude, and the young Emperor Constantine VI., who had just (780) succeeded his father Leo IV., under the guardianship of his mother, the Empress Irene. From this time Terracina no longer made part of the papal state. On the other hand, the latter increased on the side of Sabina; the abbots of St. Martin, and of St. Denis, Itherius, and Magenarius were charged to define its limits on the side of Reiti, *i.e.* towards the duchy of Spoleto.

It was probably at this time that the Pope submitted to an agreement by which he relinquished[1] the duchies of Spoleto and Tuscany, conceding the tribute formerly paid by them into the treasury of the Lombard kings.

Another very important matter was arranged between the Pope and Charlemagne. The latter had brought with him his two young sons, Pepin and Louis (both the children of Hildegard), and they were now crowned by the pontiff as kings of Italy and Aquitaine. As far as Italy was concerned, this was a second confirmation of the continuance of the Lombard kingdom, a second rejection of the distribution policy set forth in the treaty of 6th April 774. The fair dreams of the Romans were becoming fainter and yet more faint.

A few years later, at the beginning of 787, Charles returned to Rome with the idea of settling the affairs of his distant possession of Beneventum, for the Duke Arichis was continually getting mixed up with Byzantine intrigues, and was by no means a satisfactory agent. One result of this expedition was that the Pope obtained an important increase of territory in Roman Tuscia, which henceforth included Viterbo, Orvieto, Soana, and all the inter-

[1] Privilege of 817.

vening places; while on the coast the territories of *Rosellæ* (Grosseto) and *Populonia* (Piombino) were also conceded. But there were difficulties in the way. Charlemagne had taken all this from the ancient Lombard Tuscia, which really belonged to him. But, as regarded Beneventum, affairs were more complicated. In order to succeed in his plans it was necessary that Charles should enter the territory of the duchy in person. Arichis, in alarm, shut himself up at Salerno, but he agreed to the king's conditions, which included the surrender to the Pope of the left bank of the Liris, Sora, Arpino, and Arce, as well as the towns of Aquino, Teano, and Capua, on the way to Naples.

The projected marriage between Rotrude and Constantine was given up. Soon afterwards Duke Arichis died, and Charles appointed as successor his son Grimoald, who had been taken by the Franks as hostage. The connection between the Greeks and the Lombards was then severed. The latter, *i.e.* the Dukes of Spoleto and Beneventum, displayed their goodwill to Charles by vanquishing the patrician of Sicily, in the Calabrian peninsula, in 788. Charles, for his part, did not interpret the terms of the surrender of the Beneventine towns very strictly. To Hadrian this was a great grievance, but he was obliged to be satisfied with a very nominal authority in the regions beyond Ceprano.

In short, setting aside these somewhat speculative rights, one may say that Pope Hadrian succeeded in assigning to the Roman duchy limits which were preserved during the Middle Ages and up to the year 1870. He was also monarch of the Exarchy, Pentapolis, and the intermediate territories, Amelia, Todi, and Perugia; as for the duchy of Spoleto, that remained outside the papal state.

Let us now try to realise the precise nature of the papal sovereignty of the time.

Since the year 774, Charles had taken unto himself the title of *patricius Romanorum* as well as that of *rex Langobardorum*. Judging by the *Codex Carolinus* he must have attached a great deal of importance to this, and to the privileges connected therewith. Nevertheless, he does not appear to have considered that his authority over the papal states was on a level with his power over the rest of Italy, even including the duchies of Spoleto and Beneventum. Though, theoretically, the Dukes of Spoleto and Beneventum were his functionaries, in reality they were vassals. Owing to the distance, Charles was obliged to permit a kind of self-government, such as he would not have tolerated in the neighbourhood of the Alps; but the governors of these far-away provinces received and held their authority from him. Whether they came into office by inheritance or by election, it was he who confirmed their promotion, and his name in which they governed.

With the Pope it was otherwise. Charles neither appointed him nor confirmed his appointment. He had, in fact, absolutely no voice in the installation of the Bishop of Rome. Once in possession of St. Peter's See, the Pope became, in consequence, the apostle's representative in all temporal affairs, and the agent through whom he exercised his rights of sovereignty. These rights originated in two ways: 1st, the donations of the Frankish kings, in virtue of which he acquired rights over the Exarchy, Pentapolis, Sabina, and the south of ancient Tuscan Lombardy; 2nd, the ill-defined precedent, by which the Pope replaced the emperor in the government of the ancient duchies of Rome and Perugia. However they may have arisen, the papal rights were recognised by the Frankish state, and upheld by it in the face of all outside claims, in particular, from that time, against the Greek empire. It was an understood thing that the Pope's subjects should remain loyal to the Frankish state, and should, under no circumstances, enter into alliance with their enemies. These were the essential points in the compact of "love and loyalty," so often referred to in the correspondence between the Pope and the Carlovingian princes.

So far it was only a question of external relations. But, from the beginning, the Pope had bestowed on Pepin and his sons the title of *patricii Romanorum*, and we have seen that this was a sign that internal affairs were under consideration. Originally, the patriciate had a purely negative significance, its chief use being to facilitate the suppression of the Duke of Rome and the annihilation of the Exarch. At first, therefore, the Frankish princes thought very little of the honour, but by degrees his experience of Italian affairs caused Charlemagne to consider the practical advantages connected with it. He began by persuading himself that, as patrician of the Romans, he ought to have a voice in the appointment of the most important of the public officials. Among these was the archbishop of Ravenna, who, owing partly to the amiability of his disposition, had, to a certain extent, filled the place of the old Exarch. Charles claimed the right to be represented at his election, but Hadrian tried to convince him that neither by precedent, nor in any other manner, had he any rights in the matter. As far as the Pope himself was concerned, there was only one election (that of Leo III.) from the time of Charles's intervention in Italy to the end of his reign, and the king took no part in that.[1]

But there was another constantly recurring opportunity for the Frankish intervention. Whenever a pontifical official or any of the Roman nobility had any cause of complaint against their sovereign, he did not hesitate to appeal for redress to the Frankish court. That the king welcomed this attitude is clear from the frequent recriminations which occur in the Pope's letters.[2] No definite arrangement was made. The Pope complained calmly, and the king, no less calmly, remonstrated with him as he thought fit. Their relations continued quite amicable. Hadrian had sense enough to know when to give way, and not to involve himself in great conflicts or discussions under circumstances in which he would assuredly have been worsted.

No constitutional progress, in short, was made during Hadrian's pontificate. All arrangements seem to have been of a provisional and indefinite kind. When the Pope died, at the close of the year 795, Charlemagne mourned as for a friend; he even caused a beautiful epitaph to be composed and engraved, which was, at the same time, a monument of royal sympathy, and of the revival of letters, which was beginning to make itself felt under the encouragement and patronage of this great prince.

The new Pope, Leo III., was elected on the

[1] J., 2467, 2478.
[2] Especially J., 2413, 2442, 2478.

very day of Hadrian's death, the 26th of December 795, and his consecration took place on the day after, a Sunday.. He was the head of the pontifical *vestiarium*, and as such had enjoyed the confidence of the deceased Pope. During the whole of his career he had been connected with the administration, and even his elevation to the rank of cardinal had not severed his relation with it. His titulary church of St. Susanna speedily became the recipient of his lavish generosity.

Immediately upon his installation, the new Pope sent Charlemagne a copy of the deed of his election (*decretalis cartula*), together with the keys of St. Peter's confession, and the standard of the city of Rome. There was also a letter, the purport of which can only be surmised from the king's reply.[1] From one of the Frankish annalists[2] we learn that the Pope begged the king to send one of his dignitaries (*optimates*) to Rome in order to receive the oath of the Roman people. The abbot of St. Riguier, Angilbert, was chosen for this mission.

We are still in possession of Charlemagne's reply to the Pope, as well as of the instructions provided for his *missus*, Angilbert. But there is no mention of the taking of the oath. The sending of the keys and the standard was clear enough demonstration of the gratitude felt towards the Frankish prince for his protectorship of the tomb of St. Peter and his temporal domain, now become, to a great extent, political ground. It was only natural that each fresh person charged with the care of the Apostle's subjects

[1] Jaffé, *Monum. Carol.*, p. 354; *cf.* p. 353, letter from Charles to Angilbert.

[2] *Rogavitque ut aliquem de suis optimatibus Romam mitteret, qui populum Romanum ad suam fidem atque subjectionem per sacramenta firmaret.* (*Ann. Einh.*)

and his confession, should testify his allegiance to their royal protector. Nevertheless, the preceding Popes had neglected this formality; and there had been, apparently, no official notice of election given, before the time of Leo III. Whether these new manifestations were spontaneous, or whether they had been agreed upon with Pope Hadrian, there can be no doubt that they had a beneficial effect upon the relations between the two powers.

As to the taking of the oath, our evidence on this point is not very reliable, and we do not clearly understand whether it was to have been sworn by the Pope or by the king. As, however, the election itself was accompanied by promises of loyalty towards the one elected, we may surmise that in this case it was a question of swearing an oath to the king. However this may be, the intervention of a Frankish *missus* in such an affair must be regarded as a protective act. The Pope cannot be considered completely master of his subjects, when they swear political allegiance to other authorities.

The letters from Charles to Leo III. and Angilbert are full of moral exhortations. Leo is enjoined to be a good Pope, pious, faithful in the discharge of his duties, and strict in maintaining discipline, especially in repressing simony; to sustain the friendly relations existing between the Holy See and the Frankish court, and, in particular, to protect the rights of the royal patrician. In all these directions Charles displays a certain consciousness of moral authority, and of the advantage of having good ecclesiastical leaders in his kingdom.

Leo appears to have accepted this advice with much amiability. It was, after all, quite in harmony with the spirit and the needs of the time. Not long after his accession he had constructed in the Lateran a large hall or *triclinium*, the apse of which was decorated with a mosaic representing Christ and the twelve apostles. On either side of the principal scene were two groups, each consisting of three persons; Christ giving the keys to St. Sylvester, and the standard to Constantine; St. Peter giving the pallium to Leo III., and the standard to Charlemagne.[1] Nothing could more aptly have expressed the actual situation of Rome and of the Romans; they were under two masters, the Pope and the Frankish king.

[1] This mosaic is now destroyed, but there still exist old copies, made at different times, and a reproduction, also a mosaic, executed in the time of Benedict XIV., on one of the outside walls of the *Sancta Sanctorum*. *Cf. L. P.*, vol. ii. p. 35.

CHAPTER X

RESTORATION OF THE EMPIRE

Opposition to Leo III.—The Attack of the 25th April 799—The Pope in Saxony—Insurrection and Legal Proceedings—The *Purgatio* by Oath—Christmas, 800—Charles proclaimed Emperor at St. Peter's—Signification of this New Title—The Donation of Constantine.

THE year 799 was witness of a deplorable occurrence, which soon put to the proof the respective stability of the two powers, and afforded an opportunity for determining their mutual relations.

Almost from the first there had been an undercurrent of hostility to Pope Leo. As his most powerful opponents numbered among them some relations of Pope Hadrian, there is good reason to suppose that the opposition was caused by a change, either in the manner of governing, or in the distribution of favours. As early as the end of 798, Arn, the archbishop of Salzburg, who was visiting Rome, remarked a spirit of discord and unreasonable resistance to the Pope's authority.[1] A plot was set on foot, and culminated on the 25th April 799, the day of the rogations. The Pope was on his way to join the procession, which was to start from the Church of St. Lawrence, *in Lucina*. He, with his retinue, had already arrived at the new monastery of St. Sylvester, not far from their destination, when he was suddenly attacked by a body of armed men. He was thrown to the ground, and the ringleaders of the riot, the *primi-*

[1] Letter to Alcuin, Jaffé, *Monum. Alcuin.*, p. 445.

cerius Pascal and the *saccelarius* Campulus, seized upon his person. Having failed in their first attempts to scoop out his eyes and tear out his tongue, they dragged him into the convent church, where they set on him anew. The Pope, terribly wounded and half-dead from the effect from blows, was left for some time lying in front of the altar, unconscious and weltering in blood. Finally he was removed at nightfall to the monastery of St. Erasmus, on the Cœlian, where he was kept imprisoned.

The traitors were disappointed in the success of their plans, for Leo speedily recovered both sight and speech. Neither did they succeed in keeping him prisoner, for, thanks to the assistance of Albinus, a friendly chamberlain, he managed to escape by night to St. Peter's. There he was met by Wirundus, a Frankish *missus*, and Winigis, Duke of Spoleto. They conducted him safely to Spoleto, where he was soon surrounded by a number of loyal Romans.

From Spoleto, Leo proceeded to Paderborn in Saxony, where he was joined by Charles. The latter received him with enthusiasm, and, after detaining him for some time, sent him back to Rome with an escort, consisting of several counts and bishops, Hildebald of Cologne, Arn of Salzburg, and others, all charged to see the Pope reinstated, and to make an enquiry into the circumstances of his maltreatment.

The situation of the Greek empire and of Italy, at that time, was such as to preclude any reliance on outside help. The insurrectionists, therefore, after a few plundering expeditions in the Church territories (*domus cultæ*), resolved to alter their methods, and the revolutionists who had begun by sacrilegious attacks on the Pope's person, ended by instituting legal proceedings against him.[1]

If we may believe his biographer, Leo was received at Rome on 29th November with a public display of welcome and sympathy. But the Frankish commissioners immediately established themselves at the Lateran, in the beautiful new *triclinium*, containing the representation of Leo with Charles, and proceeded to institute their enquiry. It was no easy task, and, judging by certain details of the correspondence between Alcuin and the Archbishop Arn, the conspirators had not been altogether without justification for their grievances. The ringleaders, Pascal and Campulus, were sent to appear before the king.

Charles had evidently reserved his judgment in the matter, for no decision had been announced when he arrived at Rome in person, one year after Leo's return. On 1st December he convened a large assembly at St. Peter's, including, among others, the two aristocratic sections of Rome, the upper clergy and the nobles. The prince was surrounded by his bishops, abbots, and barons. He expounded the object of his journey, which was to put an end to the existing strife. This was a difficult matter, for, on the one hand, the plaintiffs were abandoning the cause, and even if their grievances were real, there was no one left to confirm them ; while on the other hand, the ecclesiastical world was strongly imbued with the notion that no one could presume

[1] *L. P.*, vol. ii. p. 6 : *post dira iniqua incendia quæ in possessionibus seu rebus b. Petri ap. gesserunt.*

to judge the Pope. The latter, therefore, remained under an accusation, which no one was qualified either to prove or to refute. Following some rather hazy precedents, he decided to justify himself by swearing a solemn oath, an undertaking which, while implying a certain amount of personal humiliation, involved no principle and repudiated no claim.

As far as the canon law was concerned, there was manifestly no higher ecclesiastical authority than the pontiff. There had never yet been any ecclesiastical tribune to pronounce judgment against a Pope. Three centuries before (in 501) the history of the lawsuit of Symmachus had demonstrated the difficulties of such a situation. But with regard to the civil law, the case was quite different. Crimes against common law, such as homicide, adultery, and high treason, were brought before the ordinary tribunal, whatever the rank of the accused, and, during the whole of the imperial régime, the Pope had formed no exception to the rule. But now the situation was changed. The Pope was a sovereign, and, as such, beyond the pale of judgment.

It would be interesting to know the exact accusation [1] brought against Leo, but unfortunately we are not in a position to judge whether it was a question of what the Roman law calls *levia delicta*, which

---

[1] From a letter from Alcuin (No. 120), we learn that he was accused of *crimina adulterii et perjurii*, but it is uncertain whether the word "adultery" is used here in the full legal sense. In another letter from the same writer (No. 127), we are told that the Archbishop Arn complained keenly *de moribus apostolici*. Fornication, even in the case of clerks, is not a punishable crime according to Roman law. Clerks who commit this sin are only answerable to the ecclesiastical tribunals. Adultery, in the strict sense of the word, is dealt with quite differently.

being committed against the ecclesiastical law, can be dealt with only by an ecclesiastical tribunal; or of offences against the common law which were formerly amenable to the imperial courts.

There is no doubt, however, that Pope Leo vindicated himself, by swearing a solemn oath before a public assembly at St. Peter's, to which all the people were bidden (23rd December 800). We still have the text of the declaration which he read from the top of the ambo, proclaiming that he was acting of his own free will, under neither pressure nor constraint, and without claiming to establish a precedent for his successors, in the event of a similar case arising.

But, notwithstanding all these reservations, the fact remained that the Pope had taken the oath, and it was patent to everybody that he had done so because Charles had considered it essential. Indeed, Leo cut but a poor figure by the side of his protector, to whose clemency he clearly owed the continuation of his reign over the Romans.

Two days afterwards, the Romans and their Frankish friends assembled at St. Peter's for the Christmas celebrations. As the king rose from his prostrations before the confession, the Pope placed a crown on his head, and the congregation, who had been prepared for this, acclaimed him with the words: "To Charles Augustus, crowned of God, great and peaceable emperor of the Romans, life and victory!" Then the assembly burst forth into the imperial *laudes*, while the Pope anointed with chrism the forehead, not of the new emperor, who had long been consecrated, but of his young son

Charles, who had accompanied him to Rome, and was standing by his side.

The Frankish king, then, emerged from this Christmas mass with the title of Roman emperor. But, according to Eginhard, a competent witness, he was ill pleased at the turn affairs had taken. To judge from the general opinion of contemporary informants, Charles seemed to have had no personal objection to this change, which, indeed, was in consonance with certain tendencies of western opinion. But he probably had his own ideas as to the best ways and means of bringing it about. At that time the imperial throne of Constantinople was occupied by the Empress Irene, a woman of marriageable estate. This alliance (afterwards sought when too late) was perhaps the means desired by the Frankish king. It may also be reasonably conjectured that the Pope's idea of an improvised coronation ceremony was hardly in harmony with Charles's conception of the form in which the new dignity should have been transmitted. There is no doubt that, as his end was approaching, he himself crowned and proclaimed his son Louis as his successor to the empire.

But the deed was done, and a precedent established. Charlemagne was emperor, and it was the Pope who had crowned him. That Christmas day, the first day of a new century, inaugurated an era in the history of the West, and of Rome in particular.

As far as the West was concerned, it was, at first, merely a question of title and ceremonial, and no change occurred in the internal politics of the Frankish and Lombard kingdoms. Externally, it is true, there were efforts made to get Constantinople to recognise this Frankish revival of the old Roman empire. But this only slightly affected the Italian questions.

At Rome, the transformation of the patrician into the emperor, gave him a more clearly defined position. No one quite knew what were the exact rights attached to this title of *patricius Romanorum*, conceived by Pope Stephen II. and his advisers. On the other hand, there could be no mistaking the meaning of the title *Imperator*. History, tradition, and written law all shed a clear enough light upon it. The emperor was monarch of Rome, and every one, the Pope not excepted, stood to him in the relation of subject. As administrator, judge, and military chief, his authority was paramount. Only in the domain of religion did he yield to another, following the example of his predecessors.

We must, nevertheless, remember that this conception of imperial rights was hardly as clear to the Romans in the year 800 as it is to us to-day. They were imbued with the traditional idea of the Pope's supremacy in the domain of local politics. Memoirs of St. Gregory and Honorius in the far past, and of Gregory II., Zachary, Paul, and Hadrian, of more recent date, arose and confronted the Justinian code with a commentary, out of harmony with the text, it is true, but for all that, irresistible.

Moreover, a great impression had been produced by the form of the coronation, and as the memory of the circumstances became fainter, there finally remained in men's minds only the significant picture of Leo III. placing the imperial crown on the head of the kneeling Charlemagne. At Constantinople this was a frequent sight, for it was the patriarch who crowned the emperor. But, still more in evidence was the fact, that the patriarch was but the humble servant of the emperor, one might almost say his domestic chaplain. His right of occasionally placing the imperial crown upon his sovereign's head was really of no more consequence than the superior part which he played in the ordinary liturgical ceremonies.

At Rome it was different. Such a sight as that of an emperor being crowned by a Pope had never been seen before. The basilica of St. Peter was henceforth regarded as the cradle of the empire, which owed its rebirth to the Apostolic Vicar, the Pope. Charlemagne had inaugurated the custom, and who was greater than he? What tradition could take the place of his?

There was, at first, no definite arrangement, no written agreement. The empire was restored without any decided plans having been made. But the false donation of Constantine, which occurred at least twenty-five years earlier, expresses clearly the conception of the new imperial régime which the Romans (and in particular the Roman clergy) adopted more and more definitely as time went on. What they desired was a benevolent and gracious protective sovereign, who would leave Rome to the Pope, and take up his own abode as far away as possible. The faithful successor of Constantine might set up his throne at Aix-la-Chapelle, or anywhere else, provided that it was at a safe distance from Rome, and that he did not interfere with the heir of St. Sylvester. At the same time he would be expected to come to the help of the Romans in the event of any special difficulty.

The donation of Constantine had already offered in 800 (for the few who accepted it at that time) an excellent judicial foundation for the Pope's intervention. According to the ideas which prevailed later, the emperor had rights over the whole of the West, holding them from his consecrator the Pope. But from whom did the Pope hold them? The donation tells us from Constantine, who had yielded to St. Sylvester, *omnes Italiæ seu occidentalium regionum provincias loca et civitates*. He was thus in a position to do what he liked with them.

Far be it from me to imply that Leo III. made such use of the donation as to infer from it his right to restore the empire and its constitutional theory. By most of the critics this document is dated back to the beginning of the year 744; it was manufactured at Rome, probably at the Lateran, the very palace where Leo was, at that time, beginning his career in the administration of the sacristy. It is more than likely, therefore, that there was something in common between the idea with which it is inspired and the conceptions of the Pope and his party with regard to the theoretical, or, at least, desirable, relations between the two powers (800). As may readily be imagined, such notions were not calculated to please Charlemagne. It is doubtful whether he had any very definite idea of the extent of the ancient imperial power. Times were changed, and not even so mighty a king as himself, not even the Byzantine successors of the true empire, could lay claim to an authority as absolute as that of a Trajan or a Constantine. In the West, especially, the military aristocracy—

the forerunners of the feudal system—were a force to be reckoned with.

In short, Christmas Day, 800, had been witness of a great and remarkable event, the full importance of which was not understood at the time. And this is not an isolated instance of the kind.

CHAPTER XI

THE CONSTITUTION OF LOTHAIRE

New plot against Leo III.—Severe repressions—Insurrection—Unpopularity of the *domus cultæ*—Stephen IV.—Louis the Pious crowned at Rheims—Pope Pascal—The privilege of Louis—Lothaire—Crowned Emperor at Aix-la-Chapelle and at Rome—More plots and outrageous repressions — Pascal an unpopular Pope — Election of Eugene II.—Lothaire comes back to Rome—Constitution of 824—Roman Council—Elections of 827—Valentine and Gregory IV.

THE Pope's relations with Charlemagne and with his own subjects do not appear to have been sensibly affected by the restoration of the empire. The Romans stood in wholesome awe of the imposing person of the Frankish king, and the Pope, in some measure, reaped the benefit of this attitude. However, when Charlemagne died, on 28th January 814, the Roman nobles began to assert themselves, conspiring to get rid of the Pope by assassinating him. It evidently did not occur to them to assail so firmly established an institution as the temporal pontificate. It was the administration of this particular Pope which was distasteful to them, and they resolved to attack him in person.

But this conspiracy came to nought. The pontifical police discovered it, and the numerous conspirators were arrested, tried for the crime of high treason, condemned to death, and executed. This event caused a remarkable sensation at the court of Louis the Pious. The Frankish law, it was said, was much less severe. Had not the Pope exceeded his power in allowing sentences of death to be dealt out with so liberal a hand ? He ought, at any rate, to have consulted the emperor. What would become of the imperial authority at Rome if such things were permitted to take place without any reference to it ?

Possibly Louis may have seen, in the Pope's attitude, a kind of protest against the manner of his accession to the empire. For Leo had had no part in the matter, and was therefore inclined to ignore an emperor whom he had not consecrated.

However this may have been, Bernard, the young king of Italy, and Gerald, count of the Eastern Marches (Austria), were commissioned to go to Rome and enquire into the affair. Gerald afterwards betook himself to the imperial court with his report of the proceedings. The Pope, in self-defence, sent three ambassadors to France, and their explanations or excuses seem to have afforded Louis satisfaction. Nevertheless, the disturbances at Rome continued. A revolt took place in the country, and the *domus cultæ* was attacked and plundered.[1] It is probable that this was an act of revenge on the militia for having assisted in putting down the conspirators. Moreover, the continual development of these *latifundia* entailed a number of dispossessions which were regarded by those who suffered them as unjust usurpations. When the rural colonies had been burned, the insurgents marched upon Rome demanding redress. Pope Leo was seriously threatened, but the rebels were dispersed by Winigis, Duke of Spoleto, whom King Bernard had sent to

---

[1] *Ann. Einh.*, 815, *prædia quæ idem pontifex in singularum civitatum territoriis noviter exstruxit ; Vita Lud.*, c. 25, *prædia omnia quæ illi domocultas appellant et noviter ab eodem apostolico instituta erant.*

his assistance. The ringleaders were banished to France.

Such was the situation when Leo III. passed away, the 12th June 816. The clergy, always in evidence at election times, were quite convinced of the propriety of choosing a more popular and accommodating pontiff than the late Pope. Their approbation fell on the deacon Stephen, the son of a noble family, and protégé of Pope Hadrian. His biographer tells us that he was much liked by the Romans. In accordance with custom, his consecration took place on the Sunday following his election (22nd June). He at once showed himself to be peaceably disposed and anxious to smooth away all traces of past discord, and freely to accept the imperial protection. He began his reign by obliging the Romans to swear allegiance to the emperor, and then sent notice of his election to the Frankish court, announcing at the same time his intention of meeting Louis. This interview actually took place at Rheims in the month of October. It resulted in the settlement of many questions, of which only two seem to have been of much consequence. Louis and his wife Ermengarde were crowned by the Pope with crowns of gold, which he had brought with him for the purpose. Thus the Roman ideas of propriety were satisfied. Whether this ceremony counted for much in the opinion of their contemporaries is doubtful, but it nevertheless constituted a second precedent, and confirmed the predominance of the papacy over the empire. Moreover, Stephen brought back with him the exiles who were in France, perhaps those of the 799 insurrection, or perhaps only those banished after the last revolt.

Stephen's pontificate thus opened with good

prospects of peace. But, alas for the frailty of human plans, the month of January 817 had not come to an end when the new Pope was called to follow his predecessor.

On the very day of his death (25th January), the priest Pascal, abbot of one of the monasteries of the Vatican, was elected in his place. He was not of the aristocracy, and seems to have been inspired with the spirit of Leo III. rather than that of Hadrian. As soon as his consecration had been accomplished, he sent to inform the emperor of his accession, protesting that he had been elected against his will.

Shortly afterwards, another papal envoy, the nomenclator Theodore, was despatched to Louis the Pious, to request an official renewal of the compact between the Carlovingian House and the papacy. This agreement had already been recorded several times, under the preceding kings and Popes, but not one of these important documents has been preserved. The compact between Louis the Pious and Pope Pascal, is the oldest of which we know the terms. It contains a confirmation of the rights of the Roman Church over those Italian territories which, in one way or another, were included in its domain, the city of Rome, Roman Tuscia as defined before 787, the district of Perugia, ancient Campania, Tibur, the whole of the Exarchy, Pentapolis, including Ancona, Umana, and Osimo, the territory of Sabina, Lombard Tuscia, as surrendered by Charlemagne, the rent formerly paid to the palace at Pavia by the rest of Lombard Tuscia and the duchy of Spoleto, and, finally, the territories beyond the Liris and the ecclesiastical estates in Southern Italy, *i.e.* domains over which the Pope had theoretical rather than practical rights. The emperor undertakes to guarantee all these possessions or claims, and promises, besides, to allow the Pope a free hand in governing, and only to interfere in the event of violence or unjust oppression on the part of the *potentiores*, which evidently means the pontifical government itself. He also renounces any right of intervention in the election of the Pope, which is to be conducted in conformity with the canons, and carried by unanimous consent. The Pope, must, however, immediately after his consecration, send representatives to the Frankish king, charged to renew the friendly alliance.

In short, this document corresponds with the actual situation, at the moment when it was drawn up : protectorate of the Frankish monarch, liberty of the Romans in the choice of the Pope, and free exercise of the papal sovereignty, except in the case of abuse of authority.

Louis had permitted Stephen IV. to officiate at his coronation at Rheims, but, like his father, he regarded the papal intervention simply as a religious consecration of rights acquired from other sources. In 817 he himself crowned his eldest son Lothaire as emperor, before a large concourse of people at Aix-la-Chapelle. At the same time he created Pepin and Louis, his two other sons, kings of Aquitaine and Bavaria. Bernard, king of Italy and grandson of Charlemagne through his deceased father Pepin, refused to accept this new arrangement. He rebelled, but with ill success. His eyes were torn out, and he died immediately afterwards, in April 818. In 822, his kingdom was entrusted to Lothaire, who set out to take possession of it. Pope Pascal, on hearing of his arrival in

Italy, took the opportunity to invite him to Rome, and in virtue, undoubtedly, of an understanding with his father, he consecrated the young prince as emperor, on Easter Sunday, 5th April 823. Already, in 821, Roman legates had journeyed to Thionville, in order to be present at his marriage. But in spite of these outward amenities the conflict did not cease. The Frankish princes objected to be beholden to the Pope for their temporal authority, and the Pope refused to yield the privilege of consecrating them. He might be trusted to make the best of circumstances, and by his perseverance, finally succeeded in establishing the tradition.

The emperor had never been seen at Rome since 800, the year in which the institution was originated. Lothaire[1] held a court of justice there, and the Abbot Farfa brought before him a grievance which he had long cherished against the pontifical administration. He won his cause, and Pascal renounced his claims to temporal power over the abbey, as well as to the right of appointing an abbot. The latter was of great importance in the Roman state. The opposition to the Pope was strengthened by the temporary presence of a young emperor, who was disinclined to submit to ecclesiastical authority, and also by the prospect of his residence in the neighbourhood of Rome. The pontiff got deeper and deeper into difficulties. Those who had grievances against him, posed as champions of Lothaire and his imperial rights, and soon after the latter's departure, two dignitaries of the first rank, the *primicerius* Theodore and the

---

[1] Compare Lothaire diploma of 840 (*Böhmer-Mühlb.*, No. 1043 ; *Registr.-Farf.*, No. 298).

nomenclator Leo, were pointed out to the *familia S. Petri* (*i.e.* the militia of the agricultural colonies), as enemies of the Pope. Their disloyalty was avenged by their first having their eyes put out, and then being killed outright.

Upon hearing of this, the Emperor Louis was about to send envoys to Rome with orders to enquire into the affair. They had not started, however, when three papal legates approached, protesting that their master had had no hand in the tragedy. Louis listened to their tale, but, none the less, despatched his envoys, the Abbot of Saint-Waast and the Count of Coire. The enquiry, however, did not lead to any important result. The Pope submitted to the formality of the *purgatio per sacramentum*. He swore, before a solemn assembly which included twenty-four bishops, that he had taken no part in the assassination of the two victims, but adding that, being guilty of high treason, they were deserving of death.

This was quite possible, but for all that, it was manifest that Theodore and Leo had been the victims of violence unsanctioned by law, and that the Pope was lacking in authority over his own followers, not to mention his opponents.

Pascal sent a second detachment of legates to the Emperor Louis, who, finding the whole affair somewhat embarrassing, accepted the explanations which they offered. On their return to Rome, they found the Pope suffering from an illness which terminated his career on the 11th of February 824. So great was the aversion with which he was regarded, that the people refused to allow him to be buried at St. Peter's.

A remarkably exciting election followed ; the

two factions—the nobles and the clergy—stood out clearly : the *exercitus Romanus* and the *familia S. Petri*, long at variance, now measured their respective forces. Neither of them had any voice in the ecclesiastical elections. Since the year 769, the papal appointment had been in the hands of the clergy only. But the clergy themselves could not agree on the practical problem of meeting the present exigencies, and the disunion became so great that two candidates were proclaimed. Happily, however, the strife did not last long. The celebrated monk Wala, an adviser of the young emperor Lothaire, happened to be in Rome at the time, and he succeeded in bringing about the election of the candidate nominated by the nobles, the arch-priest Eugene of Santa Sabina.

His first act was to send a deputation to the Emperor Louis, and he lost no time in arranging that the remains of his predecessor should be interred in a becoming manner.

The Frankish court was very much taken up with the affairs of Rome, which, since the death of Charlemagne, ten years before, had been gradually growing more and more confused. Plots, insurrections, risings, and summary executions, all these were common talk, and for the second time in one generation the people had before them the pitiable sight of a Pope compelled to vindicate his character by taking a public oath. To make matters still worse, party strife arose, an infliction which had occurred but rarely during the last three centuries. The root of the evil obviously lay in the conflicting interests and ambitions of the clergy and the nobles. This situation was not peculiar to Rome, but in other places the sovereign power was strong enough to insist on peace, while at Rome the authority was held by one of two rival parties, and moreover by just the one less able to wield it successfully.   Hence arose intrigues, schisms, violence, and abuse of power.   To the Emperor Louis it seemed that the best way out of the difficulty was to make his sovereign power felt at Rome in a visible and palpable form, for up to that time, his authority there had been of a distant and intermittent nature.   He would not, however, forcibly attack the papal sovereignty, which, after all, did not proceed merely from the concessions of his predecessors, who had not so much originated as guaranteed it, and which, although under the gracious protection of the Frankish princes, was also sustained by tradition as well as by the dignity of its representative.

Lothaire was sent to Rome under the escort of Wala.   It was a recognised fact that the present disturbances resulted from the obstinacy or the weakness of the Popes [1] Leo III. and Pascal, as well as from the rapacity of their officials.   Many of the properties which had been amalgamated with the pontifical estates were restored to their original owners.

The widows of Theodore, Horus, and Sergius, the murdered officials, were given compensation, and the exiles were recalled.[2]   A code of laws of

[1] It is true that these expressions do not occur in the two official documents of 824, which have come down to us, the *Constitutio* and the *Sacramentum*, they are only found in the Frankish annals ; but the privilege of Otto (962) which reproduces the preceding official acts, and especially those of the time of which we are speaking, contains these words : *propter diversas necessitates et pontificum erga populum sibi subjectum asperitates retundendas.*

[2] We get this detail from the *Liber Pontificalis*.   It is the only touch, in the short and inadequate account of Eugenius II., which betrays any knowledge of the grave events of 824.

which the text[1] is still preserved, was drawn up, to protect the rights of the individual. The Pope was treated with formal respect, but there can be no doubt that the new measures were, on the whole, directed against him. They may be summed up under five heads concerning: 1st, the imperial protection; 2nd, the individual rights; 3rd, the choice of functionaries; 4th, the organisation of the protectorate; 5th, the papal election.

1st. On the first point it is declared that those who are under the special protection of the Pope and the emperor are inviolable.[2] This must be taken to mean that the papal authorities have no power to bring about the execution of one of the imperial protégés. As the imperial protection was of the wide-spreading order, the Roman nobles and the ecclesiastical dignitaries found themselves exempt from the fear of execution for the crime of treason, a form of punishment which had been much abused in the past.

2nd. The Romans should be judged according to the law of their choice, *i.e.* Roman, Salic, or Lombard. These last two, being less lavish with capital punishment than the Roman law, were probably preferred by some.

3rd. The Roman magistrates should present themselves before the emperor, not to be invested by him, but in order that he might know their names and their numbers, and admonish them as to the exercise of their functions.

4th. Two *missi* should be instituted, one by the

---

[1] This may be found in Migne, t. xcvii. p. 459: Hardouin, *Conc.*, t. iv. p. 1261; M. G. Leges, t. iv. p. 545; Capitul., t. i. p. 322, &c.
[2] *Ut omnes qui sub speciali defensione domni apostolici et nostra fuerint suscepti impetrata inviolabiliter justa utantur defensione.*

Pope, the other by the emperor. They should be in permanent residence at Rome, and every year should report to the emperor on the working of the administration. They should listen to complaints and retail them to the Pope, and if the latter should not do them justice, the emperor should be called upon to intervene.

5th. The election of the Pope should be in the hands of the Romans alone. The laity as well as the clergy should vote, notwithstanding the decision of the Council of 769 ; finally, before his consecration, the chosen candidate should take a formal[1] oath before the imperial *missus* and the people.

Secondary provisions prohibit plundering, and enjoin on all the Romans obedience to the Pope, whether or not they may be under the special protection of the emperor.

The difference, not to say the contrast, between these enactments and the state of things which we have been observing, is obvious. The election of the Pope was henceforth to be subject to the confirmation of the emperor. This rule was not formally expressed, but we know from subsequent history that it became a stringent though unwritten law.[2] The

---

[1] The oath is not mentioned in the Constitution itself, but in a formula which was at that time imposed on all the Romans, and which is inserted after the text of the Constitution. The reform of the electoral system is indicated in veiled terms : *Volumus ut in electione pontificis nullus præsumat venire, neque liber neque servus, qui aliquod impedimentum faciat illis solummodo Romanis quibus antiquitus fuit consuetudo concessa per constitutionem ss. Patrum eligendi pontificem.* The ambiguity of these terms is clearly explained by the accounts of elections in the *Liber Pontificalis* and elsewhere.

[2] Before the time of Justinian neither the emperors nor the Gothic kings had interfered in the papal elections, except, in the case of schism, as arbitrators or guardians of the public peace. Under

right of choosing functionaries was restricted to the Pope, but the emperor considered himself in a position to keep them, if he so desired, at his beck and call, to admonish, and above all, inspect them, and, if necessary, to reform their decisions. Certain privileged persons were exempt from the papal jurisdiction, and submitted only to that of the emperor. Finally, the latter was to be ever present in the person of his *missus* who kept a keen watch over the whole affairs of Rome.

Pope Eugenius III. not only accepted this reform, but, of his own accord, instituted another in the ecclesiastical domain. In November 826, he assembled in conclave a council of his immediate assistants, sixty-two bishops in all, and together they drew up a code of some forty-five disciplinary rules to meet the exigencies of the present situation.[1]

The reign of this excellent and conscientious Pope was all too short. He died in the month of August 827, and, before many weeks had passed, his successor, the deacon Valentine, followed his example. The Romans then elected the priest Gregory, who bore the title of St. Mark, but he

Byzantine rule, the election had to be confirmed by the emperor before ordination could take place. This, considering the distance of Constantinople, naturally occasioned great delay. After the sixth ecumenical council (681), the emperor empowered the Exarch to deliver the letters of ratification, which expedited matters considerably. This formality, of course, vanished with the Exarchy itself. The Romans had never acquiesced very heartily in this intervention, and the Frankish ratification was just as distasteful to them. Indeed, they never neglected an opportunity of evading it.

[1] According to Deusdedit (i. p. 123) this council would also be concerned in the papal election *a sacerdotibus seu primatibus, nobilibus seu cuncto concilio Romanœ ecclesiœ.*

was not ordained until his appointment had been ratified by an imperial representative.[1] This detail is suppressed by the *Liber Pontificalis*, which, on the other hand, gives a full description of the two elections of 827, showing that, in both of them, the lay nobility took part from the outset, and that they were concerned in the choice of the individual Pope, as well as in his enthronement at the Lateran. According |to the verdict of the Council of 769, they had no right to share in the matter until both these acts had been accomplished,[2] and then they were permitted to sign the deed of election. Thus the principle of the lay participation in the appointment of the pontiff was preserved, and to say that he had been elected *a sacerdotibus seu proceribus et omni clero necnon et optimatibus vel cuncto populo Romano*, was, theoretically, correct. This is the formula employed in the *Liber Pontificalis* with reference to Leo III. and Pascal; there is no special mention of Hadrian and Stephen IV. in this connection; and in regard to Eugenius II. the vague expression *a Romanis cunctis electus* is used. After the time of Valentine, however, this part of the papal history is always given in detail and in such a way as to render prominent the part played by the lay aristocracy, so prominent, indeed, that often

---

[1] ANN. EINHARDI.—*Sed non prius ordinatus est quam legatus imperatoris Romam venit et electionem populi qualis esset examinavit.* The ordination took place on the following day, as is noted in certain manuscripts of the Hieronymite martyrology.

[2] *Et postquam pontifex electus fuerit et in patriarchium deductus, omnes optimates militiæ vel cunctus exercitus et cives honesti atque universa generalitas hujus Romanæ urbis ad salutandum eum sicut omnium dominum properare debeat. Et more solito decretum facientes et in eo cuncti pariter concordantes subscribere debent.* The alternative and meaningless reading *priusquam* is omitted by Deusdedit.

but little justice is done to the influence of the clergy.

Thus, it will be seen that, on this point, as well as on many others, the position of the nobility had been perceptibly confirmed and strengthened.

CHAPTER XII

THE SARACENS AT ROME

Dislocation of the Frankish State—The Saracens in the Tyrrhenian Sea —Gregoriopolis—Election of Sergius II. (844) — Louis II. and Drogo at Rome—Bad Government of Pope Sergius—Landing of the Saracens — Violation of the Apostolic Sanctuaries — Restorative measures.

GREGORY IV. occupied the Holy See for fourteen years. His pontificate was darkened by the grievous lack of harmony between Louis the Pious and the sons of his first wife, Lothaire, Pepin, and Louis the German. The Pope was indiscreet enough to interfere in the affair and to take the side of the rebellious sons, but he found himself in a land of disillusionment, from which he emerged humiliated, a sadder if not a wiser man.

Some years later (20th June 840), the Emperor Louis died, and, as is well known, the appointment of his successor gave rise to a great deal of strife. The breaking up of the Frankish kingdom was sanctioned by the Treaty of Verdun, and henceforward it was divided into three parts—the kingdom of Western France, the kingdom of Germany, and, between the two, the kingdom of Lothaire, extending from the mouths of the Meuse and the Rhine to the estuary of the Rhone. With this was associated the kingdom of Italy, as well as Aix-la-Chapelle, the sacred town of Charlemagne.

Since his early childhood (781), the Emperor

Louis had never set foot [1] in Rome. In settling Italy upon Lothaire, he had also confided to him the management of Roman affairs, and, in particular, the protection of the Holy See. The great events of 840–843 did not then produce any very remarkable change in the pontifical relations, nor indeed, on the whole, in the Italian situation. The newly arrived Saracens were, however, beginning to create disturbances.

The Saracens of the West had long since ceased to be subject to the same princes. Those belonging to Spain were under the dominion of the Ommiad Caliph of Cordova; those of ancient Mauritania were governed by the Edrisite dynasty, whose royal seat was at Fez or at Tlemcen; while those of Numidia and the eastern provinces of Africa (including Tunis and Tripoli), were under the Aglabites, whose headquarters were at Kairwan. It was mainly with these latter that the Italian states had to do. For a long time they confined themselves to piratical enterprises. The Sicilian patrician, supported by the fleets of Naples, Amalfi, and Gaeta, defended the Byzantine coast, together with the island of Sardinia, to the best of his ability. Corsica,[2] which was a part of the Frankish empire, was placed under the guardianship of the Marquis of Tuscany, who shared with the Pope the supervision and protection of the coasts between Luni and Terracino. This was no light task. Since 831 Palermo had been in the hands of the Mussulmans, and the whole of Sicily was, by degrees, falling under their sway. More-

---

[1] In 837 he was on the point of making the journey *ad limina*, but was deterred by a Norman invasion.

[2] For information on the situation of the islands of Corsica and Sardinia in Carlovingian times, see the Memoir of M. A. Dove, in the reports of the Munich Academy, 1894.

over, since 840, the duchy of Beneventum had been claimed by two rivals, Radelgiso and Siconulf. They both called Saracen troops to their help, thus affording the Mahometans every facility for getting a footing on Italian soil.

During the latter part of his life, Pope Gregory IV. constructed, in the neighbourhood of Ostia, a fortress called Gregoriopolis, which is still in existence. It soon became evident that this precaution, far from being unnecessary, was even inadequate for purposes of defence.

Gregory died at the beginning of 844, and the appointment of a successor gave rise to some difficulty. By one party (not the nobles), the deacon John was proclaimed, and they even succeeded in introducing him at the Lateran. But the lay aristocracy had set their affections upon an old priest who directed the property of St. Martin on the Esquiline. He was weak-minded, passionate, foulmouthed, and gouty ; but he belonged to the nobility, and was a member of the same family as Pope Stephen IV. and the future Hadrian II. His supporters escorted him from his church to the Lateran palace, in stately procession. The snow was falling at the time, a sign of happy augury in the eyes of the Romans. The unfortunate John was soon ousted from the papal residence, several of his opponents demanding that he should be cut in pieces. Sergius, however, was satisfied with ejecting him, and he himself was installed and consecrated at St. Peter's without the formality of consulting the emperor.

Lothaire was of opinion that the Romans did not treat him with enough deference. He was anxious to arrive at a proper understanding of this contested election, and was especially determined to maintain his right of confirmation, which had been so calmly ignored. He despatched to Rome his son Louis, the future Emperor Louis II., and his uncle Drogo, Bishop of Metz,[1] a natural son of Charlemagne. These two princes were accompanied by an army of considerable size, which, on arriving on Roman ground, began plundering and ravaging, as though on conquered territory. This unruly behaviour was apparently intended as a manifestation of the imperial wrath. When they reached Rome, the Pope received them at the Vatican with the customary honours. But, after the first act of ceremony, the enquiry was instituted. Besides Drogo, King Louis had been followed by twenty-five Italian bishops, belonging to the Lombard kingdom, and they had been joined by the Archbishop of Ravenna, who, though ostensibly a subject of the Pope, was always pleased to oppose him. After lengthy discussions with the diocesan bishops, and with the heads of the Roman clergy and of the lay aristocracy, they decided to recognise Sergius as the rightful Pope, and it was again settled that, for the future, no one could be consecrated as pontiff without the approval (*jussio*) of the emperor and the presence of his representatives. After anointing the young prince, Sergius and the Romans swore an oath of fidelity to the emperor, and, in order to give proof of his desire to please the latter, the Pope appointed Bishop Drogo apostolic vicar, conferring upon him a kind of supremacy over all the bishops of the various Frankish districts. He

---

[1] . . . *Acturos ne deinceps decedente apostolico quisquam illic præter sui jussionem missorumque suorum præsentiam ordinetur antistes.* —PRUDENCE, *Ann.*, 844.

refrained, however, from restoring to their sees the
Archbishops of Rheims and Narbonne, Ebbo and
Bartholomew, who were recognised as adherents
of Lothaire. Rheims and Narbonne belonged to
the kingdom of Charles the Bald, and the Pope
had the good sense not to wish to encourage ill-
feeling between Lothaire and his neighbour brother.

All this took place in June 844. When Louis,
with his army and his council, had taken his departure, Sergius began to breathe more freely. Sad
to say, his reign was one of simony. The traditions
of Eugenius II., the constitution of Lothaire, and
the decrees of the Council of 826, all these were
set at naught, and the buying and selling of dignities
soon became the order of the day. To his brother
Benedict, a rustic boor of vicious habits, the Pope
gave the bishopric of Albano, and made over to
him the cares of the government.[1] Convents, as
well as private individuals, were robbed, in order
to gratify their rapacious greed and pay their ex-
penses. Benedict, strange to say, was in high
favour with the emperor, and had obtained from
him the rank of imperial *missus*, or else the confirmation of that of papal *missus*. He always seems
to be represented as exercising at Rome a kind of
tyrannical authority, though, at the same time,
keeping within the bounds of the law.

The Roman clerk who describes this situation
can hardly speak too strongly in deprecation of the
evils caused at Rome by the reign of Sergius II.
He adds that, as no one had the courage to oppose
him, God took the matter in hand and sent the
Saracens as a scourge.

Whatever may have been the exact intentions

---

[1] *L. P.*, t. ii. p. 79 and p. 103, note 30.

of Divine Providence, it cannot be denied that the Saracens landed on 23rd August 846 at the mouth of the Tiber. Porto and Ostia, abandoned by their inhabitants, gave way before them. The chief group of pirates, following the right bank of the river, fell upon the basilica of St. Peter and plundered it. The foreign *scholæ*, a mere handful of men whom the Romans had despatched to Porto, were easily put to flight, and the Romans themselves were defeated on the meadows of Nero. Louis II., who had come to their help with an insufficiently equipped army, also received a check. The invaders extended their pillaging operations to St. Paul's, but the militia of Roman Campania gained some slight success on the left bank of the Tiber. The Saracens, giving up all hopes of forcing the town ramparts, turned their attention in the direction of Fondi and Gaeta. Another royal army, commanded, it is said,[1] by the Duke of Spoleto, followed and attacked them in a strong position, where they were entrenched. Once again the Saracens obtained the advantage, though they were prevented from following it up by the intervention of a fleet from Naples and Amalfi. Seizing their booty, they re-embarked for home, but before they reached the coast of Africa a huge tempest arose, and the plunderers of the apostolic sanctuaries were engulfed, together with their ill-gotten treasure, in the waves of the Sicilian Sea.

This was but cold comfort for the Romans. The whole of Western Christendom was aghast at the gloomy news. At Rome many clerks and monks

[1] The texts relating to this event are confused, disjointed, and difficult to reconcile. I give here what I conceive to be the correct conclusion. *Cf.*, *L. P.*, vol. ii. p. 104, note 38. M. Ph. Lauer has taken up this question in the *Mélanges* of the *École de Rome*, t. xix. (1899) p. 310 and following.

abased themselves before the divine judgment, by which the wrath of Heaven was manifested against the administration of Pope Sergius.   But elsewhere, not understanding the details of the Roman affairs, they began to reflect upon the responsibility of the emperor. The tomb of the Prince of the Apostles, the great Holy of Holies of the West, had been profaned by the enemies of Christ.   Mahomet had triumphed over St. Peter, and had waged his insulting warfare in the Apostle's own dwelling, perhaps even within his mysterious sepulchre.[1]   Was not the emperor the armed protector of St. Peter, as well as the actual ruler of Italy, and as such responsible for these events?

Lothaire, who had been joined by his son Louis, lent an attentive ear to these complaints. A large convocation was held, and it was decided[2]: 1st, that the bishops, clerks, monks, and faithful should make serious efforts to reform their conduct, and, as far as lay in their power, to correct existing abuses; 2nd, that the basilica of St. Peter should be surrounded by fortifications, of which the cost was to be defrayed by a tax, levied on all the imperial states; 3rd, that an expedition under the command of King Louis should be undertaken against the Saracens who had settled in the duchy of Beneventum; 4th, that the latter should be divided between the two claimants, who, having arranged their differences, should join forces against the enemy of the Christians.

Envoys were despatched to Radelgiso and Siconulf, while others journeyed to Rome, Venice, and Naples

---

[1] As to the damage done to the apostolic sanctuary, see Grisar, *Anal. Romana*, p. 279 (*cf. Studi e documenti di storia e diretto*, 1892, p. 344).

[2] See this enactment in the *Neues Archiv*, t. xii. p. 535, 2nd edition; *M. G. Legum Sectio II. Capitularia*, t. ii. p. 65.

to organise a union of all the Italian states in view of the new undertaking. A fast of three days was ordered to precede the expedition, which was brought to a successful issue (847). The Saracens were, for the time, completely banished from Italy, though they afterwards regained their footing. The state of Beneventum was divided into two principalities, having for their capitals Beneventum and Salerno.[1]

---

[1] Distribution Act, *M. G. Leg.*, t. iv. p. 221.

CHAPTER XIII

THE EMPEROR LOUIS II

POPE SERGIUS died on the 27th of January 847. He was interred in the desecrated basilica, and a friendly hand inscribed upon his tomb words more charitable, alas, than veracious. The Romans elected as his successor the priest Leo, of the title of the Four Crowned Martyrs, a man with a reputation for integrity and prudence. His election, for some reason or other, was carried through without any reference to the emperor, and a year and a half afterwards, on Easter Day (10th April) the consecration took place. They were, nevertheless, careful to justify themselves by the gravity of the circumstances, and formally to reserve the imperial right.

Lothaire seems to have accepted the explanations of the Romans quite placidly. Although he still maintained a mild interest in Italian affairs it was becoming increasingly difficult to prevail on him to leave his own country of Lorraine, and his residence of Aix-la-Chapelle. The Lombard kingdom was governed by his son Louis, who was made an associate of the empire, and, as such, consecrated by the Pope in April 850. From that time the pontiffs had to do with an Italian emperor, who, in virtue of his residence in the neighbourhood, was the better able to intervene in the internal affairs of the Roman state.

The first question to be settled was how best to deal with their enemies, the Saracen pirates. Since 848 they had been working on the fortified enclosure near St. Peter's. The new walls were continued as far as the castle of St. Angelo, so that the fortifications reached the town itself, communicating with it by means of the *Porta S. Petri*. The enclosed area comprised not only the basilica and its dependencies, but also the quarters, or *scholæ*, of the foreign colonies of Saxons, Frisians, Franks, and Lombards. Out of compliment to the reigning Pope it received the name of the Leonine City. Part of the cost was covered by the afore-mentioned imperial tax, augmented by gifts from France and Germany. The Pope, for his part, exacted contributions from his people; the towns of the Roman state, the monasteries, the *massæ publicæ* or *domus cultæ*, all provided materials, money, or workers. Even to-day, on the remains of this fortification, may be seen inscriptions referring to the part taken in the work by various papal *militiæ*. The dedication was performed like that of a church on the 27th June 852.

As if to prove the need for this protection, the Saracens reappeared, from time to time, at the mouth of the Tiber. In 849 they were followed thither by the squadrons of Naples, Amalfi, and Gaeta, under command of Cæsar, son of Sergius, Duke of Naples. The Pope was at first somewhat perturbed at this alliance, but his fears were soon dispelled, and he went down to the shore to speed them with his blessing. A naval battle took place off Ostia, and the Neapolitans had already gained the upper hand when a great storm arose and parted the combatants. Many of the Saracen vessels were wrecked on the Roman coast; their crews were taken captive, and made to work on the fortifications of the Leonine City.[1]

The completion and solemn dedication of this great work (27th June 852) caused no abatement of Leo's energy. At his instigation the walls of Rome were restored, a colony of Corsicans was established at Porto; and *Centumcellæ* (Civita Vecchia), which had been devastated by the Saracens and abandoned by its inhabitants, was rebuilt at a short distance from the original site under the name of Leopolis.[2] The pirates seem to have been impressed by the Pope's capability and activity, for they did not obtrude themselves for several years.

The relations between Leo IV. and the emperor were, apparently, irreproachable, but not genial. From the Pope's letters we gather that two of the imperial *missi*, Peter and Hadrian, gave him considerable cause for complaint,[3] so that he mistrusted their presence at Rome. With the help of George, Duke of Emilia, brother of the Archbishop of Ravenna, they assassinated a papal

---

[1] The Saracens are again mentioned in a letter from Leo IV. (J., 2620), probably dating from 852; but he only speaks of rumours and preventive measures.

[2] For *Leopolis* see Ph. Lauer, *La Cité carolingienne de Cencelle*, in the *Mélanges* of the *École de Rome*, t. xx. p. 147; *cf.* the inscription published by M. Or. Marucchi in the *Nuovo Bullettino di arch. crist.*, 1900, p. 195, pl. vi.

[3] J., 2602, 2610.

legate who had been despatched to Lothaire. The
pilgrims who resorted to Rome had also good reason
for dreading Italian roads,[1] for a certain Gratiano,[2]
a seeker after political power, ranged himself against
them, and became distinguished for his outrages.
All these personages appear to have been papal
officials, more or less encouraged by the imperial
government to ignore the authority of their
sovereign.

Having made his complaint Louis set off to
Ravenna[3] with the intention of assisting his ill-
treated subjects. George, Peter, and Hadrian were
taken to Rome, and, in accordance with the Roman
law, tried before the imperial *missi*. They were
condemned to death, but the execution was de-
ferred on account of the Easter festival (853), and
this gave Lothaire time to intervene. He complained that, by coming so far, the Pope had
defied the Constitution of 824. There was also
question of one Christopher, of whom very little
is known. The Pope, while protesting on behalf
of his right, and of the Roman law, demanded
that an enquiry should be made into his conduct,
stipulating that it should be entrusted to envoys
of honourable character.[4]

Our sole information on this subject is gained
from fragments of letters, which were preserved from
the disaster which destroyed the papal registers.
The *Liber Pontificalis* relates the following story
with more details.

A *magister militum* named Gratiano (perhaps the

---

[1] *Cf.* the capitulary of Louis II., *M. G. Leg.*, i. p. 405 ; *Capit.*,
t. ii. pp. 84, 86; Migne, *L. P.*, t. cxxxviii. p. 572.
[2] J., 2620.   [3] J., 2627, 2628.
[4] J., 2638, 2639, 2643, 2646.

same as the afore-mentioned), and at that time (855)
governor of the papal palace, was accused of taking
part in secret intrigues in favour of a Byzantine
restoration. " The Franks," he said, "are not only
of no use to us, but they actually entertain base
designs upon our property. Why not call upon the
Greeks to help us to expel them and their king from
our midst ? " These revolutionary sentiments were
reported to the emperor, Louis II., by Daniel,
another *magister militum*. They were the more
alarming, as Louis was at that time on bad terms
with the eastern court,[1] for, after having sought the
hand of the daughter of the emperor, Michael III.,
he had altered his mind, and married the celebrated
Engelberga instead. Suddenly, without any warning,
Louis, full of rage, arrived at Rome. The Pope
received him at St. Peter's, and they arranged to
have a formal enquiry made concerning Daniel's
representations. The affair was conducted in accordance with the Roman law, and Daniel was con-
victed of false testimony, and delivered up to his
antagonist. But the emperor pleaded for him successfully, and even received him back into favour.

Whatever may have been the truth of this
matter, the effect produced by it leads us to suppose that Rome, at that time, was the centre, if not
of an organised Byzantine party, at least of a certain
element inimical to the Frankish protectorate, which
might have been turned to profit, had the occasion
offered, by the Greek empire. Just then the power
of the latter in Italy was at a low ebb. The Sicilians
and the Calabrians were having a hard struggle
against the Saracens, as were also the practically
autonomous cities of Gaeta, Naples, and Amalfi.

[1] *Prud. Ann.,* 853.

Louis II. had twice descended upon the Beneventine territory (847 and 852), and although, in his last campaign, he had not succeeded in capturing Bari, which was a stronghold of the infidels, he had nevertheless obtained considerable success.   He might, indeed, be regarded as the defender of Christendom, and the virtual master of Italy.   Under these circumstances it was futile to think of a Byzantine restoration.

As may be readily supposed, having been so often at variance with the Frankish emperors, Leo IV. was not entirely a man after their own hearts.   They could forgive the informalities connected with his accession, but they would have preferred a Pope more intent on carrying out the constitution of 824, and more faithful to his rôle of sovereign protégé. Louis II. early began making plans for the election of Leo's successor.

According to the constitution of 824, there were to be two *missi* charged with the affairs of the protectorate, kept in permanent residence at Rome. One was appointed by the Pope, the other by the emperor.   Louis II.'s first choice fell upon the deacon John, afterwards Bishop of Rieti; moreover, he selected for papal promotion one of his most devoted adherents, Arsenius, Bishop of Orta.   This dignitary was a member of one of the most important families of Rome, and from the time of Leo IV. his influence had been predominant.   As he was already possessed of a bishopric, there could be no question of making a Pope of him, but he had two sons, Anastasius and Eleutherius, who were quite worth considering.   The latter enjoyed the pleasures of a lay life, but Anastasius was destined for the priesthood, and had received an excellent education.

Not only was his knowledge of Latin and ecclesiastical literature far in advance of his time, but he also boasted an acquaintance with the Greek language, probably acquired at the school of one of those Greek monks, who owned numerous and flourishing convents at Rome. His ecclesiastical career was sufficiently advanced at the beginning of Leo's pontificate, for the latter, in compliance, probably, with weighty recommendations, decided to ordain him priest, and entrust him with the monastery of St. Marcellus (848).[1]

As cardinal, Anastasius was eligible for the papacy, so why he did not await the ordinary course of events is not clear. But whatever may have been the reason, he vanished from Rome almost immediately after his ordination, and took refuge in Louis' domains, spending most of his time in Aquileia. This conduct excited the most lively suspicions, and Pope Leo did his utmost to prevail upon him to return. Embassies, summonses, councils, ecclesiastical sentences of excommunication, anathema, and deposition, all were, in vain, directed against the deserter. Louis II., on being appealed to, promised to deliver him up, but never succeeded in finding him. Leo, in exasperation, determined to invest his sentences with a remarkable and pompous publicity. Over the principal entrance to St. Peter's he erected a huge image of Christ and the Virgin, encircled by a series of inscriptions, reproducing the sentences successively pronounced against Anastasius, at Rome, 16th December 850; at Ravenna, 29th May 853; and again at Rome, 8th December, of the same year. These sentences—as one of them expressly notes—resulted

[1] For information regarding Anastasius the librarian, see A. Lapôtre, *De Anastasio bibliothecario* (now out of print). Paris, 1885.

from the defection of the culprit, but it is obvious that Leo regarded Anastasius as a successor to be avoided at any cost.[1]

Both Anastasius and his father Arsenius had always maintained a warm friendship with Louis II., and were his chief political agents at Rome. Although they cannot be regarded as altogether desirable persons, they seem to have atoned to a certain extent for their lack of virtue by a kind of methodical reliability, often to be found in ambitious persons who are willing to restrain their natural tendencies, when, by so doing, they can further their own ends. If Leo IV. could find another pretext for condemning Anastasius, he was not anxious to quote against him the third canon of the Council of Antioch, in reference to clerks who deserted.

Moreover, Anastasius was not a man to make light of the pontifical rights, at least as far as spiritual affairs were concerned. From the letters of Nicholas I., which he edited later, with a considerable amount of licence, we gather that he had a high idea of the papacy, its relations to the rulers and its authority over the episcopate, even when the latter might be represented by a Photius or a Hincmar.

Leo IV.'s objection to him is, therefore, somewhat difficult to understand. One can only conjecture that he regarded the accession of Anastasius as the culminating political triumph of Louis II.— the absorption of the Roman state into the kingdom of Italy. It was possible, too, that once having attained the papal throne, Anastasius might change

---

[1] *Sit illi . . . anathema et omnes qui ei in electione, quod absit, ad pontificatus honorem adjutorium præstare . . . voluerint, simili anathemate subjaceant.* Leo, perhaps, was afraid that the emperor did not mean to await his death before encouraging Anastasius as his rival. This, however, is not at all probable.

his attitude, " scorning the base degrees by which he did ascend." These revulsions are not uncommon accompaniments of satisfied ambition.

However this may be, Leo's death, on 17th July 855, afforded the priest an opportunity of showing what weight he attached to the judgment passed against him.

Louis had made an arrangement with the emperors that the election of his successors should be *juste et canonice*. The Life of Benedict III. in the *Liber Pontificalis* is our only source of information on the subject. The election, it seems, was held immediately after the Pope's death. Two factions were present, the imperial party and the adherents of the deceased Pope, who were opposed to the aggravations of the protectorate. Anastasius was nominated by the imperial party, though, according to the *Liber Pontificalis*, he kept entirely in the background. The most popular candidate was Benedict, Cardinal of St. Cecilia, but the Romans, having elected him, postponed the coronation ceremony until, in accordance with the ancient custom (*consuetudo prisca ut poscit*), they had sent his decree of election, invested with much solemnity, to the emperors. The deputies, Nicholas, Bishop of Anagni, and Mercurius, the *magister militum*, encountered Arsenius at Gubbio on their way. Strange to say, he had been absent from Rome at the time of the election, and he now took the opportunity to try to prejudice these dignitaries in favour of his son.

The decree of election was not approved by the Emperor Louis, who, by means of letters and envoys, made known his intention of sending special *missi* to Rome. They were Adalbert, Count of Tuscany, and another, named Bernard. At Orta

Anastasius joined them, and together they continued their way. As they approached the city, the leaders of the imperial party, among them Radoald, Bishop of Porto, and Agatho, Bishop of Todi, hastened to meet them. At St. Lucius,[1] some distance beyond the Milvian bridge, they encountered some ambassadors from Benedict. These they caused to be arrested and ill-treated. A large number of Romans, who had been summoned to hear the emperor's decision, were beguiled into the opposite faction, and it was at the head of a goodly procession that Anastasius made his way towards the basilica of St. Peter.

Arrived there, his first proceeding was to seize a hatchet and hurl it against the eikon erected by Leo IV. as a protest against his usurpation. He then made his entry into Rome, and was escorted to the Lateran, where he lost no time in securing the person of Benedict. This was his day of triumph. The next day things did not go so smoothly. A large assembly, presided over by the Bishops of Ostia and Albano, met in the Basilica Emiliana (SS. Quattro), and the imperial *missi* presented themselves before the Roman clergy with the object of bringing them to terms. Both threats and cajolery were employed, but the clerks held out, entrenching themselves behind the ecclesiastical law, which forbade the promotion of deposed clerks. The *missi* were obliged to yield, and, in order to cover their retreat, agreed to a fresh election. Benedict was set at liberty; Anastasius departed from the pontifical palace; and a three days' fast was proclaimed. As soon as this was over, an electoral assembly met at Sta. Maria Maggiore, and, with the full approbation of the

---

[1] At present Tor di Quinto.

imperial envoys, proclaimed Benedict Pope. Thus re-elected, he was once more installed at the Lateran, and on the following Sunday was consecrated at St. Peter's, always with the approval of the *missi*. These latter seem to have been quite satisfied that the candidate of the Romans would answer the emperor's purpose just as well as his own protégé, Anastasius, would have done.

Bishop Radoald of Porto was not allowed to take his customary part in the consecration ceremony. As for Anastasius himself, the *Liber Pontificalis* does not say what became of him; but from Hincmar, who was not well-disposed towards him, and was always careful to record anything to his disadvantage, we learn that he was brought before Benedict in the synod and degraded by laicisation. It was undoubtedly at this juncture that he was provided with the Abbey of St. Mary in Trastevere.[1]

In 855 Louis II.'s policy had received a temporary check. Not content with the possession of the two *missi* of the Vatican, the papal *missus et apocrisiarius*, he maintained the right of superintending the actual choice of the Pope, and disclaimed any other foreign interference in the Italian policy of the Holy See. Anastasius, an excellent candidate as far as his personal qualifications went, was, as regards his antecedents, absolutely unsuitable. It is difficult, indeed, to understand how such a man could have presented himself in that capacity. But, whatever

---

[1] It is hardly necessary to remark that abbots, in those days, were not necessarily, or even usually, priests. The position of the Abbot of Santa Maria, *i.e.* the head of the community of monks who chanted the services in the basilica, must not be confounded with that of the titulary cardinal. As a deposed priest, regarded as a simple believer, Anastasius was excluded from the clergy, but he might then take the position of either monk or abbot.

may be the solution of this obscure point, it is probable that from the emperor's point of view the appointment of Anastasius was of less importance than the triumph of the principles of which he was the representative.   Being unable to place him in the pontifical chair, and foreseeing that his future applications for candidateship would not be more successful than that of 855, Louis made up his mind to let him share his father's rôle of confidential adviser and guardian to the Pope.   But for this end it was absolutely necessary that he should live a life of celibacy.   Anastasius, therefore, for three years retired into private life, devoting himself to religious exercises and literary pursuits.   As for Benedict III., Arsenius, who still kept his office of *missus*, was there to keep an eye upon him.

The death of Lothaire was almost coincident with the accession of Benedict III.   It caused but little change in Italian affairs, which for several years had been under the sole superintendence of Louis II.

In 858 Louis had come to Rome for the Easter celebrations; he had already begun his return journey, when he was greeted by the news of Pope Benedict's demise (17th April).   He immediately went back to Rome, and by his influence decided the election of the deacon Nicholas.   The clergy were in favour of another candidate, but as the emperor's choice had fallen on a man of worth, the election was confirmed without more ado.   Louis took part in the coronation which was held on 24th April.   From the papal biographer we get a lengthy account of the festivities, which appear to have been accompanied by many compliments and protestations of loyalty.

Nicholas just suited Louis II.[1] He understood how to combine a nice respect for papal conventions, with an exalted idea of his duties as Pope and an intense enthusiasm for fulfilling them. As we shall shortly see, his occupation of the pontifical chair marked a season of greater activity than had been known since the days of Gregory the Great. Unlike Gregory IV., of whom he was the precursor, he contrived to live on friendly terms with his emperor. It is true that the latter had surrounded him with a well-selected circle of confidential advisers better qualified, perhaps, to help him in his political career, than to be the familiar friends of so upright a man. Besides Arsenius, who continued his functions as *missus*, and was occasionally charged with important errands, we may mention his son Anastasius, the intruder of 855. This latter, it is true, was not reinstated in his priestly functions, but he was established at the Lateran as the Pope's secretary. Then there was Radoald, Bishop of Porto, one of the ringleaders of the Anastasius conspiracy, now the one of Nicholas's confidential advisers whom he most readily despatched on the pontifical business. Certainly the Pope had, later on, to rue the day when he took Radoald into favour, and, after having experienced his treachery several times, he was obliged to expel him from the episcopate. But this was only a last resource, after having borne with his faithless ways for many a long day. Arsenius did nothing worse than rob the Pope, and they seem to have lived together for a long time on friendly terms. As far as Anastasius was concerned, no cloud seems ever to have darkened their relations, although it is

---

[1] *Nicolaus præsentia magis ac favore Hludowici regis et procerum ejus quam cleri electione substituitur.* **Ann. Prud.**

beyond a doubt that the secretary, on more than one occasion, betrayed his master's confidence, and, in the most important documents, attributed to him sentiments more in harmony with his own personal passions and prejudices than with the desires and tendencies of the pontiff himself. Fortunately for the latter, he was not only a man of letters, but a government official imbued with lofty conceptions of the papal authority.

From the standpoint of local politics, the papacy had become very dependent on the empire. Louis II. held firmly to the constitution of 824, and taxed his people as well. After the death of Nicholas in 867, Hadrian, who seems to have been elected by an unanimous vote, did not receive consecration until the emperor had investigated the documents and circumstances of the election, and accorded his sanction. The fact that John VIII. succeeded to the papacy on the very day of Hadrian's death, 14th December 872, leads us to suppose that the emperor must have been in Rome at the time, for it is far from probable that any violation of the rule which required the imperial sanction of the papal election could have occurred. Moreover, we know that John VIII. was a personal friend of Louis II., and as long as the latter lived, his favourite continued to fill the most exalted positions in the Holy See.

This system was continued until Louis' death in 875, when, as he left no children, the empire ceased to be Italian, and the papal situation was changed. It had lasted for twenty years (855–875), since the time when Leo IV., somewhat displeased at the secular guardianship, had yielded the position to the official candidates.

It must not be supposed that this imperialist

papacy was lacking in prestige. Nicholas I., the typical representative of the system, was undoubtedly one of the most influential Popes ever known in the history of the Church.

Still, there was always reason to fear that the secular guardian might some day intrude upon the spiritual domain. This actually came to pass in 864. At the beginning of this year, the Emperor Louis appeared before Rome with hostile and not friendly intent. His object was to take the part of various priests who were under ecclesiastical censure. One of these was John, Archbishop of Ravenna, who, in conjunction with his brother Gregory, continued to oppress the Pope's subjects in Emilia. These, and other misdeeds of an ecclesiastical nature, had drawn down upon him the papal displeasure. He was summoned to appear before a Roman synod, but refused to obey, with the intention of appealing to Louis II. for support. But Nicholas was not to be foiled. In a synod held in 860 or 861, he issued a sentence of suspension and excommunication against the archbishop, proclaimed anew several points of dogma, on which he (the archbishop) was accused of holding heterodox views, and, finally, without regard to the emperor's feelings, renewed the decree of the Council of 769, which forbade the intervention of any foreigner in the papal elections. As we have seen, Nicholas himself had benefited by a certain infringement of this law. He probably had reason to fear that Louis II. wished to transform the fact into a right, and to claim the power of electing, as well as confirming, the choice of the Pope. When he died, the imperial *missi* demanded a place among the electors, having evidently received instructions so to do. The Romans succeeded in eluding their claim, but the very fact of the questions having been raised, was enough to justify the fears of Pope Nicholas, and his demonstration of 861.

This demonstration was, as I have said, of a nature to cause ill-feeling between the Pope and the emperor. The Archbishop John, recognising this, immediately betook himself to Pavia, hoping to profit by the prince's annoyance. Louis indeed sent two *missi* back with him to Rome, but Nicholas was not to be alarmed. Entirely in his religious capacity, he rebuked the legates for consorting with one who had been excommunicated. He spoke kindly, but the *missi* were terrified. The archbishop was again summoned to appear before a council, convened for 1st November 861, and he afterwards returned to Ravenna. Nicholas thereupon, in response to the invitation of a large number of the people of Emilia and Ravenna, who were antagonistic to the archbishop and his brother, followed him immediately. On hearing of his arrival, John fled to Pavia, and while he was again soliciting the emperor's intervention, the Pope, in his capacity as sovereign, reorganised the Ravennese government, and made the necessary changes in the ministry. So strongly was he supported by public opinion that the emperor's hopes of defending the archbishop were soon damped. Invited to make the best terms he could with the Pope, the primate of Ravenna appeared before the Roman council in the month of November. He vindicated himself from the imputation of heterodoxy, and otherwise complied with the papal exactions.

But a forced submission is not, as a rule, a satisfactory one. The archbishop, on his return home, lay low for a time, but his disposition had not changed, and it was evident that he meant to signalise the increasing animosity between the Pope and Louis by another outburst of insubordination.

An opportunity soon presented itself, in connection with the unfortunate divorce proceedings of Lothaire II. The divorce had been pronounced by the episcopate of Lorraine, in two or three synods, and afterwards sanctioned by the papal legates at the Council of Metz (June 863). In October of the same year, however, it was annulled by Pope Nicholas, who maintained that the discarded wife was so evidently in the right, that the divorce could not, in honesty, be confirmed. He therefore deposed the leaders of the Lorraine clergy, Theutgaud and Gunther, and the Archbishops of Treves and Cologne, and awaited his leisure to deal with his own legates.

This unexpected act caused a great sensation in the episcopacy. But the right, already expounded in the writings of Hincmar, was not to be denied. The prevaricators did not arouse much interest, and then finally compromised themselves by entering into alliance with the suspended Bishop of Ravenna, and Photius, the usurping patriarch of Constantinople. Not content with this, they sought out the Emperor Louis in the duchy of Beneventum, and excited his wrath against the Pope, with whom his relations had been somewhat strained ever since the Ravenna affairs. Gathering around him all the discontented bishops of Italy, they escorted him to the walls of Rome. The gates of the Leonine city, which were still fresh with inscriptions bearing the name of Lothaire, did not refuse to allow the entry of the emperor and his son.

At Rome there were not lacking people ready

to uphold the emperor's plans and to take part in an assault on the Pope's person. But Nicholas was impervious to fear. Against his temporal enemies he fought with spiritual weapons, especially prayer. Fasts and litanies were organised, in order to invoke the aid of heaven and to subdue the imperial anger. One day, as a large procession was making its way through the Leonine city to St. Peter's, it was attacked and dispersed by Louis' followers, who ill-treated the pilgrims, and trampled under foot the sacred banners. After these outrages there was indeed cause for alarm. One night the Pope emerged from the Lateran, and evading the sentinelled gates, reached the banks of the Tiber. A boat took him across secretly and he succeeded in gaining an entrance to the basilica, where he remained for two days fasting and communing with the Unseen.

His prayers were heard. Already one of the soldiers who had thrown the processional cross into the mud had been suddenly struck down by the hand of death; and the emperor himself was attacked by fever. The Pope, in abandonment of soul, continued to pray, and only rose from his knees at the urgent entreaties of the Empress Engelberga, who begged him to accompany her to the bedside of her imperial husband. She was a proud woman, but the experiences of recent days had given her cause for reflection, and the interview which she had arranged between Nicholas and Louis ended favourably. The emperor agreed to abandon his protégés, and to leave the Pope full liberty in the ecclesiastical domain. In short, the latter returned to Rome with his position strengthened, and Louis, on his recovery, regained the north of Italy.

Henceforward the two powers continued on more or less amicable terms.   At the council of 1st November Radoald, Bishop of Porto, received his well-merited sentence of deposition from the Pope. Up to that time, through fear of the emperor, every excuse had been made for him, in spite of the fact that his guilt, in the affair of Photius, could not possibly be denied.

Old Arsenius was of opinion that the Pope took too much upon himself.   Notwithstanding the favour which his son Anastasius continued to enjoy at the Lateran, and the profitable missions on which he himself was constantly being despatched, fearing, perhaps, that he might sooner or later be called upon to give an account of his proceedings, he found himself, towards the end of the reign, somewhat in disfavour with Nicholas.

Hadrian II., in celebration of his accession, dispensed marks of favour to various compromised persons, in particular to Anastasius and Theutgaud. The former was even promoted to the position of librarian of the Holy See.   In the early days of the new pontificate there was some difference of opinion between his father and himself.   Arsenius encouraged the reaction against Nicholas, and even the rescinding of certain acts to which the Emperor Louis had taken exception.   Summoning the Archbishops Gunther and Theutgaud to Rome, he made them promises of reinstatement, which, at first delayed, ended by coming to nothing.   Anastasius opposed his father's opinions.   In the preceding pontificate he had been the advocate of strict measures, and he now saw no reason why they should be abated.   Unlike Arsenius, who was a devout imperialist, he had a natural inclination towards the papacy, and if Louis II. had succeeded in making a Pope of him, the emperor would undoubtedly have met his match. He probably found occasion more than once to thank the fates for having crushed this project. In the disagreement with his father, Anastasius ended by getting the upper hand, and the family reputation does not appear to have suffered by their difference. Arsenius retained his post as *missus et apocrisiarius, i.e.* the Pope's secular guardian, and Anastasius continued to keep a high-handed supervision over the secretaryship and the affairs of the spiritual administration.

At this period nepotism was beginning to be in evidence, and alliances with the papal family were eagerly sought. Anastasius desired promotion for his brother Eleutherius, who had aims of another kind. The nieces of Benedict III. and Nicholas I. had contracted marriages with members of the lay nobility. These unions, conspicuous for a lack of sentiment, were the stepping-stones to worldly advancement, though the wives were far from enjoying unalloyed marital bliss. Before entering into major orders, Hadrian II. had married, and his wife and daughter were still living. The latter, considering the age and position of her father, could not have been in the freshness of youth, but, in virtue of her parentage, she was looked upon as a desirable match. When Eleutherius appeared as her wooer, Hadrian had already promised her to another. Arsenius, like a prudent father, always did his utmost for the advancement of his children, realising, too, that the desired marriage would have a decidedly beneficial effect upon his own position.

Hadrian, faithful to his promise, refused his consent. Eleutherius, nothing daunted, succeeded in circumventing the object of his desire, carrying her

and her mother away by force. The scandal that
resulted may more easily be imagined than described!
But this was not yet the worst. Hadrian, sorely
wounded, applied to the emperor for help in re-
covering his wife and daughter, and in avenging
their insulting treatment. Arsenius departed with
all speed to the south of Italy, where the court was
at that time established. He took care to provide
himself with plenty of money, well realising the value
of bribery in his present situation. No sooner, however, had he joined the princes at Acerenza than he
was overtaken by serious illness. He had just time
enough to confide his wishes and his treasure to the
empress, and then died, before he could receive the
last sacraments, thus giving rise to a report that
the devil had taken possession of his soul. His
servants undertook to convey his body to Rome or
to Orta, but on their arrival in the neighbourhood
of Monte Cassino the rapid putrefaction of the corpse
obliged them to resort to a hasty burial in a neighbouring field.[1]

But this was not the last of the tragedies. The
Emperor Louis had sent his *missi* in pursuit of
Eleutherius, and the latter, hard pressed, and in a
dog-in-the-manger spirit, did not hesitate to assassi-
nate the daughter, and even the wife of the Pope.
Public opinion, reinforced by competent testimony,
declared Anastasius to be the instigator of this double
crime. Hadrian, infuriated, had him brought before
an assembly of the Roman clergy at St. Praxedes,
and renewed against him all the ecclesiastical cen-
sures which he had incurred under Leo IV. and
Benedict III., forbidding him to go beyond a radius
of forty miles from Rome. As for Eleutherius, he

---

[1] See Hincmar, *Ann.*, 868; and *Biblioteca Casinensis*, t. iii. p. 139.

was arrested and executed by order of the imperial legates.

Hadrian's anger endured but for a season. It was on 4th October 868 that he had fulminated his condemnation of Anastasius, and before the end of 869 the latter was reinstated in his position of secretary and pontifical librarian. This leads us to suppose that he had proved himself innocent of any part in his brother's crime.

In the winter of 869–870, he set out, in company with two imperial dignitaries, for Constantinople, charged to negotiate an alliance between the daughter of Louis II. and a son of the Greek monarch, Basil the Macedonian. He arrived in time to be present at the last sitting of the eighth ecumenical council, and to witness the defeat of Photius, one of his most bitter adversaries. It is, indeed, thanks to him, that the Holy See was informed of the enactments of the council, for the copy confided to the papal legates was stolen from them on the way, and Photius contrived, later, to have the others burned. But Anastasius had taken the precaution of having one specially prepared for his own benefit, and he took good care not to let it be stolen. Not only did he bring it in safety to Rome, but he had it translated into Latin, in which form this important document is still preserved to us.

These disturbances did not greatly affect the pontifical organisation, and had practically no influence on the *personnel* of the administration. Arsenius was replaced by the nomenclator George, a man as rapacious as his predecessor.

The alliance between the empire and the papacy was distinguished by a touching episode. After many struggles, Louis II. had succeeded in taking possession of Bari, thus destroying the chief resort of the Mahometans in Southern Italy (2nd February 871). He was staying at Beneventum after his campaign, when he was betrayed and taken prisoner by the Duke Adelgis, who, after having robbed him, only released him on condition that he swore not to avenge himself. After thirty-five days of captivity, the unfortunate emperor was set free, and he returned to Ravenna by way of Spoleto, sadly humiliated by this attack on the representative of the imperial majesty. The following year he went to Rome, about the time of the Whitsuntide celebrations. Pope Hadrian welcomed him sympathetically, and, in order to reinvest him, to some extent, with his former dignity, he crowned him anew, and escorted him with great pomp from St. Peter's to the Lateran. The oath which the duke had extorted from him was solemnly pronounced invalid, and Louis thereupon resumed his campaigns against the Mahometans, in the direction of Capua and Salerno.

He died on 12th April 875, near Brescia, and was buried at Milan, in the basilica of St. Ambrose, where his tomb is still preserved.

CHAPTER XIV

THE TROUBLES OF JOHN VIII

The Pope and the Carlovingian family—Candidature of Charles the
Bald—His Imperial Coronation (875)—John VIII. and the Saracens
—The Formosians—Death of Charles the Bald—John VIII. and the
Dukes of Spoleto—Council of Troyes—Destruction of the Carlo-
vingian family—Charles the Fat, Emperor—Marino—Hadrian III.
—Deposition and death of Charles the Fat.[1]

ONE characteristic of the alliance between the Carlovingian princes and the Pope was, that the latter
was regarded by them as a kind of venerable parent,
whose right, or even obligation, it was to take an
interest in their concerns, and to act as their protector in case of need. As regards external political
questions this was quite natural. The papacy was
no longer Byzantine, but Frankish, and the bare
idea of a political understanding between the Pope
and the Greek empire would have been considered a
profanity. Neither could the Frankish empire entertain any thought of allowing the Greeks to resume
the least power at Rome over the Pope. But even
in the internal affairs of the Franks the Pope had
a share. He did his best to reconcile wrangling
princes,[2] and sometimes, an even more delicate

---

[1] For information on John VIII. and his time, see A. Lapôtre,
L'Europe et le Saint-Siège à l'époque carolingienne, 1st part; *Le Pape
Jean VIII.* Paris, 1895.
[2] Stephen III. was interested in the reconciliation of Charlemagne to Carloman (J., 2380).

matter, he interfered in their matrimonial affairs;[1]
then, too, his warranty was sometimes required for
solemn acts, such as the division of the empire
arranged by Charlemagne in 806,[2] and he was often
called upon to consecrate the princes, not only as
emperors, but as kings.

When the unity of the Frankish empire had been
destroyed, these relations became still more delicate.
It was not the papacy which was to blame for this
dislocation. The fatal plan of division, which Charlemagne himself had sanctioned, was too strong for
the Pope's influence to prevent its being carried out.
Once there was, among several sovereigns, a Frankish
emperor, resident in Italy; the Pope was obliged to
live on very intimate terms with him, not only
because he was the emperor, but also on account of
his neighbourly and protective attitude towards the
Romans. Hence there was always a tendency to
favour the particular political opinions of this prince.
Gregory IV. followed Lothaire into Alsace, and supported him against his father. When Lothaire died in
855, Benedict III. interfered to prevent his sons from
disputing the paternal heritage, and he even took to
himself the credit of having brought about the peace
which followed.[3] A little later, in 857, he engaged
in a vigorous attack against one of the foes of this
peace, Hubert, the intruded Abbot of St. Maurice,
who led a jovial life in this and various other holy
places. Besides owning a principality between the
Alps and the Juras, he was master of the passages

---

[1] Stephen II. prevented Pepin from sending away Bertrade
and marrying his daughter Giseta to Leo. IV., son of Constantine
Copronymus; Stephen III. objected to the marriage of Charlemagne
and Desideria.

[2] *Annals of Eginhard*, 806. *Cf.* J., 3000.

[3] *Pacem quam munivimus* (J., 2669).

between Italy and the domain of Lothaire II.[1] The Emperor Louis II. cast a longing eye on these districts, and succeeded (859) in making Lothaire surrender them, and even, a few years later (864), in getting rid of Hubert. On the death of Charles of Provence in 863, his kingdom was divided between his two brothers, Lothaire II. and Louis II., and Pope Nicholas wrote to Charles the Bald, to Louis the German, and to their respective episcopates to pledge them not to offer any opposition to this division.[2] When Lothaire II. went to Italy (869) in order to make his peace with the Pope, Hadrian II. charged these same two kings to refrain from any attack on the penitent's states.[3] His wish was complied with, but as Lothaire did not live long after his return home, his uncles, Charles the Bald first, and then Louis the German, seized upon his estates. The Pope strongly remonstrated, by means of letters and legates,[4] for he rightly considered their behaviour as an attack upon the imperial authority. His efforts, however, were fruitless. The two uncles took possession of the coveted lands, and Louis II. was again reduced to Provence and Italy. The treaty of Mersen (870) bestowed the greater part on Louis the German, who was from that time in rather bad odour at Rome. Charles the Bald, too, was unpopular, for though he had inherited less than Louis, it was he who had instigated the plan of robbing the emperor. In 871 Carloman, one of the two sons whom he had destined for a religious life, having broken his vows and taken up arms against his father, Hadrian supported him with energy. The

[1] J., 2669 (badly arranged summary).
[2] J., 2773–5.   [3] J., 2895–6.
[4] J., 2917–23, 2926–32.

letters[1] which Charles received from the Pope on this subject were written in so bitter and insulting a style that he protested. Suspecting that the pontiff was not entirely responsible for the expression of these sentiments, Charles investigated the matter. His ambassador, Bishop Actard, succeeded in obtaining a private interview with Hadrian, and returned with a letter in which the papal opinions were candidly set forth, uncontrolled by the supervision of Anastasius, who acted as the imperial representative.[2]

The old Pope expressed, in this confidential epistle, not only his opinions with regard to his family, but also his views as to the future. Hitherto the papacy had been obliged to yield to circumstances, and to accept a close alliance with the Italian monarch, not untinged with subordination. But this could not be permanent. While Charles the Bald was so abundantly supplied with male progeny that he was obliged to devote some of them to the priesthood, Louis II., on the other hand, had no son at all. His death would involve the succession, not of a prince, but of a system of government. One of the three branches of Charlemagne's lineage was arrested in its growth, and it remained to be seen which of the two survivors would be asked to act as protector of the Holy See, and which would receive the imperial title. Charles the Bald and Louis the German, the two heads of the French and German branches respectively, seem to have been on much the same level. Louis, it was true, was the elder, as well as the son of his father's first marriage, but these considerations were not likely to have much weight with the Romans, whether they looked upon the empire as the pro-

[1] J., 2940–2, 2946.   [2] J., 2951.

tector of their various interests, or as a magistrature emanating from themselves. Each of these princes was the possessor of several sons, who had all distinguished themselves by insubordinate behaviour to their father. The kingdom of Charles was more civilised, though weaker, than that of Louis, and in facilitating its succession to the Italian crown it would be considerably strengthened. Affairs were thus tolerably well balanced, and it was probable that the scale would be turned by considerations of sentiment or personal convenience.

The Romans are lovers of antiquity. Germany, at that time, was brand new, hardly free indeed from barbarism and paganism, while Roman Gaul was the home of the best survivals of the ancient Latin civilisation. An Italian or a Roman felt quite at his ease at Arles, Vienne, or Lyons, and even towns such as Rheims, Sens, St. Denis, and Tours were not altogether foreign to him. He was familiar with their names and traditions in his own language. But Ratisbon, Frankfort, Paderborn, Halberstadt—all these were in another world, and he was inclined to think it wiser to exhaust the resources of the ancient world before compromising himself in unknown parts.

Charles, moreover, was a prince of piety, intelligence, and learning. His abilities are now cast up against him, but to the Romans they were an additional recommendation. It is probable, too, that there has been a considerable amount of romancing as to his actual valour. In the eyes of German savants his was the unpardonable iniquity of being the first king of France, and according to the chroniclers of Fulda, to whom we generously sacrifice the witness of Prudence and Hincmar, he was too much addicted to opposing the ambitions of Louis the German. The Romans were of a different opinion. We must make allowance for the prejudiced views set forth in the papal correspondence as long as it was controlled by Anastasius and, to a certain extent, by Louis II. From more reliable sources of information it is evident that, on several occasions, Charles lent his support to the Holy See in maintaining a salutary attitude with reference to the clergy of his kingdom. There can be no doubt, either, that the Holy See had designed him for the imperial crown directly there was any question of Louis II.'s succession. This was in the time of Hadrian II.

Nevertheless, as long as Louis II. remained in the land of the living, these preferences could only be expressed with great caution and in purely confidential documents. Outwardly, the papal policy outside Italy remained in harmony with that of Louis II. On two occasions at least[1] John VIII. protested against the usurpations sanctioned by the treaty of Mersen.

On 12th August 875 the settlement of the succession began. Largely attended councils were held at Pavia and at Rome. Charles the Bald set great store by his friends at Pavia, but he had an important opponent in the person of the Empress Engelberga, who had long ago set her desires on Carloman, eldest son of Louis the German, and already king of Bavaria. The assembly became divided into the opposite factions, with the result that two embassies were sent from it, one to Carloman, and the other to Charles the Bald. At Rome there was no opposition; the nobility and the clergy

[1] J., 2961, 3000.

with one voice acclaimed the king of Western France. Three bishops, Gaudry of Velletri, Formosus of Porto, and John of Arezzo, immediately set out to invite Charles to come to Rome and receive the imperial coronation.

The circumstances were momentous. The destinies of Italy were hanging in the balance between France and Germany. For the first time, too, the choice of the imperial person was being made at Rome under the auspices of the Pope. It was no longer a question, as it had been in 816, 823, and 850, of a mere consecration ceremony, nor, as in 800, of a more or less obvious external initiative, but of a genuine election. The situation was indeed changed! Since 824 the Popes had been in principle, and generally in fact, confirmed by the emperor; now the emperor was chosen by the Pope! John VIII., even in his short pontificate of ten years, twice exercised this right of choice.

Charles did not require pressing. With alacrity he crossed the St. Bernard, and appeared at Pavia before the end of September. There, probably, he received the Roman envoys. But Louis the German had lost no time in despatching to Italy his younger son, Charles the Fat, king of Swabia. Charles the Bald had no difficulty in repulsing him, but Carloman gave him more trouble. The latter had descended the Brenner Pass at the head of an imposing army. Charles brought matters to a successful issue by diplomatic artifices, which have been the scandal of Germany for over a thousand years. Meanwhile Louis the German, with his other son, who also bore the name of Louis, turned his attention to Western France, which was defended by yet another Louis (Louis the Stammerer), son of the imperial candidate.

The latter, in a hurry, arrived at Rome on 17th December. He naturally lavished rich gifts upon St. Peter's tomb, and behaved generously to the Romans, who, in accordance with custom, expected a display of bounty. It may be remarked, however, that although Charles showed himself thus munificent in December, four months had already elapsed since he had received his invitation, and longer still since his candidature had been accepted and warmly welcomed.

The coronation took place on Christmas Day, exactly seventy-five years after that of Charlemagne. According to the *Libellus de imperatoria potestate*, Charles would have introduced considerable modifications into the relations between the empire and the Holy See; in particular, he would have dispensed with the permanent *missi*. This, however, is open to question; for in 885, under Charles the Fat, the *missus* was still in office, and it is hardly likely that the function would have been abolished in 875, and re-established in 881, at Charles's accession. There is no documentary evidence of this. In the *Libellus* there is also mention of territorial transfers, such as the duchies of Spoleto and Beneventum and the cities of Chiusi and Arezzo. As far as the duchies are concerned, they undoubtedly remained in the state, and Charles the Bald even appointed a Duke of Spoleto on his own authority. Moreover, the fact that the Bishop of Arezzo was one of the three envoys despatched to Charles the Bald, presumes that Arezzo was still attached to the Roman state at the time of Louis II.'s death, for the Pope was not in the habit of employing legates, other than his own subjects, for missions of this kind.

In short, it seems probable that the author of the *Libellus* must have known of a privilege (now lost) delivered by Charles the Bald to Pope John VIII., in which the new emperor gave his sanction to certain papal claims, similar to those of which it was a question in the lifetime of Hadrian, though, as a matter of fact, very little change took place either in the extent of the pontifical state, or in the relations between it and the protective empire.

The Pope was not in a position to devote much attention to annexing territories, or making efforts to throw off the Frankish protection. In spite of some repulses, the Saracens were becoming more and more formidable foes. The Emperor Louis II. had ejected them from Bari in 871. In 876, in answer to an appeal from the inhabitants, a Greek fleet took possession of the town, and not long after (880) Tarento also gave way before one of the generals of the Emperor Basil. Before the Saracen occupation these places had been owned by the Lombard duchy of Beneventum, but as the Emperor Louis II. was no longer at hand to put forward the claims of the Lombard crown, Basil himself appropriated the conquered towns. From that time the Greek empire began to establish a firm footing on the south-east coast of Italy, meanwhile extending its influence over the Dalmatian isles, and the Croatian and Servian principalities of the interior; its position at Venice was also strengthened so that the Adriatic became Byzantine property. Being prevented on this side, the Saracens fell back upon the coast of the Tyrrhenian Sea, where they often profited by the disunion among the Greek and Lombard principalities. The heads of these little states got on much more amicably with the Mahometans than with the empire. Their egotistical spirit, and their unjustifiable claims had been an impediment to Louis II.'s plans. The Duke of Beneventum had even gone so far as to attempt the life of his sovereign, the defender of Christianity. At Naples, which owned a Mahometan garrison, the Duke Sergius openly proclaimed himself an ally of the Saracens. It was the same at Gaeta, and Campania was constantly the scene of military raids. Owing to the attitude of Duke Sergius, Louis II. effected but little during his several months' sojourn (872–873) in Capua and the neighbourhood. Finally, tired of resistance, the petty princes of Amalfi, Gaeta, Salerno, and even Capua, entered into treaty with the Saracens, who, having no further occasion for plundering in those regions, betook themselves to the north where they carried on their operations in the district round Rome.

Immediately on his election John VIII. was obliged to turn his attention to this quarter. Louis II.'s campaign had been succeeded by a series of naval expeditions of which mention is made in his letters.[1] A Roman fleet, manned by Greek sailors, had been organised at the mouth of the Tiber, and the Pope sometimes placed himself in command. In a letter addressed to Louis and his wife Engelberga,[2] he relates various exploits such as his having seized eighteen Saracen vessels, delivered six hundred Christians, and killed numerous infidels. He did

---

[1] J., 2959, 2960, 2966, 3008.
[2] J., 3008 (February 875).

not confine himself to fighting, however, but put forth all the might of his diplomacy in order to dissolve the treaties concluded between the Saracens and the Campanian principalities.[1] Finally he completed the fortifications of Rome by building around St. Paul's an enclosure, resembling the Leonine city. Following Leo IV.'s example, he desired that it should bear his own name and be called Johannipolis No trace of it remains at the present day, and even its exact site is not known.

His first request to the new emperor was for help in his crusade. Charles's kingdom, invaded by Louis the German and continually threatened by the Normans, was in no position to be left without its chief, so Lambert, Duke of Spoleto, and his brother Guy, were deputed to go to the Pope's assistance, in default of Charles himself. These dignitaries having been implicated in the plot against Louis II. (871), had been deprived of their offices, but had just been reinstated by Charles. They were thus not very reliable allies, either from his point of view or the Pope's. John VIII. made his entry into Campania under their escort. He gained some measure of success at Amalfi and Salerno, but the final triumph of the expedition was prevented by the pertinacity of the Duke of Naples, who was secretly supported by Adakis of Beneventum, and even by the Dukes of Spoleto. The Saracens maintained their footing in Italy, and they soon reappeared in the neighbourhood of Rome.

Besides these external foes, John VIII. had enemies at home. There were differences of opinion concerning the promotion of Charles the Bald. The

[1] J., 3012, 3016.

Empress Engelberga, who took the part of Carloman, had allies in the pontifical circle, particularly among the high officials who had been imposed upon the preceding Popes, by the policy of Louis II. and the influence of his wife. As long as Louis was alive the Popes had been obliged to tolerate them, but now the time had come to get rid of them, and the prospect was all the more attractive because their attitude was not favourable to the papal designs. John VIII. had a free hand, and his severity would undoubtedly have been approved by the imperial *missi*.

The adversaries suspected what was coming to pass, for they knew how things had happened at Rome on a like occasion. Rumours were already afloat of the probabilities of their being cast into the Tiber, mutilated, or having their eyes gouged out. Such things had already occurred often enough to render their repetition a possibility, and to strike fear into their hearts. One night they succeeded in escaping by the St. Pancratius' Gate, and their flight was not discovered until the next day. Among them were the nomenclator Gregory, who had succeeded the celebrated Arsenius in the office of *apocrisiarius;* the two masters of the militia, George of Aventino and Sergius; the *secundicerius* Stephen; Constantine, Gregory's daughter; and, finally, the Bishop of Porto, Formosus.

Most of these seem to have been rather a shady set of people, but there was no mistaking the genuine piety and austerity of Formosus. Pope Nicholas had confided to him the leadership of the Bulgarian mission, and his ministrations met with so much acceptance among the Bulgarians, that they vehemently desired him for their archbishop. Hadrian refused to gratify them, alleging that Formosus was already Bishop of Porto, and that translations were not admissible. Porto was at that time, as it is to-day, a more or less honorary bishopric. The king of Bulgaria was greatly annoyed at the Pope's attitude on this question of canon law, but he finally yielded to the importunities of the Greeks, and accepted an archbishop of their choice. In this way did the Latin Church sever itself from the Bulgarian mission, whereas if Hadrian had but given way on so trifling a matter, he would have gained two important advantages : the Bulgarians would have been retained in submission, and Rome would have been freed from a person who was in the future to be the cause of much discord. Already, in 872, there had been some question of raising him to the pontificate. This alone was enough to make John VIII., who was far from long-suffering, look upon him with disfavour. Whether he was opposed to the consecration of Charles the Bald, is not certain ; but if such was the case, it must be admitted that John VIII. made an odd choice in selecting him as one of the ambassadors to carry the invitation to that prince. There is no proof either that Formosus ever entertained " German sentiments." An exile from Rome, he took refuge, not in Germany, but in France. It cannot be denied that John did not like him, and that he probably had a reason for his dislike, but questions of nationality have nothing to do with this affair.

When the Pope heard of the departure of his enemies, he assembled a synod at the Pantheon (19th April), and solemnly conjured them to return to Rome. Then, as they were very far from complying, he censured them at another synod held at

St. Peter's on 30th June.[1]   Notice of this condemnation was sent to Charles the Bald and to the Synod
of Ponthieu, where the prince, surrounded by papal
legates, was just then being recognised as emperor.

Having got rid of his internal enemies, John soon
learned that they had been given shelter by the
Dukes of Spoleto and the Marquis of Tuscany.
These nobles, ostensibly his protectors, were in reality
his persecutors.   The Saracens, too, were becoming
more and more offensive, and the Pope increased his
appeals to Charles the Bald.

But Charles found many obstacles in his way.
He had profited by the death of Louis the German
at Frankfort (28th June 876), to alter the treaty of
Mersen to his own advantage, and, by annexing
Louis' share of the inheritance of Lothaire II., to
extend his frontier as far as the Rhine.   He marched
upon Cologne and seized it, but Louis (son of the
German) defeated him at Andernach and forced him
to retreat.   The following year he made arrangements to go at last to the Pope's help, and after
having taken measures to secure order during his
absence, by the capitulary of Kiersy-sur-Oise, he
crossed the Alps, and was met by John VIII. at
Pavia.   While there he received notice of the arrival
of Carloman, who, while Charles was preparing to
fight the Saracens, had come to dispute with him the
possession of Italy.   His intervention quite upset
the projected crusade, besides, the vassals on whom
Charles had counted the most, forsook him just at
this moment, and refused to cross the Alps.   Thus
baffled, he relinquished his plan.   He died on his

---

[1] In the papal circle the fugitives were ridiculed in song.   See
the *Cena Cypriani,* particularly the edition published by P. Lapôtre
in the *Mélanges* of the *École de Rome,* t. xxi. p. 321.

way back, poisoned, it is said, by his physician (6th October 877). His only surviving son, Louis the Stammerer, succeeded him without any difficulty.

The Pope's state of mind on returning to Rome may be imagined. He was in the hands of his adversaries. The Saracens might lay waste his states without fear of punishment; and the exiles would not fail to engage the services of their allies of Lucca and Spoleto against him. From the moment of John's return, Lambert of Spoleto adopted an insulting attitude, which the Pope did not lessen by humiliating himself before Carloman. In the spring of 878, Adalbert of Tuscany and Lambert of Spoleto presented themselves before the Leonine city, and insisted on effecting an entry. The Pope thought it wise to have an interview with them, and with the exiles who had followed them, but their demands were so excessive that he opposed them. He was kept a prisoner for thirty days, during which they sought to assure themselves of the Roman fidelity to Carloman by instituting the taking of solemn oaths. The Romans swore, but the Pope was inflexible,[1] and the enemy was obliged to retire without entering Rome. As soon as they were gone John's anger burst forth. He began by placing the basilica of St. Peter under an interdict as the scene of his outrage; he wrote to all the Carlovingian princes, and to Carloman himself, feigning to believe that he had had no knowledge of the affair; he even sent a protest to the Greek emperor, Basil the Macedonian, requesting him to come to his assistance. He then announced that Rome being no longer endurable, he

[1] Carloman was not emperor, and therefore the Pope was under no obligation to take the oath.

was going to take refuge in France. In order to keep the Saracens at bay during his absence, he undertook to pay them a heavy tribute. Finally, after excommunicating the two dukes, he took his departure, going first to Genoa and then to Arles.

The Pope's plan was as imposing as it was impracticable. He wished to summon a convocation of the four Carlovingian princes and their episcopates, and settle with them the important questions which had arisen. But it was far from probable that the sons of Louis the German would be inclined to meet him in France, or even to enter into serious negotiations with a Pope who, by the very choice of his place of refuge, seemed to imply that he would always support the claims of the younger and French branch. Moreover, poor Louis the Stammerer had quite enough to do at home without undertaking foreign expeditions. He himself may or may not have had cravings after the imperial office, but his people were not at all anxious for the honour. From the writings of Hincmar we see how little the episcopate, and the lay aristocracy, had appreciated the transformation of Charles the Bald into the successor of Augustus.

The Pope soon realised that he must not expect much sympathy from this quarter. It is true that he held a great council at Troyes (878), where he met Louis the Stammerer and received legates from Germany, but all this led to no serious result. He was, however, given an escort back to Italy in the person of Boson, the ambitious Count of Vienne, who the next year transformed himself into an independent monarch. John VIII., making the best of the situation, tried to arouse his interest by holding up before him the splendours of Italy.

Neither was there much to hope from the Germans. Carloman, having returned from his expedition of 877 in a feeble state of health, was afflicted with paralysis, and thus unable to govern. His brother Louis was far away in his provinces of Saxony and Franconia, while the youngest of the three brothers, Charles the Great, King of Swabia, was distinguished neither by ability nor by bravery. It was no easy matter to decide among so many and such candidates.

After the departure and death of Charles the Bald, Italy remained practically in the power of Carloman. He came to Pavia, received the oaths of the ecclesiastical and lay leaders, and spent several weeks in the north of Italy. He then retired to Bavaria, already attacked by the disease which was to cost him his life. The other Frankish princes did not as yet recognise his claims upon Italy. From Louis the Stammerer in Western France there was no very definite opposition[1]; he was content to keep Provence, leaving the German princes to settle the Italian question among themselves. The next winter the following arrangement was made: the two kings in the Rhine district, Louis and Charles the Fat, were to share the old kingdom of Lothaire II., or rather such part of it as the treaty of Mersen had allotted to the German state; on the other hand they gave up Italy to Carloman.

But, on account of his ill-health, the latter was unable to take any active part in affairs. As we have seen, John VIII. had been accompanied into Italy after the Council of Troyes by Boson, son-in-

---

[1] *Cf.* Poupardin, *Le Royaume de Provence sous les Carolingiens*, p. 92, n. 3.

law to Louis II., with whose daughter Ermengarde he had absconded. This ambitious individual had been made a duke by Charles the Bald, and deputed to represent him in the government of Italy. His appearance as bodyguard and adopted son of Pope John was calculated to arouse uneasiness. Boson, however, soon returned to France.[1] For some time affairs were in an undecided state. The Pope turned a friendly face to all parties; to Carloman, whom he treated as the actual sovereign; to Charles the Fat, who was already posing as a candidate; to Boson with whom he seemed to have some mysterious understanding; and even to Louis III., the most distant of Louis the German's sons.

In 879 things began to fall into some semblance of order. Louis the Stammerer died in April, leaving two sons, who were both too young and weak to have any designs on Italy. In October Boson caused himself to be crowned king of Provence, which usurpation brought enough difficulties in its train to keep him for a long time a fixture on the other side of the Alps. In Germany, Carloman, realising the approach of death, surrendered Italy to Charles the Fat. At the same time Louis, King of Eastern France, after having profited by the death of Louis the Stammerer to invade the kingdom of the West, rushed into Bavaria and established himself in the place of the unfortunate Carloman. The latter passed away on 22nd March 880, and his successor only survived him until 20th January 882. Three years later, at the end of December 884, the last of the two reigning sons of Louis the Stammerer died too, thus leaving the Carlovingian dynasty with no other representative

---

[1] For Boson, see Poupardin, *op. cit.*

in the Western kingdom than the posthumous son of Louis the Stammerer, Charles (the Simple)—a little boy of four years old. In Germany it was represented by the last son of Louis the German, Charles the Fat. This latter received all the Carlovingian heritage, and was recognised as sovereign all over the empire of Charlemagne and Louis the Pious, with the exception of Provence, where Boson continued to flourish. This monarchy lasted only three years, ending with the deposition and death of Charles the Fat.

But these changes had no direct effect upon the history of Italy, for after the year 879 Charles the Fat is the only Carlovingian prince with whom the Romans and Italians had dealings.

Having come to an understanding with his brother and even with the two young kings of Western France, whom he met at Arles, Charles crossed the Alps. From the month of November 879 he was recognised as king in the north of Italy. About 6th January 880 he was solemnly proclaimed at Ravenna, in presence of the Pope and the chief bishops of his new kingdom, who took an oath of fealty to him.

The Pope was anxious to take him to Rome that he might lend his aid against the Saracens. But Charles, who was in a hurry to get back to France to help his cousins in the subjugation of Boson, as usual deputed the Duke of Spoleto to take his place. He returned to Italy, however, the following autumn, in response to the urgent entreaties of John VIII., who hurled maledictions at his former friend Boson, and protested that his relations with the Greeks implied no disloyalty to the king. This was quite true, for the Pope had merely requested them to set their fleets in motion against the Saracen navy. Charles arrived there again at the beginning of February 881, and on the 12th of the same month he and his wife Richarde received the imperial consecration.

But the Pope's plans did not progress much, in spite of this event. Charles the Fat set off to the north of Italy, where he tarried for more than a year. In February 882 he had another interview with the Pope at Ravenna. As long as he was present the people of Spoleto were glib enough with their promises, but no sooner was his back turned than they declined to fulfil them. In May of the same year the emperor crossed the Alps to go and take possession of the dominions of his brother Louis, who had just departed this life, leaving Lorraine to be overrun by the Normans. John again found himself deserted and helpless in the midst of his enemies.

He died on the 15th December 882 under the most distressing circumstances. A conspiracy was set on foot against him, some of his own kinsmen actually having a share in it. They began by trying to poison him, but, in order to precipitate matters, beat him to death with hammers.[1] This was the first time that a Pope had met his death by assassination.

John VIII. had been the victim of circumstances which no effort of his had succeeded in mitigating. Of the three branches of the Carlovingian dynasty, the first, the Italian, had come to grief under his very eyes; the French branch, on which he had then relied, had failed to support him; the German

---

[1] *Ann. Fuld.,* sole account, but must have been founded on the reports sent to Charles the Fat.

branch, to which he had in desperation turned, had availed him just as little. The Saracens did not cease to ravage the Roman state, and behind the ramparts of Naples, Gaeta, and Capua there were always found Christian allies ready to protect them against the expeditions organised by the Pope, and to assist them in enjoying their spoils. On the interior frontiers, the Duke of Spoleto and the Marquis of Tuscany were always undesirable neighbours. Even at Rome the malcontents, incited by the exiles, and perhaps also by the severity of the government, renewed the opposition against which John VIII. had fought in 876. The latter was indeed the victim of defeat, but only after he had fought a brave and unwearied fight.

His successor, Marinus, was elected without disturbance. He was a man of intelligence, who had been sent three times under former Popes as a legate to Constantinople; he had even figured in this capacity among the presidents of the ecumenical council of 869, at the time of the deposition of Photius. On his last visit to Constantinople he had come across this personage again, not as a criminal this time, but as the occupant of the patriarchal throne, and not at all disposed to show favour to one of his former judges. In order to keep on the right side of the Emperor Basil, and to obtain his assistance in his perpetual crusade, John VIII. had recognised Photius; but for Marinus, Photius was not merely an ecclesiastical opponent, but a personal enemy. On this point he shared the sentiments of Formosus.

Besides sharing this opinion with the most conspicuous enemy of John VIII., Marinus, it seems, had other sympathies, which diverged from those of his predecessor. His accession was the signal for a marked reaction. Formosus, the *apocrisiarius* Gregory, and the others who had been banished, were now recalled to Rome and absolved from their sentence of excommunication. The Bishop of Troyes had sworn, at the council of Troyes, to live henceforth a secular life and never again to lay claim to his see; John VIII. had even forced him to take an additional oath, by which he bound himself never again to enter Rome. Marinus absolved them from all these vows.

Whatever may have been the sentiment which guided him in this affair—and it is quite possible that the emperor may have had some influence—there can be no doubt at least that the recall of the exiles relieved the situation of considerable embarrassment.

There had been some irregularity in the election of Marinus. When John died he was exercising the functions of archdeacon, but before that he had been for some time Bishop of Caeri (Cervetri), and though at the time no objection seems to have been made to his translation, attention was soon called to his origin by the case of Formosus. He had not been in the pontifical seat sixteen months when he was replaced by Hadrian III., whose reign proved just as brief.

Of the relations between these short-lived Popes and the empire we know but little. In June 883 Marinus had a meeting with Charles the Fat at Nonantola. Two years later Hadrian III. was summoned to Germany by the emperor, who wished the support of the papal authority in arranging for his succession. The Pope set out on the journey, but death overtook him near Nonantola, where he was buried.

There is no evidence to tell whether the ancient right of confirmation was exercised in the case of either of these Popes. Both in 882 and 884 the papal seat appears to have been vacant for so short a time that the emperor could not have been appealed to. It is possible, however, that the permanent *missus* may have been authorised to confirm the appointment. There is no doubt that in 885 a *missus* existed in the person of John, Bishop of Pavia. He it was, indeed, to whom Hadrian III. committed the government of the city of Rome before responding to the imperial summons to Germany.

The sudden death of Hadrian having left the papal chair again without an occupant, the Romans, assisted by the *missus*, chose the priest Stephen, a man of rich and noble family, who was ordained without delay (September 885). Charles the Fat, it appears, had other views on the subject, and was greatly provoked by not having been consulted in the matter. He even despatched his chief chancellor, Liutward, Bishop of Vercelli, with intent to depose the newly-made Pope. The latter, however, managed to assuage the imperial anger, and to convince him, by the presentation of his decree of election, that everything had been in order.

Two years later the emperor himself suffered deposition at the hands of his own subjects. The event took place at the villa of Tribur in November 887, but the deposed sovereign did not long survive this humiliation. Already in a few weeks (13th January 898) kindly death came and bore him away to a land where regrets for his past glories could no longer oppress him.

CHAPTER XV

THE EMPIRE OF SPOLETO

Arnulph, King of Germany—Guy of Spoleto and Berengarius—Guy and
Lambert crowned as Emperors—Embarrassment of Pope Formosus
—Agiltrude—Arnulph at Rome and Spoleto—Lambert, master of
Italy—Death of Formosus—The Council of the Corpse—The Roman
Schism—Sergius III. and John IX.—The Councils of John IX.—
Death of Lambert.

The death of Charles the Fat gave rise to many
claimants to the throne. In Germany opposition
had proceeded from a natural son of Carloman,
Arnulph, Duke of Carinthia, who, like his father,
was a brave warrior. The only surviving legitimate Carlovingian prince was the posthumous son
of Louis the Stammerer, Charles (the Simple), who
was then but seven years of age. For the time his
claim was ignored, both in France and in Germany,
and Carloman's illegitimate son received the general
support.

It was, however, impossible for the latter to
maintain the unity of the Frankish empire. He
was obliged to recognise as kings the following:—
Firstly, in France, Hugh, Count of Paris, son of
Robert the Strong, the first Capetian to reign;
secondly, in Provence, Louis (the Blind), son of
the usurper Boson, but grandson of the Emperor
Louis II., by his mother Ermengarda; thirdly, in
the Juras and Switzerland (*regnum Jurense*),
Rudolph, son of Conrad, Count of Auxerre, a
rebellious functionary; fourthly, in Italy, Beren-

garius, Marquis of Friuli, grandson of Louis the Pious by his mother, Gisèle.

Besides these four royalties who, without being actually under the dominion of Arnulph, nevertheless profited by their political intercourse with the German sovereign, we must also take account, in connection with France and Italy, of the House of Spoleto.

Guy of Spoleto was sole heir of the Dukes (or Marquesses) Lambert and Guy, whom we have seen at daggers drawn with John VIII. He did not belong, like Berengarius of Friuli and Louis of Provence, to the Carlovingian family, but he was none the less a man of parts. His ancestors, like those of Charlemagne, came originally from the banks of the Moselle, and sprang from as noble a stock as did the House of Pepin. Transplanted, about the middle of the ninth century, to the centre of Italy, this Frankish family had continued to consolidate its position. The duchy of Spoleto had become for it a hereditary principality, and this was only a centre for various *radii* of activity.

Taking advantage of the parcelling out of southern Italy, and of the weakness of the central authority in these distant regions, the Lamberts and Guys made up their minds to be masters, not only of their own affairs, but also of their neighbours'. They contracted marriages in Tuscany and Beneventum, intervened in the concerns of Capua, Naples, and Salerno, protected (and, on occasion, oppressed) the Pope, and entered into negotiations with the Greek patricians, and even with the Saracens. These latter alliances, which were always open to suspicion, had already, on two separate occasions, incurred the imperial displeasure.   Louis II. had deprived them of their principality (871–875).   Charles the Bald reinstated them, but they managed to fall foul of Charles the Fat.   In 883 Guy of Spoleto, the one with whom we are at present concerned, was arrested by order of the emperor, tried at a court of justice held at Nonantola, and dismissed from office.   He succeeded in escaping, however, and returned to his duchy, where, supported by a troop of Mussulman mercenaries, he organised so decided a rebellion that the military had to be called upon to resist it.   Berengarius of Friuli was placed at the head of the defensive army, but, though he was at first successful, the appearance of the plague among his men forced him to retire.   Not long afterwards, at the beginning of 885, Guy was received into the emperor's good graces, but he never ceased to cherish a violent grudge against Berengarius.

On hearing of the death of Charles the Fat, Guy promptly presented himself as a candidate for the crown of France.   His supporters, who were numerous, were headed by the powerful Archbishop of Rheims, Foulques, the successor of Hincmar.   Guy succeeded in having himself crowned at Langres, but the disquieting behaviour of Hugh compelled him to turn his attention immediately to Italy.   Here fighting was the order of the day, and after an indecisive battle near Brescia (888), the Duke of Spoleto gained the victory of Trebbia (889).   Berengarius, in spite of the German alliance, was obliged to content himself with his marquisate, augmented, it is true, by certain important towns, such as Verona.

Both Guy of Spoleto and his rival laid claim to

the title of king,[1] though the former had much the better right to it, being now master of Milan, Pavia, and the whole of Italy south of the Po.

The kingdom of Luitprand and Astolphus was thus reconstituted to the advantage of a family which, though certainly of Frankish origin, had rapidly become Italianised, and that, not according to the tradition of Louis II. and the Carlovingians, but that of the old Lombard kings as opposed to the Pope. There was no family understanding between the princes of Spoleto and the Holy See, and though they had sometimes lent it their support, it was in their capacity as imperial functionaries carrying out the orders of their superior officers, the Carlovingians. Still, they were more given to furthering their permanent interests by making themselves troublesome to the Pope. They found as much difficulty in living at peace with the occupant of the Holy See as Astolphus had done in respecting the Byzantine provinces.

Guy's kingship was, therefore, a serious menace for the papacy. But what could be done ? They might indeed follow the popular example, and, overlooking the fact of the illegitimacy of Carloman's son, accept him as the Roman emperor. But Arnulph, far away, was too much taken up with his own internal difficulties (in particular with his enemies the Normans and the Moravians) to be able to interfere in the affairs of Italy. At this time the star of the Greek empire was in the ascendant. Ever since it had re-established its footing in Southern Italy by settling at Bari, its successes, both military and diplomatic, had been

[1] M. G. Cap., t. ii. p. 104 ; documents on the election of King Guy by the bishops.

continually on the increase. With a more forcible
attempt, the vassalage of the Greek or Lombard
princes in the interior and on the west coast
might have been transformed into absolute subjection. Since the accession of the Emperor Leo VI.
(886) Photius had been turned out of the patriarchal see to which the Pope Marinus had again
disputed his right; the bitter dissent between the
Roman Church and the empire of Constantinople
was at an end. He might have boldly interfered
in Italian affairs, exhausted the claimants of Spoleto
and Friuli by playing them off one against the other,
and taken advantage of the weakness of the trans-
Alpine kingdoms to emulate Justinian's work in
Italy. The Greeks, however, let the opportunity
slip. After the demise of Charles the Fat, Pope
Stephen V. only had to reckon with two powers,
the new king of Italy and the heir, such as he
was, of Carlovingian tradition.

He adopted a crafty policy. Guy, who was
much to be feared, was not openly thwarted. In
order to obtain pardon for his rebellion of 883 the
duke had set out to fight against the Saracens
immediately after his restoration to favour (885),
and had even demolished their establishment between
Gaeta and the Garigliano; it was only a temporary
destruction, certainly, but one which gained him a
great deal of gratitude. Pope Stephen writing the
following year to the Archbishop of Rheims,[1] a
relation of Guy's, declares that he looks upon the
latter as his only son. This paternal tenderness, however, did not prevent him from appealing to Arnulph
for help, in 890. It is true that he avoided direct
letters, and had recourse to the medium of Zwenti-

[1] J., 3420.

bald, duke of the Moravians, who in his name begged the King of Germany "to come to Rome to visit the sanctuary of St. Peter, and to resume dominion over the kingdom of Italy which had been appropriated by bad Christians, and was being threatened by a heathen people." [1]

The following year, however, on 21st February 891, this same Pope Stephen V. consecrated Guy as emperor at St. Peter's. Formosus, who succeeded him some months later, performed the same action for Lambert, Guy's son (30th April 892). Thus the House of Spoleto stood possessed not only of the Italian kingship, but also of the imperial title.

In performing these ceremonies the Pope was acting under compulsion. Formosus, like Stephen V., was playing a double part. He consecrated the Spoletans, and in his letters to his uncle of Rheims referred to them in terms of the highest praise, with protestations of loyalty and affection.[2] But he, none the less, continued to beset Arnulph with lamentations, beseeching him to come and deliver him from the "bad Christians." [3] There can be no doubt that he alluded to the House of Spoleto and their oppression of the Holy See, for there was, at that time, no question of the Saracens. It seemed like a return to the situation of 754, and Formosus, Arnulph, and Guy, being now in precisely the same relations as had been Stephen II., Pepin, and Astolphus.

Arnulph, thus importuned, ended by coming. His first expedition, at the beginning of 894, though ill equipped with forces, succeeded in taking the

---

[1] *Ann. Fuld.*
[2] J., 3481, 3482, 3500, lost letters analysed by Flodoard.
[3] J., 3486, 3501, lost letters mentioned in the *Annals of Fulda.*

territory north of the Po. Bergamo was captured by storm and plundered, and this victory led the other towns, even including Milan and Pavia, to open their gates. The Emperor Guy, having withdrawn to the Apennines, awaited Arnulph at the mountain pass. He was a doughty warrior, who, if he had lived, would have given the emperor a troublous time in Italy. But he died the same year, soon after Arnulph, who did not deem it discreet to attack him in his own mountains, had re-crossed the Alps.

But, although Guy was dead, his cause was still in capable hands. The interests of the young Lambert were watched by the Empress-Mother Agiltrude, a woman of marked force of character. She was the daughter of that Adalgis of Beneventum who, in 871, had dared to attack the sacred person of the Emperor Louis II., and, both by family tradition and the exigencies of her present position, was the deadly foe of the Carlovingian dynasty. She united in herself the old grievances of the Lombard kings with the new feelings of resentment harboured by the princes of Spoleto. Arnulph was to find her an enemy not to be despised.

In the autumn of 895 the latter reappeared in Italy, and in the following February advanced against Rome. His army had a trying time in Tuscany owing to illness, bad weather, and the dreadful state of the roads. The Marquess Adalbert, too, was a questionable vassal. Up to Arnulph's arrival at Rome nothing had been heard of the Spoletans. He imagined that the town was in the Pope's power, and expected to see a procession advancing to meet him. But he had reckoned without Agiltrude, who, with great intrepidity, had seized

upon Rome, quite ignoring the papal protestations.
She had already invested it with a garrison, and was
making ready to receive the invading party.

But her plans were checked by a chance incident
which, contrary to all expectation, delivered the Gate
of St. Pancratius into the hands of the astonished
besiegers.   The Spoletans disappeared, leaving the
field to the Pope and the Carlovingian representatives.   Arnulph was received on the steps of
St. Peter's, and Formosus warmly embraced him,
for whom he and his predecessor had awaited as
the promised deliverer.   On 22nd February 896
the Vatican was the scene of an imperial consecration, this time celebrated with whole-hearted
enthusiasm.

It now remained to follow up their victory.
Shut up in the castle whose ruins still crown the
picturesque mountain of Spoleto, Agiltrude and
Lambert awaited the coming of Arnulph.   The
latter left as his representative at Rome, not the
peaceable *missus* of former times, but a substantial
military commander, Farold by name, and set out
on the road to Umbria.   The Pope Formosus,
countenanced by Farold, was preparing to follow
the vicissitudes of the struggle between the two
emperors whom he had consecrated, when some
terrible news reached him.   Arnulph had been
struck down by paralysis, and now had to be carried
on a litter, just as his father Carloman had been in
877.   There was no prospect that he would ever
again be strong enough to fight for the Holy See
in Italy.

Overwhelmed by the overthrow of his plans,
Formosus immediately died, on 4th April 896.
Even more than in the case of Marinus, perhaps,

his election had defied the laws of the Church, for
at the time of his promotion he still held the bishopric
of Porto. The two elections that followed, under the
auspices of Farold the *missus*, showed no greater
degree of respect for the ancient rules of discipline.
Formosus was succeeded by Boniface VI., a priest
who had twice (both as sub-deacon and as priest)
incurred sentence of deposition. He seems to have
been thrust forward as candidate by the populace.
His reign was short, and in a fortnight's time there
was another occupant of the Papal See in the person
of Stephen (VI.), Bishop of Anagni.

Meanwhile Lambert was regaining a footing in
Northern Italy. He had returned to Pavia and
Milan, and had come to terms with Berengarius
who had not been conciliated by his submissive
attitude with regard to Arnulph. The Adda and
the lower Po were agreed upon as boundaries between the kings of Italy. Lambert retained the
better part—Milan, Pavia, Spoleto, and the imperial title. There could be no further question
of Germany and its princes before the Ottos.

The affairs of Italy being thus arranged, Lambert
and his mother turned their steps towards Rome,
the final refuge of the German empire. On 20th
August 896 Farold was still supreme, and he seems
to have held his own until the end of the year.
But at the beginning of 897, Agiltrude and Lambert
again took possession of the town, though under
what circumstances there is no evidence to tell.
Then there happened an event of evil omen, which
was to be the foreshadower of a long and sad
series of disturbances in the heart of the apostolic
Church.

Formosus had betrayed the House of Spoleto,

having treacherously abetted and consecrated the barbarian candidate. He had now been dead and buried for nine months, a fact which would have sufficed to disarm any ordinary avenger on the principle of *jam parce sepulto*. But even the mysteries of death and the tomb were not sacred before the unholy rage of the daughter of Adalgis, for she, almost beyond a doubt, was the real instigator of the crime carried out by Pope Stephen VI., the pitiable tool of her vengeance.

The withered corpse of the aged pontiff was dragged from its sarcophagus, and exhibited before a synod presided over by the Pope. Still dressed in pontifical garments, it was propped up on a throne, and by its side was installed a deacon, who, pale with terror, had to reply in the name of the deceased Formosus. The legal accounts of this abominable trial were burned the following year, but we get some of the details from contemporary writers. The whole history of his past, his quarrels with John VIII., his oaths, his ambitious conspiracies, the perjuries imputed to him, were all brought up to his disadvantage. They revived old ecclesiastical canons, long forgotten by every one, including the president of this gruesome council, and ended by proclaiming the unworthiness of the accused, the irregularity of his promotion, and the invalidity of his acts, especially his ordinations. On this point, however, they confined themselves to the annulment of the Roman ordinations, continuing to recognise those outside. Not one of the Roman clerks thus deposed was reordained.[1] In accordance with the ancient ceremony, the papal mummy was stripped of its insignia, and of all its

---

[1] Auxilius, App. *Dümmler, Auxilius and Vulgarius*, p. 95.

clothing except the haircloth which still clung to the withered flesh. It was then thrown into an unconsecrated tomb, among the bodies of strangers. But the brutal populace, anxious to have a share in those outrages on the man before whom they had long grovelled, had the corpse cast into the Tiber.

In order that nothing should be lacking to the horror of this gloomy time, the old Lateran basilica collapsed. This catastrophe possibly preceded the ghastly council; it seems almost a pity that it did not occur just at the time of it, and that the venerable building, which had so often been witness of the prayers of Sylvester, Leo, Gregory, and Nicholas, did not crash in upon the head of their unworthy successor.

The latter, however, did not live long to enjoy the horrible triumph of which he had been the instigator rather than the hero. Whatever may have been his exact motives for taking part in this grim comedy, there can be no doubt that he thought it would be to his own advantage. The judgment pronounced against Formosus would have been his own fate, if by a revolting casuistry he had not been careful to have the ordinations of his predecessor annulled. It was Formosus who had consecrated him Bishop of Anagni, but, the acts of Formosus being repealed, this episcopal ordination vanished with them, so that it could no longer be said that Pope Stephen VI. had been transferred from one See to another.

But Stephen was to meet with his deserts. A rebellion arose, evidently incited by horror at his proceedings, and he was cast out of the papal See. As he had caused Formosus to be stripped while dead, so was he stripped while alive ; a monkish garment was flung over his shoulders, and then he was thrown into a prison.   But this was not considered punishment enough and before long they strangled him.

The reigns of the next two pontiffs, Romanus and Theodore II., were extremely brief.   Romanus occupied the papal chair for four months, and Theodore for only twenty days.   But under the latter reparatory measures were begun.   The body of Formosus had been cast up by the Tiber near the church of St. Acontius, in his old diocese of Porto.   A monk, warned, it is said, in a dream by the shade of the unfortunate Pope, found it and bestowed upon it a temporary burial.   Several months later, Theodore II. having been elected pontiff, decided to restore it to its original tomb in the atrium of St. Peter's, in the midst of the other Popes.   Clothed anew in his pontifical adornments, Formosus was conveyed, with chanting and prayers, to the last long home, of which he had been deprived by unholy rancour.[1]

Theodore did more still.   He restored the clerks deposed by the council of Stephen VI. to their lost positions.   A special assembly was convened for this purpose, but its provisions, unfortunately, have not been preserved.

Thus, in efforts to repair some of the ills that had been incurred, the year 897, one of the darkest in the long annals of the papacy, came to a close. But the spirit of unrest was abroad, and peace was

---

[1] The paintings in St. Peter's had been restored by order of Formosus.   According to a legend related by Luitprand, when his body was brought back to the basilica, the statues of the saints bowed towards it.

not yet to be established.   There was strife over
the tomb of Theodore II., two Popes, Sergius III.
and John IX., being elected at the same time.
The imperial authority appears to have supported
John, who was a lover of peace.   Sergius was a
fierce and radical adherent of Stephen VI. and his
council.   The Emperor Lambert had the upper
hand, and the idea of resorting to the transalpine
protection could not be entertained.   To extenuate,
as far as might be possible, the scandalous behaviour of the council of Stephen VI., to lessen the
internal dissensions of the Roman Church, and to
confirm the legitimacy and positions of the emperor,
the bishops, and the cardinals, such was the self-
imposed task of John IX.   With this end in view,
he held three councils, of which we only know the
details of two, one held at Rome[1] and the other
at Ravenna.   Bishops from every part of Italy were
present.   The decrees of Stephen's council were
read and repealed, while those of Theodore's council
were sealed with approbation.   It was also decided
that in future no corpse could be brought up for
trial.   The ordinations of Formosus were recognised
as valid, as were also his decrees in general, with the
exception of the " surreptitious consecration of a
barbarian "—*unctio illa barbarica, per surreptionem
extorta.*   Finally, the rights of the emperor in connection with the jurisdiction over the Romans were
solemnly ratified.   As regards the papal elections,
it was declared that any disorders that had occurred,
proceeded from the lack of the imperial participation
in the choice of the Pope, and that, consequently,
no future elections could be followed by consecra-

[1] For this council, reference must be made to Mansi's account,
which is more complete than others

tion without the presence of the emperor's legates—
præsentibus legatis imperatoris.

In this way the Church of Rome returned, on
her own initiative, to the régime of the constitution
of Lothaire.   She recognised that, outside these rules,
to which she had with so ill a grace resigned herself
under Lothaire and Louis II., there could be no
security, either for the papal elections or for the temporal government of the Roman state.

The Pope's hopes, like those of the rest of Italy
outside Berengarius's kingdom, thus began to centre
upon the young Emperor Lambert.   Unfortunately,
however, he was killed by a hunting accident on
15th October, not many weeks after the council
of Ravenna.   Like his predecessors, John VIII.,
Stephen V., and Formosus, John IX. had to gaze
upon the ruins of the hopes which he had built on
the empire.   He died in January 900, having no
doubt realised more than once the truth of the
psalmist's words, *Nolite confidere in principibus filiis
hominum, in quibus non est salus.*

CHAPTER XVI

THE HOUSE OF THEOPHYLACT

The Empire annihilated—Theophylact and Sergius III.—John X. and the Expulsion of the Saracens—Alberic of Spoleto—End of the anti-Formosan quarrel—Marozia—Accession of Alberic II.

BERENGARIUS immediately assumed authority over the kingdom of Lambert, and took possession of the palace of Pavia. In the following year (899) the Hungarians penetrated into Italy for the first time, and laid waste everything not defended by fortified walls. The new king took up arms against them, but while trying to cut off their retreat, he sustained a crushing repulse on the Brenta—an unlucky omen for his future reign. On the 8th December Arnulph died; he was succeeded by his very youthful son, Louis the Child.

Towards the beginning of the year 900, John IX. was succeeded by Benedict IV., a man who shared the same theories of government. Berengarius, whose defeat had brought him into disrepute, had now to struggle against a rival, King Louis of Provence, whose mother was daughter to the Emperor Louis II. The success of the newcomer was great enough to cause him to be recognised at Pavia and even at Rome, where he was consecrated emperor by Pope Benedict in February 901. But his prosperity did not last long. Berengarius regained the upper hand in 902, and compelled him to retreat beyond the Alps, after having sworn never to reappear in Italy. This oath was broken in 905, when Louis was besought to come to the support of those Italian nobles who were ill-content with Berengarius's government. He even succeeded in wresting Verona from his rival, but fell into his power through treachery, and after having his eyes put out, was banished for ever.

Rome took no part in these quarrels. The particularistic spirit prevailed more and more strongly. Nothing could be expected from the transalpine dynasties, and the King of Italy was too weak and beset by foes to be of any substantial support. But help came from within. From the very heart of the local aristocracy there issued an influential family, which straightway placed itself at the head of affairs, a position which it maintained for nearly sixty years under one form or another.

At the time of which we are speaking, it was represented by the papal *vestararius* or *vestiarius* Theophylact, his wife Theodora, who bore the title of *vestararissa*, and his two daughters, Marozia and Theodora. The office of *vestararius* was one of the most important in the whole of the pontifical administration. It was early secularised, and its incumbent seems to have been specially charged with the supervision of the government of Ravenna and the neighbouring provinces. Theophylact was both duke and *magister militum*, and at Rome the titles of consul and senator were his in an exclusive fashion—he was not *a* consul, but *the* consul,[1] not *a* senator, but *the* senator.

[1] Eug. Vulgarius (ed. Dümmler, p. 147) calls him *dominus urbis*. In 900 he appears for the first time at a court of justice, held by the Emperor Louis of Provence (*Memorie di Lucca*, t. iii. p. 639); his name appears second among the lay nobility. In a document of 915 (Gattola, *Hist. Abb. Cassin. Acc.*, t. i. p. 111) he

Upon the death of Benedict IV., towards the end of July 903, they elected a priest *forensis* (*i.e.* one who was not a cardinal). He was known as Pope Leo V., but in less than two months he was supplanted by another priest, Christopher, by whom he was cast into prison. Hardly had the following year begun, when who should turn up again but Sergius, the exiled rival of John IX. (898). His return was supported by the "Franks," probably, that is, by Berengarius or the Marquess of Tuscany, whose help was claimed by one Roman party. His first proceeding was to send Christopher to keep Leo V. company in prison. These two unfortunates dragged out a wretched existence for some time longer, when it was decided, "out of pity," to relieve them of the burden of life.

With such a beginning, the pontificate of Sergius III. seemed to shadow forth a period of passionate reaction against Formosus, John IX., and his successors. He revived in all its severity the tradition of Stephen VI., with whose ecclesiastical position he had much in common. He had indeed received episcopal ordination at the hands of Formosus, and that, too, for the See of Caeri, which had already in 882 supplied Rome with a Pope. Certainly Formosus was allowed to rest in his tomb, but on that of Stephen was engraved an epitaph exalting him for having "checked the licentiousness of the haughty and intrusive Formosus": *Hic primum repulit Formosi spurca superbi, culmina qui invasit sedis apostolicæ.* A convocation was summoned in

is spoken of as *senator Romanorum,* and named the first; at the imperial consecration of Berengarius (fin. 915), his son appears under the title of *filius consulis,* together with the brother of the Pope (John X.), quite in the same rank, and above all the other Roman nobles.

order to annul once again the ordinations of Formosus, and its decisions were carried out with
merciless severity. Bishops, priests, and deacons,
all who had been consecrated by Formosus, were
obliged either to resign their positions or to submit
to reordination. It was forbidden to use the title of
priest (*sacerdos*) with reference to Formosus, even in
correspondence, and there is still preserved a letter
from Sergius III. to Amelius, Bishop of Uzés, in
which the latter is vehemently reproached for not
having complied with this rule. John IX. and his
successors, who were looked upon as usurpers, were
designated on the epitaph of Sergius as "ravening
wolves." Sergius himself also uses the same expression when he refers to them in the monumental
inscriptions which he had placed in the Lateran
basilica, restored during his administration.

The unpleasant effect produced in the ecclesiastical world of Italy by these measures may easily be
imagined. Apart from the Roman clergy, strictly
speaking, who appear to have been too much alarmed
to make any show of resistance, there were in pen-
insular Italy a number of bishops who had been
consecrated by Formosus during his five years'
pontificate. Not only were these consecrations rendered null and void, but the ordinations celebrated
in their own dioceses by these bishops themselves
were also annulled. In such places as Naples and
Beneventum, which were not under the temporal
power of the papacy, some resistance was manifested. There was even a series of polemical
writings directed against the Pope, several of which
have come down to us under the names of Auxilius
and Eugenius Vulgarius.[1] These latter defended

---

[1] Some of these writings have been published by Morinus,
Mabillon, and Bianchini ; others have been collected by E. Dümmler,

the ordinations of Formosus; Sergius III. wrote on behalf of the opposite side, but his writings have not been preserved.

Eugenius Vulgarius appears to have steered a middle course between the two parties; although he assailed Sergius III., there came a time when he deemed it prudent to ingratiate himself with him, lavishing flattery and compliments both in prose and verse. He also addressed himself to influential

who has devoted to them "an ensemble study"—*Auxilius and Vulgarius*, Leipzig, 1866. Auxilius, a priest of French origin, wrote to Naples. He had been summoned to attend the council of Sergius III., but refused to comply. He wrote three works upon the ordinations of Formosus : (*a*) *In defensionem sacræ ordinationis papæ Formosi*, in two volumes (Dümmler, pp. 59–95), with an appendix on the history of the Popes from Marinus to Sergius III. ; this work must have been published in 908 ; (*b*) *De ordinationibus papæ Formosi*, a collection of texts (Migne, t. 129, p. 1059), of which Dümmler has found a rather more extensive edition (*op. cit.*, pp. 107–116); (*c*) a dialogue on the same subject (*Infensor and Defensor ;* Migne, t. c. p. 1070), addressed with the preceding work to Leo, Bishop of Nola. These last two books date from 911, or a little earlier. Besides these three works, Auxilius published an apology for the ordinations of Stephen, Bishop of Naples, who died in 907, or rather sooner, and who, like Formosus, had been transferred from a bishopric.

Vulgarius, it seems, was a grammarian, a professor of a school at Naples, or some other Greek town in southern Italy. Unlike Auxilius, he was not deeply versed in ecclesiastical literature, but, on the other hand, he had an extensive acquaintance with the classics, and tenderly cultivated the various poetical metres and forms of dialectic. His first work (Dümmler, p. 117) was issued in the form of a letter addressed to the Roman Church by a council of Gauls, held at Lutetia, the year 17 of the Emperor Charles IV., *i.e.* Charles the Simple (910); the second is in the form of a dialogue (*Insimulator, Actor ;* Migne, p. 1103); it was composed at the request of a deacon, Peter. Mabillon had published it under the name of Auxilius, but Dümmler discovered that of Vulgarius at the beginning of both works. Besides the letters and the pieces of verse mentioned in the text (Dümmler, pp. 139–156), we must also quote the *Invectiva in Romam*, published under John X. (*i.e.* between 914 and 928), the last of the known arguments on behalf of Formosus ; the latter was published by Bianchini (*Anast. bibl.*, t. iv. p. lxx).

persons in high places at the Roman Court, the *apocrisiarius* Vitalian, the *vestararissa* Theodora, and many others.

From his letter to Theodora, and also in one from Ravenna, discovered a few years ago,[1] we gain some idea of the influence and power of the *vestiarius* and his wife. They made common cause with the Pope, dealing out his favours, and generally behaving as if they were the real masters of the Roman state. The understanding went further. Sergius III. was on terms of intimacy with Marozia, one of Theodora's daughters, and he even had a son by her, who, later on, rose to the papacy as John XI. There seems to have been no secret as to his paternity, for not only the chroniclers, such as Luitprand, but also the semi-official catalogues, by means of which the *Liber Pontificalis* was continued, do not hesitate to make mention of it. From this we see how openly vice was tolerated among the most exalted personages at that time.

Pope Sergius was spiteful, brutal, and a scoundrel,[2] but it must be admitted that he knew how to retain the papal throne at a time when its occupants came and went in rapid succession. He held it for seven years, and then died a natural death. He also had the power of making himself feared and obeyed, in which he was greatly assisted by Theophylact and his family. Neither must it be forgotten that his pontificate was distinguished by the renewal of the Lateran basilica, in which he displayed the most lavish generosity possible.

---

[1] *Neues Archiv.*, t. ix. p. 517.

[2] Sergius had been promoted to the sub-diaconate by Pope Marinus (882-84); he was therefore over forty years of age when his pontificate began (904). Marozia, who was married for the third time in 932, could hardly have been born before 892. There was thus a great disparity of age between her and Sergius III.

The two Popes who succeeded Sergius were Anastasius III., who reigned rather more than two years, and Laudo, who was in authority for less than six months. We know nothing of their history, and it seems improbable that they could have opposed the influence of Theophylact, who was the virtual temporal ruler. John X., who came after them, maintained his position during fourteen years (914–928).

It was even claimed that his promotion, due to Theodora, was the consequence of his adulterous relations with this woman, who, as Luitprand remarks, governed Rome with vigour, *Romanæ civitatis non inviriliter monarchiam obtinebat.* However this may be, there can be no doubt that John's government was conspicuous for its force and virility.

The great question of the day was how best to bring about the expulsion of the Saracens. Since their defeat of 885, they had renewed their strength, and, always welcome at Naples and Gaeta, had established a fortified centre of plundering operations in the mountains commanding the lower course of the Garigliano. This was extremely unpleasant for the important possessions of the Roman Church in their vicinity. Moreover, the Saracens, invading Roman Campania, had set up at Sabina a kind of branch of their Garigliano establishment on the site of the Abbey of Farfa, which had been taken from the monks in 898. John X. directed all his energies towards the destruction of these two Mussulman resorts.

He undoubtedly had this end in view when, about the month of December 915, he invited Berengarius to Rome, and bestowed upon him the imperial crown. Louis the Blind (died 928) was still living in his kingdom of Provence. No attention was paid to his claims, which went back to Pope Benedict IV., unrecognised by Sergius III. The poet by whom the *Gesta Berengarii* were celebrated with so much pomp, has left us a description of the fêtes with which his hero was honoured in 915. Berengarius, however, took no part in the struggle against the Saracens; after his coronation he returned to the north of Italy, leaving his subjects of Tuscany and Spoleto to help the Pope in his schemes for their overthrow.

This time their help was really worth having. The governor of Spoleto, the Marquess Alberic, acted in concert with the Romans. The infidels were defeated at Baccano and at Trevi, and forced to abandon their establishment, and to fall back upon the Garigliano. But this was not all. John X. was well adapted for such an undertaking, and he succeeded in organising in Southern Italy a league of all the Christian principalities. Naples and Gaeta, indemnified at the expense of the pontifical estates, broke off their alliance with the Mussulmans; the Greek strategist of Langobardium, Nicholas Picingli, appeared in the Tyrrhenian Sea at the head of an important fleet; round him rallied the squadrons of Naples and the neighbouring ports, not to mention the pontifical vessels; the Lombard princes of Beneventum, Capua, and Salerno, all lent their aid; and the Roman state, Tuscany, and the duchy of Spoleto, sent a considerable contingent under the command of the Senator of the Romans, Theophylact, and the Marquess Alberic.[1] So well managed

---

[1] The treaty signed near Garigliano is still preserved with all its signatures in a charter of 1014, published by Gattola, *Hist. abb. Cass. Acc.*, t. i. p. 109.

was the whole undertaking that in August 916, after a two months' siege, the Saracens, hemmed in on every side, were utterly defeated. The Pope, who was a worthy successor of John VIII., did not hesitate to risk his own life in the fray, for on two occasions we hear of his charging into the ranks of the enemy. He himself does not disdain to boast of his prowess in a letter written shortly afterwards to the Archbishop of Cologne.

The Marquess Alberic has equal claims to distinction; he fought *ut leo fortissimus*, and to his share fell the greater part of the laurels of the war. He had been, for a long time, a conspicuous character. Already in the time of the Emperor Guy he had been one of the chief captains of Italy. He afterwards entered Berengarius's service, and received the spoils of the Lambert family in the duchy of Spoleto. He was by no means scrupulous as to the methods he employed, and the last member of this family, the Marquess Guy, was murdered by him on one of the Tiber bridges.[1] Both Spoleto and Camerino were in subjection to him, and like his predecessors in the same situation, he cast longing eyes at Rome. The Romans, thanks to his prowess in the Saracen war, looked upon him with favour, and, after the Garigliano episode, Theophylact bestowed on him the hand of his daughter, Marozia, who, as we have already seen, had been the mistress of the late Pope Sergius III.

John X., strong in his temporal supporters, recked little of the scruples of those who considered (and not without reason) that his promotion was illegal. As deacon of Bologna, John had been nominated as the successor of the Bishop Peter, but

[1] *Gesta Berengarii*, ii. 29, 89.

the metropolitan throne of Ravenna being vacant at the same time, he preferred to accept the more important post. He retained the office for several years until, by the favour of Theodora, he was promoted to the chair of St. Peter. The *Invectiva in Romam*, which blazed forth from Naples, and the chronicles of Monte Cassino, treat him as an *invasor*. The Roman catalogues, which are more discriminating, place him in his due rank, but otherwise pass over the circumstance without remark. John, like his predecessor Sergius, refused to recognise the ordinations of Formosus. They were strangely inconsistent, these popes—Stephen VI., Sergius III., and John X. They were all three tarred with the same brush as Formosus, having all of them been bishops before their accession to the papacy, and yet they with one accord condemned him, his promotion, and his ordinations.[1]

The disagreement on this point of canon law came to an end in the course of time. Towards the end of John X.'s reign, serious events were happening in Northern Italy. Rudolph II., king of transjuran Burgundy, was called upon in 922, by the Marquess of Ivry and other local potentates, to fight against the Emperor Berengarius. This unlucky prince was assassinated at Verona, after many ups and downs of fortune, including the Hungarian invasion incited by himself. But Rudolph was not long to enjoy his success unmolested. Another rival appeared in the person of Hugh, Count of Provence, the successor of Louis the Blind, and grand-

---

[1] It is probable that, like Stephen VI. and Sergius III., John X. got out of the difficulty by the shifty theory of his first episcopal ordinations having been annulled. If this is the case, his consecration as Archbishop of Ravenna must have taken place before the time of Sergius III., *i.e.* 904.

son of Lothaire II., and Waldrade, by his mother Bertha. Recognised at Pavia in 926, Hugh immediately attracted the attention of the Romans. Dissension again arose round the person of John X. Theophylact and Alberic were both dead. There could no longer be any question of the male descent of the former, of that *filius consulis* who had made such a brilliant figure at Berengarius's consecration. Theophylact's daughter, Alberic's widow, however, was still alive, and had taken to herself a second husband, Guy, Marquess of Tuscany, without in any way yielding her claims upon the Roman state.

But her ambitions were thwarted by the Pope, supported by his brother Peter, who had also taken part in Berengarius's consecration, in 915. Relying on his position as head of a principality at Orta, as well as on the papal influence, he sought to counterbalance the authority of Marozia. The Hungarians, whom he had bidden, took the Saracens' place in the Roman district, and made it the scene of all kinds of horrors. To these dangerous allies the Pope was anxious to add, or to substitute, the support of the new king of Italy. He met him at Mantua, and they concluded a treaty of which the details are unknown.

This attempt at emancipation was not calculated to please Marozia, and owing to the united efforts of herself and her husband, a revolt sprang up at Rome. The rebels, strengthened by the Tuscan troops, seized Peter and murdered him in the sight of his brother. The Pope himself was cast into prison and shortly afterwards stifled under a cushion (928).

As the monk of Mt. Soracte remarks, in his strange Latin : *Subjugatus est Romam potestative in manu feminæ.* Marozia employed her power in bestowing the Holy See on her tools, first on Leo (Leo VI., 928), priest of St. Susan's, then on Stephen (Stephen VII., 929–931), priest of St. Anastasius'; and finally on her own son John (John XI.), formerly incumbent of St. Maria in the Trastevere. It was only his youth, probably, which had kept him from promotion before.

Meanwhile, Guy of Tuscany had died. Hugh, King of Italy, who lived like a sultan in his palace at Pavia, also lost his legal wife. Marozia, bursting with ambition, and not content with reigning at Spoleto and Lucca, saw no reason why she should stop short of becoming queen, or even empress. She, therefore, offered her hand to King Hugh, who accepted it with alacrity. The wedding was celebrated at Rome, at the Castle of St. Angelo, where Marozia appears to have taken up her abode. There was every reason to expect that John XI., like a dutiful son, would adorn the heads of the newly married pair with the imperial crowns. Things, however, turned out differently.

In addition to John XI., who was illegitimate, Marozia had had another son—the young Alberic— by her first marriage with the Marquess of Spoleto. He was displeased at his mother's new matrimonial alliance, particularly as King Hugh was imprudent enough to insult him publicly in the midst of the festivities. Alberic, goaded to desperation, rallied round him a number of the discontented Romans, and immediately laid siege to the Castle of St. Angelo. Hugh, with difficulty, succeeded in escaping, but Marozia was taken captive.

When all is said and done, this event was nothing but a change of person. The power passed out of the hands of Marozia into those of Alberic, her son.

Marozia herself had inherited it from her father, Theophylact, and the dynasty was continued. The Pope was obliged to submit to circumstances, and to confine himself more and more to his ecclesiastical province. After John XI. (931–935) came Leo VII. (936–939), Stephen VIII. (939–942), Marinus II. (942–946), and Agapitus II. (946–955). Neither of these Popes exercised any temporal authority; they were princes merely in theory, like the last of the Merovingian kings. This had been the real state of affairs ever since the time of Sergius III. (904). The Roman state had, from its constitution in 754, been placed under the direction of the Pope and the clergy, though evidently contrary to the inclinations of the lay aristocracy. After many ineffectual efforts, the latter had succeeded in obtaining a place on the staff of management, but only by means of allying themselves with the protective government and taking advantage of its support. When the Carlovingian line had come to an end, and it had become obvious that the title of emperor was no longer synonymous with practical power, the lay aristocracy had no difficulty in getting the upper hand. The important question of who was to be the *primus inter pares,* then the master, was solved by Theophylact; circumstances with which we are but imperfectly acquainted favoured his plans, and for long generations the power was centred in the family of the clever and ambitious *vestararius.*

CHAPTER XVII

ALBERIC AND JOHN XII

Alberic, Senator of the Romans—Limits of his Principality—Character
of his Authority—Relations with the Byzantine Court—Monastic
Revival—Octavian, Alberic's Son and Successor—He is elected
Pope—His Disorderly Life—Otto is summoned by him to Rome
and consecrated Emperor—Quarrel between the Pope and Otto—
Deposition of John XII.—Election of Leo VIII.—Otto's Privilege—
The Papal Election annulled by the Emperor—Return of John XII.;
his Death—Benedict V. and Leo VIII.

ALBERIC, upon becoming prince of the Romans,
immediately set himself to defend his principality
against outside attacks. There was no longer anything to fear from the Saracens, and the relations
with the Greek empire had long been of a diplomatic
nature only; under Alberic they seem to have been
peculiarly amiable. He had no trouble with his
neighbours of Spoleto or Tuscany, for his ambitions
did not soar beyond the limits of the old duchy of
Rome. As for the transapennine provinces of the
Exarchate and Pentapolis, they were, as a matter of
fact, already in the power of the King of Italy.
Alberic did not attempt to interfere with them,
but devoted his attention to plans for defending
his territory against the king's claims, and for
strengthening his newly acquired power in the
interior.

Hugh of Provence made several attempts (933,
936, 941) to take possession of Rome, and to gain
access to the Vatican, *i.e.* to receive the imperial
coronation. Alberic, however, was more than a

match for him.   After several truces, brought
about by the intervention of St. Odo, the worthy
Abbot of Cluny, Hugh finally agreed to cede all
the rights which had accrued to him through his
marriage with Marozia.   The same year he returned
to Provence, leaving the kingdom in the charge of
his son Lothaire.   The latter, however, died in
950, while still in the prime of early manhood,
leaving behind him a widow, Adelaide, as youthful
as himself.   Thereupon Berengarius, Marquess of
Ivrea, whose importance had remarkably increased
during the last few years, had himself proclaimed
king.   But Adelaide was not a person to be
ignored.   She resisted Berengarius on the strength
of rights acquired through her husband and her
father, Rudolph of Trans-juran Burgundy, who had
reigned between Berengarius and King Hugh.   She
was defeated, and imprisoned in a tower on Lake
Garda, but managed to escape and take refuge at
Reggio, when she appealed for help to Otto, the
powerful king of the Germans.

Otto responded to some purpose.   On the 22nd
September 951, while Berengarius was taking refuge
in a fortress, he appeared at Pavia, and took to wife
Lothaire's young widow.   Henceforward, for many
a long day, the destinies of Italy were to be closely
bound up with those of Germany.   Alberic was
anxious not to encourage any resumption of the
ancient tradition of the imperial protectorate, and
coldly repulsed Otto's desire to come to Rome,
even though the latter sent him an embassy conducted by the Archbishop of Mainz and the
Bishop of Coire.

Otto was not importunate.   Returning to his
kingdom, where there was still work enough to

occupy him for a long time, he decided to commit the government of Italy to his rival, Berengarius, who accepted the position of vassal king.

The Roman situation was not affected by these external events. Except for a slight family conspiracy, which was checked and severely punished, Alberic's sway remained undisputed. Public acts were still dated with the papal year, but on the coinage the emperor's name was replaced by Alberic's,[1] which appeared in conjunction with that of the Pope. As in the past, the judicial assemblies were held with the co-operation of the dignitaries of the papal palace and the lay nobility. In former times the pontiff rarely intervened, although the usual place of meeting was the Lateran palace, in a hall called *ad Lupam*, after the famous bronze she-wolf popularly known as *mater Romanorum*.[2] When the emperor was present these assemblies were held in the Vatican; under Alberic's rule they sometimes took place at his own dwelling in the palace of the Via Lata, which probably corresponded with the Colonna palace of to-day. In all this there was no essential alteration as regards outward forms, but, apart from the inscription of Alberic's name on the coinage, the real change that had taken place was well symbolised in his title of *princeps et omnium Romanorum senator;* to the title of *princeps* he himself added the qualification of *humilis*, others that of *gloriosus*.

In the early part of his reign Alberic had taken advantage of favourable circumstances to enter into family relationships with the Byzantine empire. The

---

[1] Benedict of Mt. Soracte.
[2] *Libellus de imp. pot. Cf.* Jaffé, 2633.

actual emperor at that time in Constantinople was
Romanus Lecapenus. He was the father of several
sons, one of whom, Theophylact, he intended for
the patriarchal throne. The child was then only
thirteen years of age, and, as his promotion was
strongly opposed at Constantinople, Lecapenus
begged that legates might be sent from Rome
with the Pope's sanction, in order to prevent
further protest. John XI. did send four ambassadors, among them two bishops, and these, on 2nd
February 933, by their presence at St. Sophia, in
company with the patriarchal child, countenanced
a tremendous breach of ecclesiastical law. Affairs
at Rome had been conducted on the principle of
Do ut des. Marozia, the possessor of a considerable line of ancestors, offered a daughter to the
Greek emperor, who, for his part, was plentifully
provided with male offspring to be settled in life.
These negotiations had most probably been begun
as early as 932, before the revolution which had
substituted Alberic for Marozia. Our chief information about this affair is procured from a letter
written by Romanus Lecapenus to John XI., and
recently published by Cardinal Pitra.[1] We gather
from it that the Greek emperor, satisfied with the
concessions relating to Theophylact, was not at all
anxious to recognise them by making an alliance
with the prince of the Romans. According to
him the journey from Constantinople to Rome is
too long for his son, though Marozia may bring,
or even send, her daughter. If she has no ships
suitable for the undertaking they can be provided
for her.

According to Benedict of Mt. Soracte, it was

---

[1] *Analecta novissima,* t. i. p. 469.

Alberic himself who had set his affections on a Greek princess. He was even prepared to furnish her with a whole staff of maids-of-honour, chosen from among the aristocratic ladies of Rome, when the plan fell through. Whether there were two successive plans of marriage, or whether we only admit the one of 932–933, there can be no doubt that the ruling family of Rome sought alliance with the imperial parvenus of Constantinople. Moreover, this fact has all the more weight when we remember the determination with which Alberic severed all links with Provence, Germany, and Italy. Like the Popes Stephen and Paul before him, he preferred a distant protector to one close at hand. It was the principle of the Donation of Constantine, only with a different application.

As regards Alberic's government we have nothing but favourable, not to say edifying, accounts. The four Popes who owed their promotion to him, seem to have been most estimable persons. He took an active part in founding and reforming monasteries, that of St. Mary on the Aventine being established in one of his paternal mansions. He also founded the convent of St. Cyriacus in the Via Lata, and endowed and remodelled those of St. Gregory, St. Paul, St. Lawrence, and St. Agnes. The famous abbey of Subiaco, laden with memories of St. Benedict, was, under his auspices, changed from a mere country chapel to a great monastic establishment. At Farfa he succeeded in restoring discipline, a feat which, considering the extreme decadence of conventual life, and the attitude of the monks, necessitated nothing short of military measures. In all this Alberic was led by St. Odo, Abbot of Cluny, who, during his long stay at

Rome, made of him the instrument by which he carried out his much-needed reforms.

In order that such an administration should produce any very permanent good effects, Alberic must have lived to a good old age, and have left behind him a capable successor, imbued with the same spirit. This, however, was not the case. While not yet in his fortieth year, the prince of the Romans recognised the approach of death. Possibly he imagined that his son, who bore the ambitious name of Octavian, would one day become Augustus, and that a native Roman empire would spring from his principality and family. He must have been much alarmed at the appearance of Otto upon the scene. So powerful a prince, once established at Pavia, could not fail to be stirred by thoughts of Charlemagne, whose memory was still green in the ecclesiastical world of Rome. This could bode no good to the lay aristocracy, of whom Alberic was the triumphant leader and head. The papacy, monarch of the past, had less reason than ever to fear the future. It was manifest to Alberic that the only resource of his family when he was dead would be in the possession of ecclesiastical power. Octavian, therefore, was now destined for the pontificate instead of for the empire. Alberic assembled the Romans at St. Peter's, and made them swear that his son should be elected Pope on the death of Agapitus II. Octavian was, at this period, in his sixteenth year. Some time after, in the year 954, Alberic died, and his son immediately succeeded him as *princeps et omnium Romanorum senator.*

It would have been well for Rome and for the Church, if Pope Agapitus could have postponed his departure until his successor had had time to gain a little wisdom. Unfortunately, however, he died towards the end of the following year, and, on the second Sunday in Advent, 16th December 905, the young prince of the Romans became Vicar of St. Peter's, and head of Christendom, under the title of John XII. The fact of his promotion put an end to the struggle for supremacy between the nobles and the clergy of Rome. There was no longer even a titular emperor, nor a foreign protector, *patricius Romanorum.* It was like a return to the days before Sergius III. and Theophylact, Nicholas and Louis II., Eugene II. and Lothaire, to that state of unstable equilibrium, in which the temporal sovereignty of the Popes had had its rise. John XII., except for certain changes introduced by a tradition of two hundred years, was in much the same position as had been Pope Zachary, or Stephen II. before the expedition to France. The difference lay in the fact that while the young Pope's only substantial support lay in the memory of his father, the papacy of the eighth century had behind it a long past of service and influence.

The situation was rendered still more unsettled by the danger resulting from the extreme youth of the new Pope. In his rash inexperience he set out upon a venturesome enterprise against the Lombard principalities of Southern Italy, but was defeated and obliged to sign a treaty. The indiscretion of youth displayed itself in yet another way, and Rome soon became witness of the most revolting scandals. The young Pope took very little interest in the offices of the Church and was never seen at Matins. His days and nights were spent in the society of women and young men, and in the midst of the pleasures of the table and the chase.

His illicit amours were a matter of public knowledge, for they were restrained neither by ties of blood nor by respect of persons. The Lateran became a resort of persons of ill-fame, and no virtuous woman could remain in safety at Rome. The ecclesiastical treasury was, at that time, maintained by the practice of simony, and was employed for such illegitimate purposes as the support of these licentious proceedings. We hear of a bishop consecrated at the age of ten, of a deacon ordained in a stable, and of dignitaries blinded or mutilated. Cruelty and impiety were conspicuous, and it is said that in the Lateran festivals the Pope even went so far as to drink to the health of the devil!

It is true that, from force of habit, the pontifical administration was carried on in the usual way, like well-organised machinery, from force of long custom. John XII. even issued a document in which he enjoined that the monks of Subiaco should every day chant a hundred *Kyrie Eleisons*, and as many *Christe Eleisons* for the salvation of his soul. He certainly was in a position to need the devout prayers of all earnest Christians!

Strangely enough, the very person who was to put an end to these scandals was summoned to Rome by John himself. His relations with the Italian kingdom were not altogether satisfactory, and there seem to have been a few frontier disputes. There was certainly no great need for alarm, but the good people of Rome, not knowing which side to take, were not at all sorry for the interposition. John chose from among them two ambassadors, the deacon John and the protonotary Azo, and despatched them to Germany with complaints of his royal neighbours. There is no doubt that they took advantage of the occasion to lodge (though unofficially) their own grievances against the Pope. They were not alone in their protestations. Many of the Italian princes were growing restive under the government of Berengarius II. and his son Adalbert. The Archbishop of Milan who had been expelled from his See, the Bishop of Como, and many others, joined with the Romans in begging Otto to interpose.

Towards the autumn of 961, Otto bore down upon Italy and entered Pavia without opposition. Berengarius and his wife Willa took refuge in a fortress in the Apennines, while Adalbert set out to find assistance. In the middle of winter the King of Germany started for Rome, after having made arrangements with the Pope as to the conditions of his stay, and the results that might be expected to follow his demands.[1]

The coronation took place on 2nd February 962. The Pope and the emperor signed an agreement by which John XII. swore that he would be loyal to Otto and never lend his support to Berengarius and Adalbert. Otto, for his part, guaranteed to the Pope all his temporal claims and possessions. At the same time he stipulated for the imperial rights over Rome and the papal elections. There still exists a celebrated document relating to this compact. It is known as " the Privilege of Otto,"

---

[1] The formula of the agreement, preserved by Bonizo of Sutri (cf. L. P., t. ii. p. 354), contains a clause which throws some uncertainty upon this : *In Romam nullum placitum aut ordinationem faciam de omnibus quæ ad te aut ad Romanos pertinent sine tuo consulto.* Certainly the privilege set forth *after* the consecration presupposes quite a different relationship. The formula *de futuro* might, however, bear more than one interpretation.

and dates from 13th February 962, a few days after the imperial coronation.[1]

John XII. and Otto parted on excellent terms, and the emperor returned to Pavia.[2] He had hardly left Rome, however, when the Pope began to enter into conspiracy with the claimants to the Italian throne. On hearing of this, Otto, not disposed to hurry matters, affected indifference and set himself to quell the opposition which he still encountered in his new kingdom. But, the following year (963), while he was besieging Berengarius II. and his wife Willa in the Castle of Montfeltro above Rimini, he received news that John XII., displaying his true colours, had welcomed Adalbert to Rome. He now hesitated no longer, and, on the 3rd November, appeared before the town. John XII.

[1] "The Privilege of Otto" (M. G. Diplom., t. i. p. 322 ; cf. Lib. Censuum, No. 82) has been the object of an official investigation by M. de Sickel (Das Privilegium Ottos I. für die römische Kirche), who has discovered that we possess a contemporary copy of this document, at present preserved in the Vatican Archives. It is, however, possible that this copy has been tampered with in this passage : Et ut ille qui ad hoc sanctum et apostolicum regimen eligitur nemine consentiente consecratus fiat pontifex priusquam talem in presentia missorum nostrorum vel filii nostri seu universæ generalitatis faciat promissionem qualem domnus et venerandus spiritalis pater noster Leo sponte fecisse dinoscitur. According to M. de Sickel's idea (cf. Ottenthal, in Böhmer, Regesta imp., 2nd edition, t. ii. p. 153) the Leo referred to is Leo III., and the Privilege of Otto here slavishly reproduces the terms of a promise made by this Pope to Charlemagne or Louis the Pious. Others think that it is Leo IV. who is meant. M. B. Simson (Neues Archiv, t. xv. p. 577) points out the strangeness of applying the formula domnus et venerandus spiritalis pater noster to any other Pope than the contemporary one, in which case it would refer to Leo VIII. The same phrase, however, recurs in the privilege delivered by Henry II. to Benedict VIII., which is practically but a reproduction of Otto's formula, while the latter, although it may have borrowed something from previous documents, is undoubtedly in the main original. It is evident that the privilege of 962 is not yet free from obscurities.

[2] He set out from Rome on 14th February and celebrated Easter at Pavia (30th March).

and Adalbert, powerless in face of the reaction caused by the emperor's arrival, speedily took flight. The Romans opened their gates and took an oath of fidelity, swearing that they would never again *elect* or *ordain* any Pope without the *consent and choice* of the Emperor Otto and his son Otto II.[1]

On 6th November a huge conference was held at St. Peter's. The emperor presided, around him being ranged his court, both ecclesiastical and lay, including German and Italian priests, the episcopate from the neighbourhood of Rome, the Roman clergy, and the local aristocracy. Many complaints were lodged against the Pope, and the council decided to summon him to appear. Legates were sent with the message, but John returned a disdainful and threatening response.[2] A second summons was despatched on 22nd November to his residence at Tivoli, but this did not affect him personally. Finally, on 4th December, after a month of waiting, the council pronounced on him a sentence of deposition. Thereupon the Romans, with Otto's full consent, elected as Pope the *protoscriniarius* Leo. In accordance with custom he was introduced at the Lateran, and on the following Sunday (6th December) his consecration was celebrated at St. Peter's.

To return to the privilege of Otto. It was perhaps at this juncture that it adopted the form in which it has been handed down to us. The second

---

[1] *Fidelitatem repromittunt, hoc addentes et firmiter jurantes, numquam se papam electuros aut ordinaturos præter consensum et electionem domni imp. Ottonis cæsaris aug. filiique ipsius regis Ottonis.* (Luitprand.)

[2] *Johannes episcopus, servus servorum Dei, omnibus episcopis. Nos audivimus dicere quia vos vultis alium papam facere. Si hoc facilis, excommunico vos de Deo omnipotente ut non habeatis licentiam nullum ordinare et missam celebrare.*

part, which relates to imperial rights, is practically a replica of the constitution of 824. As far as the papal election is concerned, it seems to be a revival pure and simple of the law of the ninth century. One point alone does not seem quite clear. By the privilege of Otto, the Romans were bound not to allow the consecration of any Pope until he had sworn, in presence of the people and of the imperial *missi*, an oath in conformity with that which *domnus et venerandus spiritalis pater noster Leo sponte fecisse dinoscitur*. As regards words and signification, this part of the privilege is a reproduction of the prescribed form of the *Sacramentum Romanorum* attached to the text of the constitution of 824. It refers to a promise made in 824 by Pope Eugenius II., as well as to another made by a Pope Leo, perhaps Leo VIII. As, however, we do not possess the actual wording of these stipulations, we are not in a position to judge. It may, however, be asserted that the general tenor of the privilege of Otto does not imply any progress in the imperial authority at Rome,[1] either in the elections or in any other connection.

This being the case, it is somewhat surprising that Luitprand should have spoken of a veritable renunciation of the right of election, for, according to the passage quoted above, the Romans actually relinquished their claims to the choice of the Pope. And this is not the only reference to the subject. In his account of the council of 964 at which the deposition of Benedict V. was pronounced, Luitprand

---

[1] No theoretical progress, be it understood, for since the death of Lambert the constitution of Lothaire had become a dead letter. But from the imperial standpoint, the mere reinforcement of the regulations of 824 was an enormous advance.

relates that the archdeacon addressed the following
reproach to the accused Pope: "Canst thou deny
having, with the other Romans, taken a solemn oath
before the emperor that thou wouldst neither elect
nor ordain any Pope without his consent and that of
his son, King Otto?" It must here be pointed out
that this evidence on the part of Luitprand is much
more reliable than his prattle about Theodora and
Marozia. It is the testimony of one of the most influential bishops on the council, the confidential friend
of the Emperor Otto, and one who actually saw and
heard that to which he bears witness.

This account, twice repeated in the same terms,
obviously produces quite a different impression from
that of the privilege. I have, nevertheless, no hesitation in maintaining that it is the correct one.
With it accord all the statements concerning the
elections during a period of nearly a century from
the events of 963. As long as there was an emperor
capable of doing so, he it was who actually chose
the Pope; when the imperial power was monopolised at Rome by a patrician, or any other representative of the emperor, it was still, so far as one
can tell, the responsible factor in the papal elections.
This election was merely a formality, and did but
confirm a choice made independently of those who
appeared to take part in it.

As for the privilege, it was not what it seemed
to be. In the first part it recognises the Pope's
right to a territorial domain as large as that of which
it was a question in the life of Hadrian I. Otto, if
we are to take the words literally, was to guarantee
to the papacy the possession of Tuscany, Parma,
Mantua, Venice, Istria, and the duchies of Spoleto
and Beneventum, and was even ready to promise

the Byzantine territories of Naples and Gaeta. No one will venture to maintain that these professions were put into practice. One might also suggest that, even in the second part, as far as the papal elections were concerned, there was a considerable discrepancy between the theory sanctioned by the document and the actual facts. This idea is confirmed by Luitprand's evidence as well as by what we know of the elections under the new régime.

That this was a very great change may be both affirmed and denied. As far as the Romans were concerned, it was not, for they had long exercised their right in appearance only. Ever since the beginning of the century there had always been a chief elector in the person of Theophylact, or Marozia, or Alberic. On the other hand, when we take into consideration the fact that the nationality of this dominating influence, up to and including John XII., had always been Roman, we realise that a serious change was taking place. The ruling power was now to be a foreign one, that of the Saxon family, which was, for the time being, charged to preside over the destinies of Germany.

It must, of course, be clearly understood that all this is true, and is proved, in spite of the apocryphal documents[1] by which it was later on sought to confirm the pretensions of the kings of Germany, by an alleged compact entered into between Otto and Leo VIII., to the right of investiture in general, to the appointment of the Popes, and to certain

[1] J., 3704–6. Of these and other documents it may be said that they bear a striking resemblance to those charters of donation which the monks took upon themselves to manufacture in place of the originals, which had been lost. The forged documents, attributed by them to Leo VIII. and other earlier Popes, correspond with those of the period of 960–1060.

portions of the temporal estates of the Holy See.

But John XII. and his followers did not meekly accept the sentence pronounced against him. When the Christmas festivities were over, the emperor dismissed part of his army, and himself prepared to undertake the siege of Montefeltro. On the 3rd January 964 a rebellion burst forth, and barricades were erected on the bridge of St. Angelo. The Romans expected to have no difficulty in dispersing Otto's frail forces, but they soon found out their mistake. The barricades were swept away, and a huge massacre was set on foot. The vanquished Romans the next day presented themselves in sorry plight before the emperor and delivered up their hostages, Leo being artless enough to interfere. The emperor had only just taken his departure when John XII. reappeared. His rival immediately decamped. A council, of which the records are still preserved, was held at the Lateran in the early part of February. Heavy sentences were passed on all adherents of the imperial Pope (now regarded as an usurper) who would not retract their opinions. There were two very weighty arguments against the promotion of Leo: first of all, the prevailing idea that the Pope could not be judged by any one, *sancta sedes a nemine judicatur*,[1] and, consequently, that the deposition of John having been pronounced

---

[1] Owing to this principle, Leo III. and Pascal had avoided the courts of justice, their innocence being established simply in virtue of their own oaths. It was quite different with John XII., who was involved in a notorious and permanent scandal; the Pope would have been with difficulty made to undergo the *purgatio per sacramentum*, and even had he done so, it would have been universally considered an additional sacrilege. There was nothing for it but a trial extraordinary.

by an incompetent assembly, was null and void. Moreover, the appointed Pope did not belong to the clergy. It is not absolutely certain, though very probable, that his office of *protoscrinius* presupposed the tonsure; but there is no doubt that at the time of his election he did not possess any ecclesiastical orders, not even that of door-keeper. Ancient tradition required that the pontiff should be elected from the cardinal clergy, among the priests or deacons, and no deviation from this custom was allowed to pass without protest.[1]

From the Roman point of view it seemed that the council of February 964 had avenged the ancient right: John XII. was the rightful Pope, the representative of tradition, as well as of what may be called the national sentiment. Otto, of course, was far from seeing things in the same light. Nevertheless he did not think fit to interrupt his military proceedings, with the result that John XII. was able to enjoy his success for several weeks. He was still in possession of the Holy See, when death overtook him on 14th May 964.

Pope John XII. died, alas, as he had lived, his last hours being passed in the gratification of an illicit passion—in the bed of a young married lady. Luitprand maintains that he was struck mortally on the temples by the devil himself, but Gregorovius justly surmises that it was more probably the injured husband who acted as the avenging instrument of the prince of darkness! However this may have been, by some means or other the chair of St. Peter was disencumbered of a most unworthy occupant.

It might have been supposed that the Romans

---

[1] Silverius, Constantine II., Leo V.—John XII. himself was cardinal deacon at the time of his promotion.

would now rally round Leo VIII. But nothing of the kind occurred. So far from troubling about the imperial Pope, they immediately took unto themselves another—the Deacon Benedict. He was a suitable person, and of some literary attainments (*grammaticus*), and was apparently ordained on the 22nd of May. The Romans were even good enough to send notice of his accession to the emperor, who was already advancing against Rome. The gates of the city were closed, but the defence did not last long. On 23rd June Otto and Leo VIII. having obtained the mastery, convened a new synod at the Lateran; the unfortunate Benedict was brought before it, and, having received sentence of deposition, was despatched to Germany, where he was placed under the charge of the archbishops of Hamburg.

The opposition being thus quelled, Leo VIII. was able to hold his own up to the time of his death, which took place shortly afterwards.

CHAPTER XVIII

THE POPES OF THE EMPIRE

TOWARDS the month of March 965, the Holy See was once more without an occupant. The Romans dared not run the risk of an election, and communicated with the Emperor Otto,[1] whose choice fell upon a relation of Pope John XII., named John, Bishop of Narni, son of Theodora II., and nephew of the celebrated Marozia. It was a return to the family of Theophylact, but with the imperial countenance. John XIII. was installed on the 1st October, but in less than three months a rebellion broke out at Rome, caused, it was said, by the severity of the new Pope, but, in reality, directed against the imperial authority. John, after having suffered ill-treatment and insults, was imprisoned in the castle of St. Angelo, and finally banished from Rome. He took refuge in Lombard territory, at Capua, and then

---

[1] *Cont. Reginonis: Legati Romanorum . . . imperatorem pro instituendo quem vellet Romano pontifice in Saxonia adeuntes suscipiuntur et remittuntur.* The election took place at Rome, under the supervision of two *missi*, Otger, Bishop of Spires, and Luitprand, Bishop of Cremona.

returned by way of the Abruzzi, Sabina, and Tuscany, at the head of such an imposing army, that the Romans decided to receive him back. He made his re-entry with much pomp on 14th November 966. This change of front was in great part due to the report that the Emperor Otto had crossed the Alps, and was advancing for the fourth time on Rome. The monk of Mt. Soracte saw his army pass, and thereupon terminated his chronicle with lamentations on the decline of Rome, once mistress of the world, and now in bondage to the Saxons.

He was quite right. The Saxons had abolished the ancient form of the papal elections, and the Romans had now to learn what remained to them of the political power.

The chief instigator of the revolt, Count Rofred, had been killed in the reaction which followed, but some of his associates were still left at Rome. Several "consuls" were arrested, and banished to the other side of the Alps, and the twelve district chiefs were sent to the gallows, to serve as deputies for the common people. The prefect, who was deeply implicated, was handed over to the Pope for punishment. John had his beard shaved,[1] and ordered him to be hung by the hair to the *caballus Constantini*, the celebrated equestrian statue of Marcus Aurelius, which at that time adorned the Lateran palace. After having been made to ride a donkey, face backwards, with the animal's tail between his hands, he was cast into prison until the departure of the emperor, when he was also banished to Germany. Finally Otto had the bodies

---

[1] This ceremony, according to Byzantine custom, was the symbol of degradation. Even now, in the East, priests, on being suspended, have their beards cut off.

of Rofred and the *vestiarius* Stephen exhumed, and thrown into the public sewer.

Thanks to these severe methods of repression, the authority of John XIII. was maintained without any further difficulty. In April 967 he held a synod at Ravenna in conjunction with the emperor, who then restored to him (in theory) his transapennine territories, which had long been outside the power of the Holy See. On Christmas Day of the same year the young Prince Otto II. received the imperial coronation at the hands of the Pope in the basilica of St. Peter. John XIII. passed peacefully away on 6th September 972, and Otto appointed in his stead Benedict, a cardinal deacon, whose ordination did not take place until January 973. This long interval is the only existing proof of the imperial intervention on this occasion, but, considering the circumstances, it is quite conclusive.

The great Otto died in Germany, 7th May 973. The Romans, at first, did not make any disturbance, but a fresh revolution broke out a year later, when the young Otto II. was occupied in contending against the Duke of Bavaria and other of his vassals. The leader of the rebellion at Rome was Crescentius, the son of Theodora, and brother of John XIII. Benedict VI. was taken prisoner and confined in the castle of St. Angelo, and replaced by a so-called " national " Pope—Boniface VII., son of Ferruccius, and formerly the deacon Franco. All in vain did the imperial *missus*, Count Sicco, protest against the turn affairs were taking ; his objections only served to hasten matters. By order of the usurper, Benedict was strangled in his prison. Sicco, nevertheless, managed to gain the mastery, and succeeded in ejecting Boniface VII. In place of the unfortunate

Benedict VI., they elected a new Pope, who adopted the name of Benedict VII. Franco, some time afterwards, fled from Rome, and took refuge at Constantinople.

This was already the third time since the accession of Leo VIII. that the Romans had openly rebelled against the new order of things. They strongly objected to having their Popes appointed for them, and had not yet come to an end of their powers of resistance. Benedict VII. had a tolerably easy time of it during his reign, which lasted until his death on 10th July 983. The Emperor Otto came to Italy at the end of 980, and from that time he often stayed at Rome, making it the headquarters for his campaigns in Southern Italy. He died there on 7th December 983, just as he was preparing to avenge a serious defeat sustained the year before in Calabria.

On the death of Benedict VII. Otto had appointed in his place a bishop of his kingdom of Italy, the Chancellor Peter, who took the name of John XIV. This new Pope attended him on his deathbed, and permitted his interment in the atrium of St. Peter's, a ceremony which was the precursor of sad days to come. There were only two representatives of the imperial family—a child of three years old, proclaimed in Germany under the name of Otto III., and the Greek Princess Theophano, widow of Otto II., and grand-daughter of the Emperor Constantine Porphyrogenetis. Theophano was a strong-minded woman, as was soon made manifest. But circumstances did not allow her to stay at Rome; she was obliged to hasten to rejoin her son in Germany, leaving the Pope to the mercies of the Romans.

Franco thought that his chance had come; in

April 984 he came back from Constantinople, seized upon John XIV., and threw him into prison at St. Angelo, where the wretched victim died four months later, possibly from hunger. Boniface still regarded himself as the rightful Pope, and reckoned the years of his pontificate from the deposition of Benedict in July 985. Rome put up with him for more than a year, and in July 985 he died unexpectedly. His death gave rise to a temporary reaction; his corpse was treated with disrespect, dragged through the town, and finally left in a nude condition in front of the "horse of Constantine."

Crescentius, who had raised him (974) to the papal throne, and played an important part in his restoration (984), had died immediately after the latter event. His epitaph[1] is still to be seen at St. Alexis. The authority was boldly seized by his son Crescentius, who assumed the new qualification of *patricius Romanorum*. There was no longer any prospect of a complete independence. Though the emperor was but a child, the empire remained solid, and to attack it too severely would have been indiscreet. Crescentius, in adopting the title of patrician, appears to have posed as a kind of lieutenant or provisional manager during the interregnum. His name appears, together with the Pope's, in certain documents of the time; possibly it figured on the coins as well, but of this there is no evidence.

---

[1] He was a monk at the time of his death, and richly endowed the monastery. His epitaph recommends him to the prayers:

ut tandem scelerum veniam mercatur habere.

His conscience, indeed, must have been heavily burdened, for he and Franco between them had caused the overthrow and assassination of two Popes.

THE POPES OF THE EMPIRE

John XV., who succeeded Boniface VII., probably owed his promotion to Crescentius, but we have very little accurate information as to the pontifical history of this period. At the close of 989 the Empress Theophano reappeared at Rome, comporting herself as if she were the sovereign. The documents are dated with her imperial year, and sometimes even dignify her with the masculine title of emperor. As we hear of no resistance, it is reasonable to suppose that she was on good terms with Crescentius, and did not dispute his patriciate.

John XV. seems to have shed as dim a lustre round the papal throne as did the Pope appointed by Marozia and Alberic. But meanwhile the young king of Germany was growing up, and when, in 996, he reached his majority, he made up his mind to visit Italy where his presence was greatly desired. The Pope himself, who was beginning to weary of Crescentius, had invited him to come to Rome. He had not, however, the pleasure of receiving him there, for he died at the beginning of April 996, when Otto III. had got no further than Pavia.

Crescentius did not venture to appoint John's successor, and a solemn embassy was despatched to Otto at Ravenna, begging him to undertake the responsibility. The young emperor was at this time barely sixteen years old, and he selected one of his cousins, Bruno, son of the Duke of Carinthia, to take the vacant post. He was a clerk, a young man of only twenty-three. His consecration took place at Rome, on 3rd May, under the title of Gregory V., and then, on the 21st of the same month, he celebrated the imperial coronation of his cousin. Though this was not the first time that the Romans had suffered the infliction of a young and immature pontiff, it was the first time that they had had one of transalpine origin foisted upon them by the Roman court. After Gregory V. came Sylvester II., so that, thanks to Otto III., the chair of St. Peter was occupied successively by the first of the German and the first of the French Popes.

Otto's arrival heralded the fall of Crescentius, who had to render an account of his misdeeds before the imperial tribunal. His trial resulted in a sentence of banishment, which, however, through the ill-advised intervention of Gregory V., was never carried out.

Three months after the emperor's departure, when he had only just crossed the Alps on his homeward way, a rebellion broke out against the German Pope. The latter was probably not altogether blameless: a contemporary writer, John Caneparius,[1] speaks of him as *multum fervidæ juventutis.* But it is evident that the old national leaven was fast fermenting. The movement was headed by Crescentius himself, and Gregory V. fled ignominiously. The emperor was just then busy fighting against the Slavs, and the Pope was not in a position to do more than hurl denunciations against the insurgent. A council was held at Pavia, in February 997, at which Crescentius was solemnly anathematised. He, however, in no way disconcerted, brought forward a rival to Gregory V., in the person of Philagath, Bishop of Piacenza, who was passing through Rome on his way back from Constantinople, where he had been sent on an imperial embassy. He was a Calabrian Greek, who owed everything to the favour of Theophano and her son, but at the instigation of Crescentius he consented to turn traitor to his benefactors, and, in the

---

[1] *Life of St. Adalbert, M. G. Scr.,* t. iv. p. 591.

month of April 997, he was installed as Pope under the title of John XVI.

But, less than a month afterwards, Otto came back, in company with the German Pope. Rome opened her gates ; Philagath took flight, and Crescentius shut himself up in the castle of St. Angelo. While they were preparing to besiege it, according to rule, the unfortunate John XVI. was caught on one of the Campanian roads. His captors hastened to cut off his nose and his ears, and to tear out his eyes and tongue. In this pitiable plight he was brought before a council at the Lateran, formally deposed and delivered over to the populace, who subjected him to the humiliating process of riding backwards on a donkey. In vain did the venerable St. Nilus, the patriarch of the Greek monks of Southern Italy, intercede on his behalf. His life was spared, but that was all. He managed to survive his ill-treatment for another fifteen years, when he died, probably at the abbey at Fulda, in the year 1013.

To return to Crescentius. The assault on the castle of St. Angelo was successful, so that on 29th April 998 the fortress was seized by the Germans. Crescentius, taken prisoner, was beheaded on the battlements, and then his body and those of twelve other Romans were hanged upon gibbets erected on Mte. Mario (*mons Malus, mons Gaudii*).

But this torture did not succeed in suppressing the patrician race. There still remained, in addition to the collateral branches, a son called John Crescentius, of whom we shall presently hear more. The Romans had been profoundly impressed by the hardy resistance and tragic death of Crescentius, who soon passed into a legendary hero.

Otto, from that time, made Rome his permanent abode. His presence was absolutely necessary to keep the Romans within bounds, although he applied himself to winning them over by means of all kinds of flattering attentions, and by reviving for their benefit a sort of imperial court in the fashion of bygone days. On 18th February 999 Gregory died, either from poison, or in some even more tragic way. Otto thereupon raised to the pontificate his former tutor, Gerbert, at that time archbishop of Ravenna. Sylvester II., as he was called, does not appear to have been any more at ease than his predecessor as chief shepherd of the Roman flock, and no sooner did Otto leave him for a moment than he implored him to come back.

The young emperor had a propensity for pious companions, and he devoted much time to pilgrimages. Close to his residence on the Aventine arose the convent of Saints Boniface and Alexis, just then in all the first fervour and enthusiasm of its foundation. Otto was on terms of friendship with the monks there, some of whom were compatriots of his own. He was known to perform his devotions at Beneventum before the shrine of the Apostle Bartholomew; at Monte Cassino and at Monte Gargano amid the solitudes of Campania, where St. Nilus, hunted out of Calabria by the Saracen invasion, had found a temporary refuge. At Ravenna he visited another monkish patriarch, St. Romuald. Sometimes these devout pilgrimages led him farther still to Aix-la-Chapelle, allured by memories of Charlemagne, or to Gnesen, in the south of Poland, where reposed the remains of his friend St. Adalbert of Prague, who had been murdered on the shores of the Baltic by the uncivilised Prussians.

These journeys seemed very long to Pope Sylvester, but they had no disastrous consequences. The danger lay in another quarter. In the immediate neighbourhood of Rome there were at that time several important seigniories. Various branches of the family of Theophylact were in possession of large estates, of which Tusculum, on Monte Albano, Praeneste, Arci in Sabina, and Galera on the Tuscan road, were the chief centres and fortresses. The abbot of Farfa was likewise a baron of the first rank. But the one and only city which lived its own life was Tivoli. Thanks partly to a certain degree of preservation in the municipal institutions of ancient Tibur, as well as to the progress of the local organisation under the auspices of the bishop, Tivoli was of considerable importance. Not only did she exist by the side of Rome, but she also had the power of irritating the Romans by the very fact of her existence and prosperity. The Romans loathed Tivoli, as, later on, they loathed Tusculum, with a loathing as deadly as it was irresponsible. When, in 1001, the inhabitants of Tivoli were misguided enough to rebel against the imperial authority, the emperor, assisted by the Romans, who hoped for a share of the spoil, set out to quell them. The Pope and Bishop Bernard of Hildesheim[1] urged the rebels to submit, and the emperor, having them at his mercy, spared their lives. This was the very step to displease the Romans, and, soon after his return to Rome, Otto III. saw the rebellious populace surging to the very doors of his palace in the Aventine. With difficulty he succeeded in escaping to

[1] His life, by Tangmar, is full of interest (*M. G. Scr.*, t. iv. p. 754).

Ravenna, taking with him the Pope Sylvester. This was on 16th February 1001, and from that time Otto never went back to Rome, although his military expeditions against the southern provinces must sometimes have led him to pass within sight of the ramparts. On 24th January of the following year, he died at Paterno, near Mt. Soracte. Rome, the city which he so loved, was closed against him, so that his body could not find a resting-place by the side of his father, Otto II., and they were obliged to take it to Aix-la-Chapelle. As he had never been married, the male issue of Otto the Great was now extinct, and the Germans rallied round Henry, Duke of Bavaria, grand-nephew of the great emperor.

Italy, for the last time, appointed a national king, Arduin, Marquess of Ivrea, who was proclaimed at Pavia on 15th February. At Rome the power, without any pressure from outside, became once more centred in the family of Crescentius. It is probable that John Crescentius, son of the criminal executed in 998, had been in some way connected with the rebellion of 1001, and that from that time the Romans had vested the chief authority in him. After Otto's death he assumed the title of *patricius Romanorum*, which he maintained without any difficulty.

History was repeating itself. For thirty years Ottos and Crescentiuses had succeeded one another alternately. Though the actual individuals varied, it was always the same conflict between the national chief and the foreign prince.

Sylvester II. returned to Rome, where the patrician allowed him to die in peace. This event took place on 12th May 1003, and the next Pope appointed was John XVII., who, after a reign of six months, was succeeded by John XVIII. This latter occupied the papal See until the year 1009, when his place was taken by Sergius IV. (*Buccaporca*), who, from being the son of a Roman shoemaker, had risen to the rank of bishop of Albano. He died on 12th May 1012, the patrician having preceded him to the grave by a few weeks.

Owing to the party strife among the aristocracy the vacancy of the Holy See gave rise to a double election. In opposition to the Crescentius family was the increasing influence of the Counts of Tusculum, who were connected with the family of the great Prince Alberic, as well as with the far-away ancestor Theophylact. Gregory, the head of the house, figures in the time of Otto III. under the title of *præfectus navalis*. To him, doubtless, was due the restoration and transformation of the acropolis of the old Latin city, which had been abandoned for centuries. He was the father of three sons, Alberic, Romanus, and the Cardinal Theophylact. There can be no doubt that this influential family had long cherished the ambition of succeeding the Crescentii in the government of the Roman state.[1] But there were obstacles in the way. The power was in the hands of the Crescentii, who represented the tradition of independence, as far as this had been possible, since the advent of the Saxon kings in Italy. According as the German authority was strong or weak, the Crescentii regulated their behaviour, resigning themselves or objecting, as the occasion

[1] The chief country strongholds of the Crescentius party were between the Tiber and Farfa, at Monticelli, Nomentum, and Arci. At Rome they held the castle of St. Angelo, which was apparently inherited by the family of Theophylact.

seemed to demand. In one way or another they managed to express the attitude of the people, or rather of the aristocracy, the only class which had any weight at that time. The Tusculans, in order to counter-check them, assumed a special devotion to the German interests, but, in point of fact, this was very little beyond assumption, though it undoubtedly made them more favourably regarded on the other side of the Alps.

The patrician of the Romans being no longer alive, the two papal candidates, Gregory, supported by the waning Crescentian influence, and Theophylact, the third son of the Count of Tusculum, turned to King Henry II. This latter had already made a campaign in Northern Italy in 1004, and had even gained an entry into Pavia, but the old Lombard capital had risen up in arms against him, so that, although the rebellion was checked by fire, Henry had thought it wiser to curtail his sojourn in the Italian kingdom.   After his departure, Arduin, the national king, had regained his footing, and the internal difficulties of the German kingdom, combined with the diplomacy of John Crescentius, had sufficed to keep Henry II. on the north of the Alps. The present position of affairs seemed more promising.   Henry spoke encouraging words to Gregory's ambassadors, but withheld his decision, which was clearly affected by the fact that Theophylact, who, through the influence of his father and brothers, had been proclaimed Pope under the title of Benedict VIII., had succeeded in consolidating his position.

At the end of February 1013 Henry II. made his entry into Italy, thus causing Arduin to disappear from public view. On 14th February of the following year, the king of Germany and his wife, Queen Cunegunda, were crowned by Benedict VIII. at St. Peter's. Arduin made a last effort to reassert himself a little while afterwards, but with so little success that he was reduced to entering a monastery, where he spent the remainder of his days.

Pope Benedict VIII., who reigned twelve years —to the 7th April 1024—left behind him a satisfactory record. He seems to have always maintained amicable relations with the emperor. He led a naval expedition against the Saracens, who had seized upon Luni (1016), paid a visit to Germany in 1020, accompanied the emperor to the south of Italy in 1022, and the same year united with him in holding a synod at Pavia, where the long-forgotten regulations concerning celibacy were once more brought to light.

Benedict had plenty of time to occupy himself with religious matters. The burden of the temporal government was assumed by his brother Romanus, who bore the title of *Senator omnium Romanorum*, revived in the time of Alberic, so that the whole power of the papacy, spiritual as well as political, was vested in the nobles of Tusculum. They had, however, to reckon with the supreme authority of the emperor as far as temporal affairs were concerned. Like the Crescentii, they were in the position of vice-governors, or permanent *missi*, rather than that of independent princes. Alberic had been free from any such restraint, for there had been no emperor in his day to impose it upon him. But the situation had utterly changed since the consecration of 962. Under the Crescentii, especially the first two, the lay chiefs of the Roman aristocracy had tried to resist the imperial authority, but with the

Tusculans things were on a more friendly footing. When the emperor, as constantly happened, was away from Rome, the governing power was left in the hands of the Tusculum family ; but when he was in the city, he naturally took the headship of affairs, presiding at the courts of justice, and modifying the legislation if necessary. Thus we have an edict of the Emperor Conrad II.[1] addressed to the Roman judges, by which the personal right of the Lombards over Roman territory is annulled. This point of personal right had not been inserted in the privilege of Otto I., which reproduced so many conditions of the constitution of 824. Nevertheless, the abbot of Farfa, in an action brought before Otto III., appealed successfully to the Lombard law. But the curious documents from which we derive our information concerning this suit show how very few and far between were the Roman magistrates who really understood the Lombard legalities. Conrad brought things into better order, and commanded *ut quæcumque negotia mota fuerint tam inter Romanæ urbis mœnia quam etiam de foris in Romanis pertinentiis, actore Langobardo vel reo, a vobis dumtaxat Romanis legibus terminentur.*

This fact demonstrates how the emperors of the eleventh century, like those of the ninth, regarded themselves as genuine monarchs at Rome, particularly in connection with legislation. Certainly the privilege documents give no hint of this degree of authority, but that only proves how little these are to be relied upon in a question of defining the precise circumstances. Henry II. issued one for the benefit of Benedict VIII. on the occasion of his consecration, and that is an exact reproduction of the privilege

[1] *Mon. Germ. Leges,* ii. 40.

of Otto. It is probable that a document of this kind was produced at every imperial consecration.

When Benedict died, the senator, without more ado, calmly established himself in his place, taking the name of John XIX. It was the counterpart of the accession of John XII.—the family traditions were being carried out. The new Pope, who, according to one of the chroniclers, *uno eodemque die præfectus fuit et papa*,[1] was not well adapted to fulfil the ideas of Benedict VIII., or rather of the Emperor Henry II., on ecclesiastical reform, and the old abuses cropped up again more vigorously than ever. John XIX. reigned until 1032, the most conspicuous event of his pontificate being the coronation of the Emperor Conrad II., successor to Henry.

The only survivor of Count Gregory's three sons was the eldest, Count Alberic, who had no inclination to assume the papal authority. He had four sons. On one of them, Gregory, he bestowed the temporal government, together with the title of *Consul Romanorum* ; another, bearing, like his distant ancestor and Benedict VIII., the name of Theophylact, was appointed to succeed his two uncles in the pontifical chair. That he was only twelve years old was no obstacle, and he was proclaimed Pope under the title of Benedict IX. To the German princes there was nothing objectionable in this hereditary transmission of the Apostolic Chair. They had recognised John XIX., who, though a layman, was a full-grown man, and they tolerated Benedict IX., a mere urchin, who was before long to become actively offensive.

Indeed, as time went on, the young Pope revived

[1] John XII., at any rate, was a cardinal at the time of his election.

at the Lateran the rule of revelry which had flourished under his ancestor John XII., eighty years before. Conrad II., who understood how to manage this papal puppet, not only encouraged him, but overwhelmed him with attentions. He benefited by this attitude in his struggle against the archbishop of Milan, when, on two occasions, at Cremona 1037, and at Spello 1038, Benedict went to meet him, and at his request, pronounced sentence of excommunication against the Archbishop Heribert. Not until seven years had passed did Henry III., who succeeded Conrad in 1039, interfere and put a stop to the gross scandals over which every earnest-minded person in Christendom was obliged to lament in helpless silence.

The Romans themselves were the first to grow weary of their Pope's proceedings. During the autumn of 1044 they rose in rebellion and expelled him from his See,[1] together with his brother the consul, and all connected with the House of Tusculum. However, the pontifical party succeeded in maintaining their own in the Trastevere, while Rome herself and the Leonine city remained in the power of the rebels. The latter, on 7th January 1045 made an onslaught on the Trasteverans, but were put to flight by the vassals of Tusculum, under the leadership of Gerard, Count of Galeria. They fell back in disarray on the Saxon gate, which, however, was not forced, so the Romans, emboldened, elected a successor to Benedict. This was John, Bishop of Sabina, who took the name of Sylvester

---

[1] *Ann. Rom.* (*L. P.*, t. ii. p. 331). It is perhaps to this event that Raoul Glaber's account refers iv., 24 (*cf.* 17), only he confounds the dates. The Roman annalist mentions a solar eclipse of 22nd November, immediately after having spoken of the expulsion of Benedict IX.

III. The chief electors had been heavily bribed, but, as far as the new Pope was concerned, it was money wasted, for at the end of forty-nine days Rome had succumbed to her besiegers, and Sylvester returned to his bishopric. In order for him to live peacefully in Sabina, which was in the country of the Crescentii, the powerful members of his flock must have defended him against the re-established Pope, Benedict IX. There is every reason to suspect a revival of the Crescentian influence in the revolt of 1044 and the election of Sylvester III.

Benedict, forcibly reinstalled, and yet not able to prevail against the discontented attitude of the Romans, made up his mind to resign the pontificate. This he did on 1st May, in favour of his godfather, John Gratian, Archpriest of St. John-before-the-Latin-Gate. A charter of resignation was drawn up,[1] but that probably did not prevent a counterfeit election. The new Pope, who took the title of Gregory VI., was not a cardinal, but he had other greater disqualifications than that. Benedict had not yielded the papal seat for nothing, and Gregory had been obliged to pay down ready money as the price of his promotion. The papacy had been sold, and that not by the electors as had been done sometimes before, but by the actual Pope himself.

Gregory VI., who was an elderly man, found no difficulty in leading a steadier life than his predecessor had done. He took Hildebrand under his protection, so that the chroniclers connected with the latter speak of him with respectful consideration.

His accession was, at any rate, welcomed by

---

[1] *Per cartulam refutavit Johanni, &c., Ann. Rom.* This extraordinary document has not come down to us.

people worthy of respect. From the recesses of his convent in the Apennines, St. Peter Damian wrote greeting him as the dove bringing back the olive branch to the Ark; Hildebrand, who was at that time residing in the monastery founded by Alberic on the Aventine,[1] became his chaplain and adviser. These friendships do him credit, and we can only suppose that these worthy persons were, at first, ignorant of the simony involved in his promotion. Moreover, it cannot be denied that the papal morality had fallen to such an extremely low level under John XIX. and Benedict IX., that people were not now disposed to criticise Gregory VI. too severely.

[1] S. Maria del Priorato.

CHAPTER XIX

THE GERMAN POPES

ALL these changes had been brought about by the Romans ; Benedict IX. had been disposed of, and with him the House of Tusculum, without the slightest interference on the part of the King of Germany. The substitution of Gregory VI. for Benedict IX. presented two different aspects ; from one point of view it was the end of a scandal which for years had put all Christendom to the blush ; while, from another, it was an attack against a family which, for the last fifty years, had represented the German influence at Rome, and even against the rights that the German crown claimed in the election of the Popes. Things were arranged amicably by a written and signed agreement; but there can be no doubt that the rebellion of 1044, together with the invincible antipathy of the Roman people, had greatly influenced Benedict's decision.

Having regard to these occurrences, Henry III. thought it well not to commit himself at first. The next year (1046) he came to Italy, and began by holding a great council at Pavia, in which simony was condemned in unmeasured terms.[1] At Piacenza he had an interview with Gregory VI., who came to meet him. He welcomed him graciously, but made no definite assertion as to his rights. Arrived in Roman Tuscia, he held a council at Sutri on the 20th December, which resulted in the deposition of Gregory VI. and Sylvester III. Both of them seem to have been quite resigned to their fate. Sylvester embraced a religious career; and Gregory was detained that he might be transported to the other side of the Alps on the king's return. Benedict IX., who, from the height of his fortress at Tusculum, was quietly waiting for the storm to blow over, also received sentence of deposition, but not until a few days later, at a synod held at St. Peter's on the 23rd and 24th of December. Henry III. evidently considered Benedict more legitimate than his rivals.

Having thus cleared the ground, they set about electing a new Pope. Henry III. appointed Suidger, the Bishop of Bamberg, who took the title of Clement II., and was ordained the next day (Christmas). At the same time he consecrated Henry and his queen, Agnes, as emperor and empress.

Among the oaths taken at this season figured, as in 963, the renunciation by the Romans of the right of election. This fact is confirmed by the witness of the Roman *Annals*, as well as by that of St. Peter Damian, not to mention other less reliable sources. It was a new consecration of the established tradition of eighty years.

Nevertheless, the German princes and their

---

[1] This is the council mentioned by Raoul Glaber, v. 25.

substitutes, the Crescentii and the Counts of Tusculum, had, as a rule, chosen Roman Popes. The occasional election of a foreigner, such as Gregory V. and Sylvester II., had not been enthusiastically received. It might, perhaps, have been more prudent to select a Roman, or even to retain Gregory VI. who had his good points. Henry III., however, thought otherwise, considering himself powerful enough to maintain a transalpine Pope at Rome. And, indeed, he succeeded in thrusting four upon her: the Bishops of Bamberg, Brixen, Toul, Eichstädt, who became respectively Clement II., Damasus II., Leo IX., and Victor II.

But it was no easy task. Pope Clement II. followed the emperor into Southern Italy, summoned by the continual disturbances of the district. On his way back he was seized by sudden illness near Pesaro, and died on 9th October 1047. There is every reason to suspect that his death was caused by a poisonous potion, served at the instigation of the deposed Pope, Benedict IX. The emperor had already got to the other side of the Alps. Benedict reappeared at Rome, where, with the help of Boniface, Marquess of Tuscany, he was soon re-established. It was then 9th November, and he succeeded in retaining his position until 17th July of the following year (1048).

Two new powers now appeared upon the Italian horizon, one to the north of Rome, the other to the south. The first was represented by the House of Tuscany, which had been founded in the last century by Azzo, the chatelain of Canossa in Emilia; the same who had posed as the protector of Queen Adelaide on her escape from imprisonment by Berengarius II. He and his son Tedald had been reckoned among the most faithful adherents of the House of Saxony, and were very popular in the north of Italy (Mantua, Ferrara, Brescia, Reggio, Modena); finally, Tedald's son, Boniface, had become Marquess of Tuscany. The great Countess Matilda, so famous in the Gregorian annals, was his daughter. Altogether, Boniface was too influential a vassal not to be formidable.

In Southern Italy the Saracens were keeping fairly quiet, except for some raids upon the coasts of Byzantine Calabria. The rest of the country had long been the scene of struggles carried on by the Lombards, either among themselves or against the Greeks. Of the three Lombard principalities of Capua, Beneventum, and Salerno, the latter was predominant at the time. It owed its prosperity to the arrival in the country of several bands of adventurers from Basse-Normandie, substantial warriors, not over-scrupulous as to their methods. While ready to work for any one who would pay them, they sought at the same time to further their own ends and to obtain a solid footing in the land. They had already succeeded in founding two establishments—one at Aversa, near Capua, and the other at Melfi, between Beneventum and Byzantine Apuleia. These Norman colonies, formed by Frankish subjects (though for their own advantage, it is true), would have had no political position if the Prince of Salerno had not taken them under his feudal responsibility. The Normans of Melfi and Aversa were subject to Salerno, but the pre-eminence of the latter was destroyed as a result of Henry's expedition. The German emperor, however, extended his immediate protection to the two little principalities (1047).

This did not tend to increase their popularity. The newly arrived Normans, who were always enlarging their borders at other people's expense, were regarded with great distrust. They were as much hated as the Saracens had been, and indeed were often designated by the same name of *Agareni*, as though they too were the disciples of Mahomet.

These two new powers of Tuscany and Normandy played an important part in the period which followed. Henceforth Boniface, by supporting the cause of Benedict IX., acted in open opposition to the emperor. As soon as the death of Clement was made known, those of the Romans who had remained loyal to Henry III. had sent to ask the emperor to appoint a Pope. His choice fell upon Poppo, Bishop of Brixen, who took the name of Damasus II. The Marquess of Tuscany refused at first to escort him to Rome, on the pretext of Benedict's reinstallation, and only after many importunities and threats did the enthronement of the new Pope take place, 17th July 1048. His reign, however, was speedily terminated by death, and the 9th of August saw him committed to his last resting-place at San Lorenzo. Benedict IX. passed, more or less, into oblivion; according to one report he became a monk at Grotta Ferrata; another, which seems more likely to be true,[1] states that he came to an early grave in consequence of his continued dissolute way of living.

The Emperor Henry replaced Damasus II. by Bruno, Bishop of Toul, who assumed the name of Leo IX. He was a man of great piety and full of zeal for ecclesiastical reform. Hildebrand, who had

---

[1] See the legend related by St. Peter Damian, *De abdicatione episcopatus*, c. 2. This supposes that the unfortunate Pope died in a state of impenitence.

followed Gregory VI. into exile, was now brought back to Rome. Later on it was said that he remonstrated with Leo on his promotion, and that the latter defended himself by reference to the Roman freedom of election. If there is any truth in these stories, they can only refer to external formalities. Leo must have waited to be elected and installed at Rome in due form before being invested with the pontifical insignia. Indeed, like his two predecessors and his successor, he was actually chosen by the emperor, and the Romans could do no more than confirm this choice by a simulated election.

It is certain that Leo displayed much energy on behalf of ecclesiastical reform, and that he was continually journeying about, preaching, excommunicating, and holding councils, even visiting Rheims for the latter purpose. He also made it his aim to rid Italy of the new Saracens—the Normans—and headed a kind of crusade against them. This, however, was a failure; at the battle of Civita in Capitanate (1053) the Pope's army was put to flight, and many of his men were massacred before his very eyes. He himself was forced to surrender to the conquerors, and to withdraw the sentences of excommunication which he had lavished upon them. They took him to Beneventum, which had for two years been a papal possession; the inhabitants, finding in their Dukes Pandulph and Landulph inadequate protection against the Normans, had banished them from power and put themselves under the Pope's governance (1051). The Emperor Henry III. had sanctioned this change in return for the papal retrocession of the bishopric of Bamberg, which had been offered by his predecessor, Henry II., to St. Peter. It was from the Pope's new position as sovereign of Beneventum that the struggle between himself and the Normans had arisen.

In the spring of 1054 Leo returned to Rome, but only in time to die. Gebhard, Bishop of Eichstädt, succeeded him as Victor II. He was accompanied by the emperor to Verona, where his stay was signalised by certain arrangements in connection with Tuscany. Beatrice, widow of the Marquess Boniface, had taken for her second husband Geoffrey, Duke of Lorraine, a rebellious vassal of the Emperor Henry. Geoffrey had a brother Frederic, who, under Leo IX., had become cardinal and chancellor of the Roman Church. Just then he was performing the function of papal legate at Constantinople.

The ducal family of Tuscany had every reason to dread the emperor's arrival. Geoffrey did not wait for him, but repaired to Lorraine, and began operations there, hoping in this way to relieve Italy. Henry III. seized upon Beatrice and her daughter Matilda, then went in person to Florence, and appointed the Pope as his vicar in Italy, charging him to arrest the Cardinal Frederic on his return from the East. Warned in time, Frederic took refuge at Monte Cassino, where he took the Benedictine habit, and succeeded in getting sent to Tremiti, an obscure little island in the Adriatic. Thus sheltered, he let the storm rage on.

The next year, 1056, Victor II. betook himself to Germany, hoping to arouse the emperor's interest in his plan of resuming the aggressive policy of Leo IX. with regard to the Normans. But death intervened, and the Pope had the grief of seeing Henry III. pass away on 5th October, leaving as his successor a little son, Henry, only six years old, and still under the guardianship of his mother, the Empress Agnes.

This event seriously affected the Pope's situation. After spending several months in Germany, striving to support the regency which was just beginning, he returned to Italy, where he, in his turn, died, 28th July 1057. On being deprived of the powerful protection of Henry III., he had at once realised the necessity of being on good terms with the House of Tuscany. He began by reconciling it with the empress. Duke Geoffrey was restored to favour, and his wife, daughter, and estates were given back to him, while his brother Frederic was appointed abbot of Monte Cassino and cardinal priest. The whole aspect of things was completely changed.

Hildebrand had always united with the Popes Leo IX. and Victor II., whose counsellor he had been, in waging war against ecclesiastical abuses, though he had never unduly troubled about the incompatibility between ancient custom and the origin of his patrons. But in his inmost heart he cherished schemes for the enfranchisement of the papacy and the freedom of the election, or rather for its devolving upon those who could hardly do otherwise than choose wisely.

When the Pope breathed his last at Arezzo, Hildebrand was with him. Without waiting for his return, the Romans proclaimed, as Victor's successor, the Cardinal Frederic of Lorraine, who happened to be in Rome at the time. He was elected on 2nd August, and consecrated on 3rd August, without any reference to the court of Germany. This was a serious infraction of the agreement of 1046, but, as the choice had fallen on a man both honourable and powerful, and the brother of the chief German vassal in Italian territory, the acquiescence of the queen-regent might not unreasonably be anticipated. Hildebrand was despatched, in the hope of disarming her displeasure, and seems to have accomplished his mission with success. During his absence the new pontiff experienced a desire to confer with his brother Geoffrey, and set out for Tuscany. Before starting, however, he took the precaution of assembling the clergy and the faithful of Rome, and making them swear that, in the event of his death during the journey, they would await Hildebrand's return from Germany before electing a successor to the Holy See.

But it was one thing to take an oath and another to keep it. Stephen IX. never came back, but died from poison in Tuscany. His death was reputed to have been brought about by the Romans, probably the leaders of the aristocracy, who had been obliged to bend under the yoke of the Emperor Henry III. as well as under that of the Duke of Tuscany, and who were strongly opposed to the government notions of reform. Their ideas on the freedom of election differed greatly from those of Hildebrand and his party. Both sides wanted to throw off the German supervision and to have the Pope to themselves; but while Hildebrand's party desired a pontiff who would have regard for the spiritual dignity of his position, and encourage ecclesiastical reform, the others wanted a sort of papal phantom, who would act as an external screen for the maintenance of abuses of every kind, both in the government of the Roman state as well as in the moral domain.

Each of these two parties were soon provided with a Pope. The Roman aristocracy were first in the field, and, on 5th April 1058, installed at St. Peter's, John, Bishop of Velletri, surnamed "the

Thin."[1] He took the title of Benedict X. The
Crescentii, the Tusculans, the Count of Galeria,
all seemed in accord, and almost the only dissentient
voice was that of a Trasteverian noble, Leo, son of
Benedict the Christian, so called because he had been
converted from Judaism. These were the leaders of
the Pierleoni family, who rose to such renown in the
following century. The faithful clergy, who were at
that time headed by the holy monk, Peter Damian,
Cardinal Bishop of Ostia, had, it must be understood,
taken no part in the proceedings.

The ecclesiastical chiefs succeeded in escaping;
they rallied round Hildebrand in Tuscany, on his
return from Germany. The latter seems to have
come to an amicable understanding with Duke
Geoffrey, and, probably, also with the German
court, which was represented in Italy by the chancellor Guibert; they united in choosing as their
Pope, Gerard, Bishop of Florence, who took the
name of Nicholas II. Guibert, Geoffrey, Nicholas,
and Hildebrand, together with the representatives
of the clergy and the faithful laity, betook themselves to Sutri in January 1059, and assembled a
solemn conclave, at which Benedict was deposed,
and Nicholas recognised. Then Hildebrand and his
followers, aided by the internal disputes of the
aristocracy, as well as by Leo's financial wealth,
succeeded in gaining an entrance to Rome. Benedict X. was obliged to flee for shelter to his friends,
the barons of the Campagna, and Nicholas II. was
solemnly installed at St. Peter's, 24th January
1059.

The names of both Benedict X. and Nicholas II.

---

[1] The description of his person is by St. Peter Damian (*cp.* iii.
4), and seems to be somewhat forced.

appear in the papal lists, but that is no criterion of their legitimacy. Benedict was certainly regarded by Hildebrand, and by Nicholas II. and his successors, as an intruder, an *invasor*, but then what claim had Nicholas II. to be considered legitimate ? It is not a question of his personal qualities, with which St. Peter Damian seems to have been so deeply impressed. That an oath had been sworn to Stephen IX. cannot be denied. It was quite within the province of a Pope, during his lifetime, to arrange the conditions of his succession, always provided that they did not interfere with the liberty of the electors. It is obvious that Nicholas II. was not freely elected by the Romans, but that he was foisted upon them without their consent. Where then lies the explanation of his legitimacy ?

There is only one reasonable answer to this question. The legitimacy of Nicholas II., like that of Clement II., Damasus II., Leo IX., Victor II., and Stephen IX. himself, hinged upon the co-operation of the German court. Ever since the time of Leo VIII. this had been the external guarantee of legitimacy. The signature of the chancellor Guibert, the future anti-pope, represented the official stamp, which enabled the world to distinguish between usurpers and others.

As time went on, the incongruity of this situation became more and more evident. Such a position might be tolerated for the Sees of Spires or Salzburg, but that the papacy should remain indefinitely in the condition of a German bishopric, within the nomination of the king and his council, could hardly be expected. Hildebrand had foreseen that, although the question of reform might be the most urgent, and that it might even be promoted with the support of the imperial Popes, there was another no less serious question to be settled, that of the re-conquest of the papacy by the Church. Since the days of Otto and Theophylact, or one might say, since Lothaire, or even Pepin and Charlemagne, the spiritual papacy had been adversely affected by the strife and contention connected with the temporal papacy. It would never be free, either in thought or action, until the day when it should have thrown off the authority of its temporal masters.

Thus, by the logical and chronological sequence of events, the head of the reform party came to the conclusion that a stronger force than that which had hitherto been employed was needed, and that the case was urgent. But what was to be done? To re-establish a prince of the Romans, an Alberic, a Crescentius, or a Count of Tusculum, or to deliver Rome over to the Duke of Tuscany, would have been to create round spiritual Rome a temporal Rome of much stricter limitations than had been the case under the intermittent protectorate of the transalpine kings. Hildebrand never recognised the much loathed rule of the barons of Rome; he could resign himself to the kings of Germany, and even to the Tuscan princes, but that was the extent of his forbearance. He was haunted by the phantom of Benedict IX., and on beholding it embodied anew in Benedict X., he became exasperated. He thereupon ventured upon a remarkably bold measure, and threw himself into the arms of those "Christian Saracens," the hated Normans, who had been not only excommunicated by the Popes, under his influence, but actually combated by Hildebrand himself.

As we have already mentioned, these Normans

had established two colonies, one at Aversa, near Capua, and the other at Melfi, in Apuleia. It was to the former that Hildebrand first made application. Richard, Count of Aversa, had just taken possession of Capua, putting an end, as Leo, IX. had done before him, to one of the three Lombard principalities, which, up to that time, had existed in those regions. Thanks to his help, they succeeded in taking the castle of Galeria, where Benedict X. was taking refuge ; or rather, by dint of many solemn oaths as to the safety of life and limb, and the comparative liberty of the unfortunate Pope, they prevailed upon him to deliver himself into the hands of Nicholas II. Meanwhile, a large conference was held at the Lateran, which resulted in the promulgation of an edict on the papal elections. This important act[1] preserved the honour and respect due to King Henry, in virtue of the concessions granted him, and the honour and respect which might be due to his successors by reason of possible personal concessions ; at the same time it defined the respective rôles of the various categories of electors. The lead was to be taken by the cardinal bishops, who, after deliberation, were to combine with the other cardinals, and then with the remainder of the clergy and the people. The choice must fall on a member of the Roman clergy, if there was one suitable, if not they must seek further. Finally, if Rome itself was in too great a state of disturbance to permit of the

---

[1] There are two editions of this act ; one in which the imperial rights are accentuated, figures, according to the *Vatic.* 1984, in the M. G. Leges, t. ii. app. p. 177, and in *Watterich*, t. ii. p. 229 ; the other has been preserved by the canonists of the eleventh century, and is to be found in the Council collections. This is the more reliable, that of the *Vatic.* 1984, having been touched up by the Guibertists.

election's taking place there, the cardinal bishops and the pious laity might, even though they formed but a very small number, proceed to hold the election outside the city. In that case, the successful candidate, without being enthroned, would nevertheless have full possession of all the papal rights and dignities.

This decree, after all, was nothing else than the legal transformation of all the circumstances which had brought about the promotion of Nicholas II., and it seemed exactly calculated to meet the needs of the present situation. It was clearly directed, first and foremost, against the feudal aristocracy of the Roman state ; its chief opponents would be the Crescentii, the Counts of Tusculum, Praeneste, Galeria, and Sabina ; but others also regarded it as an injury. Notwithstanding the outward and intentional demonstrations of respect for the imperial authority, the cardinal clergy were credited with an initiative and an eligibility which overstepped the bounds prescribed by the German authority, and seriously violated the traditional rights of the successors of Otto I. and Henry III. Not only were Popes like Benedict IX. or X. debarred, but also such as Gregory V., Clement II., and Leo IX., were excluded from the powers symbolised by the tiara and the cross keys.

But Hildebrand was not the man to make the serious blunder of issuing such a manifesto without having regard to the opposition which would follow. After having relieved him of Benedict X. and the Roman aristocracy, the Normans were commissioned to try to find a means of thwarting the plans of the German court, or, at least, of adopting towards it an awe-inspiring attitude.

On 23rd August of this same memorable year, 1059, Nicholas II. held a council at Melfi. The Norman chiefs of Aversa and Apuleia, Richard and Robert Guiscard, presented themselves before him, and were invested with the principality of Capua, and the duchy of Apuleia and Calabria respectively. The very fact that the Pope performed this act shows that he must have looked upon himself as the sovereign of the country. Now, with the exception of Beneventum, which he had not yielded to the Normans, his rights were confined to the theoretical claims mentioned in the compacts or privileges of the French or German kings since Pepin and Charlemagne, but which had never been realised. Moreover, the emperors and kings of Germany arrogated the same rights over these provinces as the old Lombard sovereigns had done —the rights of the Italian crown, which they had exercised on several occasions, and in particular under the Emperor Henry III.

Thus, over the question of the sovereignty of Southern Italy, as well as that of the papal elections, a contest arose between the Holy See and Germany. It must be stated that in return for their recognition by the Holy See, the Norman princes held themselves henceforth in duty bound to support the Pope. They were his vassals, and he was their lord. Provision was even made for the event of rivalry among several claimants to the tiara — the Normans would then lend their countenance to the one upheld by the " best cardinals." [1]

As might have been expected, the enactment

[1] The wording of these promises has been preserved by the pontifical canonists, Deusdedit, Albinus, and Cencius.

concerning the elections and the alliance with the Normans excited the keenest opposition in Germany; a council was called to pronounce the decree invalid, and when the Pope despatched a cardinal to explain matters, he was not even granted a hearing.

On the 27th July 1061 Nicholas II. ended his days at Florence. This was the signal for the outburst of a violent conflict. The Roman party, who were not in favour of reform, communicated with the German regency, which, in accordance with ancient custom, appointed Cadalus, Bishop of Parma, Pope, under the name of Honorius II.; Hildebrand, on the other hand, acted in consonance with the decree of 1059, and the voting favoured Anselm, Bishop of Lucca, who assumed the title of Alexander II. The struggle between these two rivals was long and bitter, but finally, thanks to a change of opinion on the part of the German government, Alexander gained the day. By dint of making certain concessions in the form of election, he obtained, in 1064, the royal recognition, which was solemnly awarded to him at the council of Mantua.

In this last circumstance, just as at the accession of Gregory VII. in 1073, the right claimed by the German crown was, in some measure, taken into account. We know how affairs had become entangled, and how Henry IV., after having recognised Gregory VII., tried to get him deposed. But the days of Otto and John XII. were over and past, and Christendom no longer followed the lead of the German crown. The latter was engaged in a dangerous game, by which she finally lost all her authority over the papal elections. For the future she was only concerned with the election of anti-popes. The legitimate pontiffs, Victor III., Urban II., Pascal II., Gelasius II., and Calistus II., were all installed without any reference to her. When peace was concluded at Worms, 1122, the question of the papal elections[1] was not even considered, and from that time neither emperors nor kings were involved in them.

This ultimate triumph of liberty was, however, quite a different thing from the particular success of Nicholas II.'s decree. This latter seems shortly to have been abandoned, not in its general tenor, but with regard to its characteristic feature, *i.e.* the predominant rôle played by the cardinal bishops. In its general drift and by what it had in common with the tendencies of the reform party, its aim was to free the papal elections: 1st, from all interference on the part of the Roman feudal aristocracy; and 2nd, from undue and harmful interference on the part of the kings of Germany. As far as these two points were concerned, its object was attained, and even surpassed as far as the German kings were concerned, for they did not even succeed in retaining the position marked out for them by Nicholas II.

[1] They seem, rather, to have been disposed of in these words appended to the rules on episcopal and abbatical investitures: *exceptis omnibus quæ ad Romanam eçclesiam pertinere noscuntur* (Jaffé, 6986).

CONCLUSION

To prolong this account would be to exceed the limits which I have sketched out. Moreover, with the advent of the Gregorian papacy begins a new epoch in the history of the temporal power as well as in general history. This pontificate realises the potential might of its religious and moral power, and, with one vigorous stroke, rises above all the political considerations of the West. As a result of this great change, the relative importance of the little principality is somewhat diminished. It was by no means destroyed, however, but, like all other rights connected with the Holy See, adhered to with tenacity. Sometimes it provided a temporary refuge from outside attacks; even in times of depression, when suffering the imperial occupation, hardly any change was made in the manner of government; it was always the pontifical estate. Gregory VII., Urban II., and Gelasius II. might be compelled to live and die away from Rome, but in the interval it was occupied by the anti-popes. It was in their capacity of vicars of St. Peter that they posed as sovereigns of Rome. Although in and after the twelfth century the papal dominion was often interfered with (at least as far as Rome was concerned) by the commune, its claims were quite in accord with the theory of the pontifical sovereignty.

The Pope, therefore, held the sovereignty after the time of Gregory VII. as before; one may even say that the conditions were the same, with the double anxiety of his untractable subjects at home and of the empire abroad. But, though the sovereignty did not change, the same cannot be affirmed of the sovereign. Formerly he had been the high priest of the Roman pilgrimage, the theoretical head of the episcopate, the dispenser of benedictions and of privileges, and of anathemas. But, over the Church as a whole, his influence was lacking in vigour and continuity. True, he had been known to organise or instigate certain missions, and occasionally, as in the time of Nicholas I., energetically to interpose in the general affairs of the Church ; but these cases were exceptional. He had had no part in furthering the somewhat evanescent reforms brought about under the early Carlovingian princes, though the author of the " Forged Decretals," recognising their decline, sought to make out that they were placed under the protection of the earliest Popes, without succeeding in arousing in their successors any sustained interest. These latter, as we have seen, were drawn from an environment which, to put it mildly, bore but an indifferent reputation. Indeed, even if we eliminate the gross scandals which are on record, it must be admitted that the personal character of almost all of the Popes of those days was very far removed indeed from the apostolic ideal.

What a contrast do they present with later times, when we have to deal with such men as Gregory VII., Urban II., and Alexander III. !

With so extensive a papacy it was impossible to avoid difficulties in connection with the old temporal establishment. There were often quarrels with the emperors, in which the Romans displayed but little interest, although they suffered considerably from their effects. When once they were organised into a commune, their wishes had more than ever to be reckoned with. On the other hand, the pontifical *curia* was gradually becoming less Roman. German Popes were no longer appointed, but there were several of French, and even one of English nationality. It naturally followed that the members of the second and lower degrees of the clergy were drawn from various nationalities. This fresh set had but few ties with Rome. The cardinals had long since ceased to take any personal interest in their churches, and rarely came into contact with the native population. As time went on, the *personnel* of the Holy See became more and more distinct from that of the old Roman days. Many complications arose, but, notwithstanding these, the combined pressure of external influences, the emperors, the anti-popes, and especially the commune, finally succeeded in moving this venerable and weighty mass. By dint of constantly changing place it became accustomed to a wandering existence. Theoretically the centre of Catholicism remained at Rome, the Lateran being the official residence of the Popes. But, as a matter of fact, those who wished to come into touch with the head of the Churches, had generally to go further afield—to Anagni, Viterbo, Perugia, Cluny, Sens, or even to Avignon, not to mention the high roads of Italy and France, where the papal retinue often made a halt.

As regards the finances, it is not to be supposed that pilgrimages or the revenues, such as they were, of the duchy of Rome, could afford adequate means of subsistence. Like the papal staff, the funds, as well as warrants of security, were drawn from various sources. The travelling Pope might meet with adventures on the way, but he could always make sure, wherever he might go, in the whole of Latin Christendom, of finding places where he could remain in absolute safety. As long as he was in opposition to the emperor, the Normans of Italy were on his side, and more than one common Italian had the happiness of giving him shelter. In France, too, the kings, the monks, and the bishops always welcomed him with sympathy.

It is easy to understand that, under these circumstances, temporal politics should have been relegated to the background. Not that they were altogether forgotten, but they suffered from a certain neglect. It was not until the end of the fourteenth and beginning of the fifteenth centuries that they regained their former position of importance.

Enough has now been said to justify the break that I have introduced in this history. It now merely remains for me to sum up the main points of the pages dedicated to the earlier period.

The temporal power had its origin in the repugnance of the Romans to becoming Lombards, and in their inability to organise their autonomy unless the Pope was placed at its head. From the very outset the new state felt and displayed a twofold weakness, an external incapacity to cope with the Lombards and Greeks, and an internal lack of cohesion, due to the constant dissensions between the lay aristocracy and the clergy. A protector was necessary to defend the Roman state against outside attacks, as well as to help the Roman clergy in the struggle against their rivals at home. The external enemy speedily ceased to give cause of offence, and indeed, except perhaps for the Saracen inroads of the ninth century, the Romans had very little to complain of on this score after the year 774. But the internal situation became more and more strained, as is evidenced by the tragedies which followed the death of Pope Paul, and the riots in the times of Leo III. and Pascal. But the crisis did not pass, and it became necessary to deal with it effectively. The sovereign protector intervened, and in 824 the new order of things became incorporated in the constitution of Lothaire.

That this arrangement had been submitted to, rather than initiated by the clergy, is not to be gainsaid. On several occasions they sought exemption from it, but as long as the emperor's authority had any weight, they were obliged to put up with it. Moreover, the clergy themselves, after some experience, ended by recognising its inevitability.

The charter of 824 was concerned with the protectorate, and implied the presence of a resident, and the existence of a protector. At the close of the ninth century, however, these two essential elements were conspicuous by their absence, and the Roman clergy found themselves defenceless against the lay aristocracy. The nobles thereupon made themselves masters of the state, and for the space of a century and a half the House of Theophylact provided them with a succession of leaders, who undertook the direction of the political destinies of the pontifical estate. First of all they ruled alone, unimpeded by the Carlovingian heirs, but after the time of the Ottos they were obliged, in some measure at least, to submit to the guardianship of the kings of Germany. In the main they managed to keep the upper hand, and if they had confined themselves to the retention of the political power, things would have turned out differently. But they took upon themselves the right of choosing the dignitary who was, at one and the same time, their theoretical sovereign and their bishop, and the Pope, therefore, was appointed by this incongruous company of feudal barons.[1] After their first encroachments the conclave of 769 had excluded them from the electoral council, but they returned to it in 824 in company with the emperor, who was invested with the right of verifying and confirming the papal elections, a right which had been exercised by the Greek sovereigns since the time of Justinian. This intervention of a higher power might have acted as a check on the unsuitable elections made by the nobility; certainly the Popes of the ninth century, who were elected under this régime, seem to have no blot upon their fair fame. The empire, however, underwent some eclipses; the princes of the House of Saxony either could not or would not intervene as often as was desirable. They apparently cared little for the holiness of the pontificate, so long as it remained in subjection to them, and it was for his intractability rather than for his unexampled licentiousness, that John XII. was deposed. Otto immediately took upon himself the actual choice of the Pope—not merely the confirmation of the choice of others. Afterwards the system became elaborated. The German emperor appointed his intimates, Gregory V. and Sylvester II., and then some of his own bishops. In the hierarchy of the Church under German influence the Pope was promoted from the

---

[1] Almost everywhere the same effects were produced by the same cause. Monopolised by the feudal aristocracy, the episcopal sees were often occupied by very unworthy bishops. With the lapse of time they have passed into oblivion, one result of which is that the scandals created by the feudal Popes stand out all the more conspicuously. It is only right to place these things in their proper perspective and not to represent the Roman *milieu* in a darker light than the others.

lower ecclesiastical ranks, rather than from the cardinalate.

But this state of affairs could not last indefinitely. On Gregory VII. fell the onus of setting matters on a different basis, and great was the scandal and affront among those who had long been nourished on the traditional abuses. But Pope Gregory VII. had confidence in the ark which he was steering through such devious ways—a confidence which was not misplaced, for the bark of Peter responded willingly to the guidance of her captain.

INDEX

A

Abbon, governor of Provence, *patricius Romanorum*, 39

Abbots not necessarily priests, 154 *note*

Abruzzo attacked by Romans for Trasimund, 9

Acolytes distributed among priestly offices, 65

Acontius, St., body of Pope Formosus cast up near church of, 201

Actard, Bishop, ambassador of Charles the Bald, 170; interview of, with Hadrian II., 170

Adalbert, Count of Tuscany, *missus* of Emperor Louis II., 152

Adalbert, Marquess, questionable vassal of Arnulph, 196

Adalbert, son of Berengarius II., 225; welcomed in Rome by John XII., 226; flies before Emperor Otto from Rome, 227

Adda, the, one of boundaries between kings of Italy, 198

Adelaide, widow of Lothaire of Provence, 218; resists Berengarius, 218; defeated, and imprisoned on Lake Garda, 218; escapes, and appeals to Otto, King of the Germans, 218; marries Otto, 218; Azzo, chatelain of Canossa, protects, 255

Adelchis, son of Desiderius, leads revolt at Verona, 93; when revolt subdued, seeks Byzantine refuge, 93

Adelgis, Duke of Beneventum, takes Louis II. prisoner, 166, 196

Administration, diaconal, 63

Administration, financial, at Lateran, presided over by *arcarius*, 64; funds of, drawn from many sources, 272

Adriatic, the, becomes Byzantine, 175

Adultery, judged at ecclesiastical tribunals, 115 *note*

Advocates of the Lateran, 64

Afiarta, Paul, pontifical chamberlain, 82; confederate of Desiderius, 82; at daggers drawn with Christopher (*primicerius*) 83; inhuman treatment of Sergius (son of Christopher) by, 84–5; Stephen III. takes standpoint of, 85; sent by Hadrian I. to Desiderius, 88; undertakes to arrange interview between Hadrian and Desiderius, 89; denounced to Hadrian, 89; arrested by Archbishop of Ravenna, 90; executed, 91

Agapitus II., Pope, 216; Romans swear to elect Octavian on death of, 222; death of, 223

Agareni, Normans often called, 257

Agatho, Bishop of Todi, leader of imperial party, 153

Agiltrude, Empress-mother (widow of Emperor Guy), 196; marked character of, 196; daughter of Adelgis of Beneventum, 196; watches interests of Lambert of Spoleto, 196; deadly foe of Carlovingians, 196; seizes Rome, 196–7; plans checked, 197; shut up in castle of Spoleto, 197; retakes Rome, 198; institutes mock trial of dead Pope Formosus, 199

Aglabites, Saracens of Numidia and East Africa under the, 137

Agnellus, Life of Sergius, Archbishop of Ravenna, by, 99 *note*; reverses names of Popes Paul and Stephen II., 100 *note*; incomplete account by, of revolt at Ravenna, 101 *note*

Agnes, Empress (wife of Henry III.), consecrated by Clement II., 254; guardian of Henry IV., 259; Victor II. reconciles House of Tuscany with, 260

Agnes, St., convent of, remodelled, 221

Aistulf, Lombard prince, full of piety, 25

Aix-la-Chapelle, sacred town of Charlemagne, 136; much frequented by Emperor Lothaire, 144; visited by Otto III., 242

Alamanny, duchy of, loosely bound to Frankish kingdom, 6

B

of, 84 ; honourable burial of, in St. Peter's, 91

Chrodegang, Bishop of Metz, escort of Pope Stephen II., 33

Chronicle, Moissac, on meeting of Pepin and Stephen II., 36

Chronicle, Bavarian, valuable details in, 83 *note*

Chronicler succeeding Fredegarius, 32 *note*, 39, 41 ; use of term "*respublica*," 38 *note*

Church, Frankish, rather supports iconoclast emperors, 57

Church property, depredations in, 24, 66 ; pontifical revenue drawn from landed, 66 ; plunders in, 113

Churches, Byzantine and Roman, reconciliation of, 20 *note* ; East and West, no difference between, in 767 ; on Holy Spirit, 59 *note*

Citta di Castello (*Castellum Felicitatis*), people of, proclaim allegiance to Pope, 94

Clausula de Pippino, title of "*patricius Romanorum*" used in, for Pepin, 39 *note*

Clergy, Roman, recruited from two sources, 65 ; rivalry of, with army, 70 ; meet army in friendlier spirit in convocation, 73 ; interests and ambitions conflict with those of nobles, 129 ; election of John XII. ends struggle of, with nobles, 223 ; Pope to be chosen from, 265

Cluny, St. Odo, Abbot of, 218

Code of Lothaire, 131–2

Codex Carolinus, letters in, 33, 58, 73 *note* ; correspondence in, on Desiderius, Sergius, and Christopher, 81 ; on Charlemagne and title "*patricius Romanorum*," 106

Coire, Count of, envoy of Louis the Pious, 128

Cologne, Archbishop of, deposed by Pope Nicholas I., 160

Columba, St., Irish party lay stress on patronage of, 30

Comacchio, yielded by Astolphus, 45 ; named in list of territories given to Holy See, 46 ; taken by Desiderius, 89 ; Lombards to evacuate, 97

Comita, Roman noble, sent by Pope to Pepin, 44

Como, Bishop of, begs interposition of Otto I. with Berengarius, 225

Compact between Louis the Pious and Pascal I., 125

Conrad II., Emperor, edict of, 248 ; annuls personal right of Lombards over Roman territory, 248 ; corona-

tion of, 249 ; knows how to manage Benedict IX., 250 ; Benedict IX. excommunicates Archbishop Heribert at request of, 250

Consiliarius, functions of, 64

Constantine, brother of Toto, plots for Pope Paul's death, 73 ; proclaimed Pope, 73 ; ordained subdeacon, deacon, and priest, 74 ; consecrated by Bishops of Prenesto, Albano, and Porto, 74 ; is treated with treachery, 77 ; takes refuge in chapel after chapel, 77 ; undergoes humiliations, 78 ; declared to have forfeited papal dignity, 78 ; eyes put out, and cruelly treated, 79 ; death of, result of cruelties, 79 ; indignities suffered at trial, 80 ; ordinations and enactments declared illegal, 80

Constantine V., Emperor, Pope Zachary sends envoys to, 19 ; an iconoclast, 19 ; besieges Artavasde in his capital, 19 ; designs of, on Ravenna, 56 ; makes overtures to Desiderius, 56 ; death of, 102

Constantine VI., proposed alliance of with Rotrude, daughter of Charlemagne, 103–4 ; alliance of, given up, 105

Constantinople, Emperor of, replaces Gothic kings, 1 ; Romans look for help from Rome, rather than from, 18 ; Constantine V. reinstated in, 19 ; little realisation in, of Roman changes, 22 ; collisions of Holy See with Emperor of, 28 ; Empress Irene occupies throne at, 117 ; efforts made in, to get recognition of Roman Empire, 117–8 ; Patriarch of, crowns Emperor, 118–9 ; ecumenical council (eighth) in, 165 ; bitter dissent between Roman Church and empire of, ends, 194 ; Emperor Lecapenus at, 220 ; John XI. sends four ambassadors to, 220 ; presence of ambassadors in St. Sophias' at, breach of ecclesiastical law, 220

Constitution of Lothaire, 122–35

Consul of Rome, Theophylact *the*, 205

Convention, national, at Braisne, in 754, 42 ; at Kiersy-sur-Oise at Easter, 754, 42

Convocation, after death of Pope Paul I., 73

Corbi, Desiderius and Ansa confined at, 96

Council, ecumenical, at Constantinople, 165

INDEX

Boson, 190 ; succeeded by Hugh, Count of Provence, 213

Louis the Child succeeds Arnulph, 204

Louis the German, lack of harmony of, with father, 136 ; Pope Hadrian II. reproaches, for seizing estates of Lothaire II., 169 ; treaty of Mersen bestows lands on, 169 ; in ill odour at Rome, 169 ; head of German branch of Charlemagne's lineage, 170 ; sends to Italy younger son, Charles the Fat, of Swabia, 173 ; death of, 180

Louis, son of Louis the German, defeats Charles the Bald at Andernach, 180

Louis the Pious, Emperor, Frankish Church under, 57 ; crowned by father, Charlemagne, as successor, 117 ; conspiracy against Pope causes sensation at court of, 122 ; crowned by Pope Stephen IV. with wife Ermengarde, at Rheims, 124 ; crowns eldest son Lothaire Emperor, 126 ; crowns Pepin and Louis Kings Aquitaine and Bavaria, 126 ; despatches envoys to Rome, 128 ; resolves to make power felt in Rome, 130 ; lack of harmony with sons, 136 ; Gregory IV. concerned by quarrels in family of, 136 ; death of, in 840, 136 ; strife subsequent to death of, 136 ; had not visited Rome except in childhood, 136-7

Louis the Stammerer succeeds father, Charles the Bald, 181 ; not inclined for secret negotiations with Pope, John VIII., 182 ; content to keep Provence, 183 ; death of, in 879, 184 ; death of last two reigning sons of, 184 ; Charles the Simple, posthumous son of, 185

Lucca, Anselm, Bishop of, Alexander II. *See* Alexander II.

Luitprand, King of Lombards, successes of, 4 ; Christian prince, and experienced politician, 6 ; overwhelms St. Peter's with gifts, 6 ; desires to make power felt in Spoleto and Beneventum, 5-6 ; Dukes of Spoleto and Beneventum assume independent attitude to, 8 ; expels Duke Trasimund of Spoleto, 8 ; seizes Ameria, Orte, Bomarzo, and Blera, 8 ; Gregory III. asks to restore the four towns, 8 ; comes to understanding with Pope Zachary, 11 ; interviews Pope at Pavia, 11 ; seizes Cesena, 11 ;

yields to peaceful tactics of Zachary, 11 ; death of, 11 ; arranged peace of Terni, 16

Luitprand (author) on renunciation of right of election, 228 ; on deposition of Benedict V., 228-9 ; prattle of, about Marozia and Theodora, 229

Luni, protection of coasts between Terracino and, 137 ; seized by Saracens, 247

Lupam, ad, hall in Lateran palace, called after famous bronze she-wolf, 219

Lutri, Luitprand yields claims on, 7

Lyons, Bishop of, meets dignitaries in Rome and tries Pope Constantine, 80

M

Mabillon publishes polemics against Sergius III., 207 *note*

Magenarius, Abbot of, to define certain limits of Papal State, 104

Magistrates, Roman, to present themselves before Emperor (Constitution of Lothaire), 131

Magra, position with regard to Frankish kingdom, 96 *note*

Mainz, Bishop of, meets dignitaries in Rome, and tries Pope Constantine, 80 ; Archbishop of, envoy from Otto I. to Alberic, 218

Mantua, Azzo and Tebald of Tuscany popular in, 255-6

Maria Antica, Santa, Byzantine church of, connected with Palatine, 61 *note* ; countless attempts to trace origin of, 61 *note*

Maria, Santa, of Farfa, Abbey of, 68 ; transferred to papal jurisdiction, 69

Maria Maggiore, Santa, Pope and court often present at ceremonies in basilica of, 64 ; Waldipert, Lombard priest, vainly seeks refuge in, 79 ; Pope Benedict III. proclaimed in, 153-4

Marin plots against Paul I., 70 ; promoted to French bishopric, 70

Marinus I. elected Pope, 187 ; had been three times legate to Constantinople, 187 ; recalls Formosus, 188 ; absolves Bishop of Troyes from oath, 188 ; some irregularity in election of, 188 ; had been Bishop of Caeri (Cervetri), 188 ; meets Charles the Fat at Nonantola, 188 ; replaced by Hadrian III., 188

115 ; question from whom holds rights, 120 ; election of, according to constitution Lothaire, 132–3 ; election of subject to imperial confirmation, 132; lay participation in election of, confirmed, 134 ; choice of emperor, for first time, under auspices of, 173 ; held sovereignty, from time Gregory VII., as before, 270

Popes, of sixth, seventh, and eighth centuries, relations of to Emperor of Constantinople, 13–14 ; of seventh century, have troubles with Ravennese, 97–8 ; John XI., Leo VII., Stephen VIII., Marinus II., and Agapitus II. exercised no temporal authority, 216 ; of the Empire, 234–252 ; German, 253–269 ; French, 272 ; one Englishman, among, 272 ; often away from Rome, 272

Popes, Anti-, Germany concerned in election of, 268–9 ; Rome occupied by, 270

Poppo, Bishop of Briscen, Damasus II. *See* Damasus II.

Populonia (Piombino) conceded to papal territory, 105

Porto, colony of Corsicans at, 146 ; Radoald, Bishop of (*see* Radoald)

Possessor, Bishop, Frankish ambassador, 102

Poupardin, "Le Royaume de Provence sous les Carolingiens," 183 *note*

Præfectus navalis, 245

Præneste, in possession of Theophylact family, 243

Prefect of Rome, humiliating degradation of, by John XIII., 235

Prenesto, George, Bishop of, confers tonsure on Constantine, declared Pope, 74 ; consecrates Constantine, 74 ; paralysed in right hand, 75 ; death of, regarded as token divine displeasure, 75

Presbyteræ, wives of clergy, 66

Presbyteral churches, 68

Primicerii, rank of, 61

Primicerius, Christopher, 70–86

Primicerius of notaries, with chief priest and archdeacon, makes up governing triumvirate Roman church, 63

Primiscrinius (or Protoscrinius) succeeds Primicerius, as head of chancellor's office, 64

Princeps, et omnium Romanorum, senator, title of Alberic, 219

Prior vestiarii, at Lateran palace, 63

Property, church, depredations in, 24, 66 ; pontifical revenues drawn from landed, 66 ; arrangements for, in Privilege of Otto, 229–30

Protoscrinius (or Primiscrinius) real head of chancellor's office, at Lateran, 64

Provence, invaded by Saracens, 9 ; Louis the Stammerer keeps, 183 ; "Le Royaume de, sous les Carolingiens," 183 *note* ; Boson crowned king of, 184 (*see* Boson) ; Louis the Blind of, 190 ; King Louis of, rival of Berengarius, 204 ; Louis of, consecrated Emperor, 204 ; Berengarius compels Louis of, to retreat, 204 ; Louis of, wrests Verona, but falls, through treachery, 205 ; Theophylact at court of justice held by Emperor Louis of, 205 *note* ; Berengarius proclaimed King of, 218 ; Berengarius resisted in, by Adelaide, 218

Q

Quinto, Tor di (St. Lucius), 153 *note*

R

Rabigaudus, Abbot, Frankish ambassador, endeavours to reconcile Pope Hadrian I. and Duke Hildeprand, 102

Radelgiso, claimant to duchy Beneventum, 138 ; envoys sent to, regarding expedition against Saracens, 142

Radoald, Bishop of Porto, 153 ; did not take customary part, in consecration Benedict III., 154 ; ringleader in the Anastasius conspiracy, 156 ; now confidential adviser, Pope Nicholas, 156 ; treachery of, 156 ; expelled from episcopate, 156 ; receives sentence of deposition from Pope, 162

Ratchis, King, succeeds Luitprand, 11 ; grants Pope's desire for twenty years' peace, 12 ; abandons siege of Perugia, 12 ; abdicates, 12 ; succeeded by Astolphus, 12

Ratchis, brother of preceding king, Astolphus, claims Lombard throne, 47 ; a monk at Monte Cassino, 47 ; Pope exhorts to return to monastic life, 48 ; complies, and leaves field to Desiderius, 48

Ravenna, Gothic Kings of, 1 ; engaged in struggle in mid-Italy, 4 ; port of, Classis, yields to Luitprand, 4 ; succumbs to Lombards, 7 ; receives different treatment from that given Rome, 16 ; restitution of, demanded by Stephen II., 34 ; Astolphus forced to deliver up, 42 ; Pepin refuses to restore to imperial government, 45 ; name on list of territories given to Holy See (Stephen II.), 46 ; Archbishop of, and Bishop of Reggio, consecrate churches and oratories, 52 ; designs of Constantine V. upon, 56 ; George, chief secretary, plots with Desiderius against, 58 ; Desiderius meditates descent on, 89 ; leaders of, conspicuous for greed, 97 ; Pope's intervention for, gladly received, 98 ; people of, welcome Pope Zachary, 98 ; decapitalisation of, 98 ; formerly residence of Lombard kings, 98 ; Charlemagne claims voice in election of Archbishops of, 107

Ravenna, Archbishops of, Gerbert, afterwards Sylvester II., 242 (*see* Sylvester II.). John of, summoned to appear before Roman Synod, 158 ; accused of heterodox views, suspended, and excommunicated, 158 ; papal action against, 158–60. John X., formerly of, 212–13. Leo of, claims cities, as property St. Apollinarius, 101 ; visit Charlemagne, whom he treats falsely, 101–2. Michaelius of, appointed by people, 100 ; Stephen III. refuses to acknowledge, 100 ; eventually ousted, 101. Sergius of, aggressive influence of, 99 ; appoints officials, without reference to Rome, 99 ; summoned to Rome, 99 ; returns to Ravenna, 99 ; invested with authority over Exarchy and Pentapolis, 99 ; later, on good terms with Pope, 100

Reggio, looks to Sicily for help, 3 ; consecration of church and oratories, by Bishop of, 52 ; Azzo and Tebald popular in, 255–6

Régions de Rome, au moyen age (Mélanges de l'École de Rome), 60 *note*

Reiti, limits of Papal State on side of, 104

Relic of body of St. Sylvester taken from Rome to Nonantola, 53 ; question of authenticity of, 53

Relics, frequent thefts of in eighth century, 24

Remedius, brother of Pepin, sent to Italy, 55

Republic, the Holy, no mean thing to be member of, 26

Respublica, unsuitable expression as used in Chronicles, 38 ; sense in which used by Didier, 45 *note*

Rex Francorum and Rex Langobardorum, title used by Charlemagne, 40

Rheims, Bishop of, with other dignitaries, tries Pope Constantine, 80 ; Stephen IV. crowns Louis the Pious and Ermengarde at, 124 ; Ebbo, Archbishop of, adherent of Lothaire, 140 ; belonged to kingdom, Charles the Bald, 140 ; Foulques, Archbishop of, supports Guy of Spoleto, 192

Rialto, Venice beginning to rise on island of, 4

Richard, Count of Aversa, applied to by Hildebrand, 265 ; has possession of Capua, 265 ; presents himself before Nicholas II. at Council Melfi, 267 ; invested with principality of Capua, 267

Richarde, wife of Charles the Fat, imperial consecration of, 186

Rieti despoiled by Romans, for Trasimund, 9 ; Abbey of St. Saviour at, 68 ; Christopher and Sergius retire to Abbey at, 75–6 ; possibility of Popedom for John, Bishop of, 149

Riguier, St., Angilbert, Abbot of, sent to Rome by Charlemagne, 109

Robert, the Strong, 190

Robert Guiscard, Norman chief, 267

Rofred, Count, instigates revolt against John XIII., 235 ; killed in reaction following revolt, 235 ; body exhumed and thrown into public sewer, 235–6

Roger, Norman King, 20

Romans establish Italian unity, 1 ; undertake to subjugate Spoleto, 9

Rome, Duchy of, 13–20 ; extent of Duchy of, 15 ; Duchy of a self-governing state, 20 ; Bishop of has exceptional position, 13 ; election of Pope at, 14 ; treated very differently from Ravenna, 17 ; people of called " peculiaris populis," 18 ; reconciled with Byzantine Church, 20 *note*; sort of protectorate created at, 22 ; Astolphus levies poll-tax on people of, 22 ; copy of treaty, broken by Astolphus, fastened to stational cross at, 23 ; even as part of Lombard kingdom would have been Holy City, 25 ; no wish for

THE END

M